JOHN WHITGIFT
AND THE ENGLISH REFORMATION

THE HALE LECTURES · 1953

JOHN WHITGIFT AND THE ENGLISH REFORMATION

by

POWEL MILLS DAWLEY

Sub-Dean and Professor of Ecclesiastical History
The General Theological Seminary, New York

1954

CHARLES SCRIBNER'S SONS

New York

PRINTED IN THE UNITED STATES OF AMERICA

TO
CHARLES SMYTH

CONTENTS

PREFACE ix

I THE NATIONAL CHURCH 1

II THE ELIZABETHAN SETTLEMENT 31

III CAMBRIDGE AND CONTROVERSY 64

IV WHITGIFT AT WORCESTER 101

V THE CHALLENGE OF PURITANISM 133

VI THE DEFENSE OF THE ESTABLISHMENT 161

VII THE LAST DECADE 195

EPILOGUE 229

BIBLIOGRAPHY 231

INDEX: *Selected Names and Topics* 243

THE HALE LECTURES 253

vii

JUSTICE is seldom done the Church of Elizabeth Tudor. Contemporary Puritan and Romanist opponents perceived little virtue in a Reformation settlement which suffered in the eyes of each by its manifest affinities with the other, and, unlike either, was tailored out of materials almost wholly English. Even those within the Anglican tradition in succeeding generations have not always understood the Elizabethans and their Church. The ecclesiastical history of the Queen's reign is too often viewed as an indeterminate phase in the life of the English Church, preparatory to the hardening of Anglicanism into more coherent and well-defined patterns. One suspects that here might have been the greatest success of Puritans and Romanists—in persuading men that between their respective positions lay little ground where Christian doctrines and institutions might be firmly rooted in the authority of Scripture or the appeal to history. Yet the forty-five years of Elizabethan England were precisely those in which this ground of Archbishop Parker's "reverent mediocrity" was explored, and in it was found the distinctive and unique place that Anglicanism occupies in the Christian tradition. It may well be that the critical importance of these years during which Elizabeth I insisted that "none should be suffered to decline either on the left or on the right hand" is obscured by complexities characteristic of the Tudor age. It is not easy now to understand the Tudor ideal of the National Church, nor to think the thoughts of men who did not know "the Church" and "the State" as separate entities. Hooker's famous remark, "By the goodness of Almighty

God and his servant Elizabeth, we are," is only an embarrassment to those who fail to grasp the sixteenth-century conception of the proper functions of the "Godly Prince" and the "True Obedience" owed him. Consequently, Royal Supremacy is seen as an intolerable tyranny by the power of which religious convictions and loyalties were subordinated to the demands of the national welfare, *politique* considerations, and the dictates of secular policies. The temptation, therefore, is to distill out of this complex of sixteenth-century ideas the useful spiritual and intellectual perceptions of Richard Hooker; virtually all the other features of the Elizabethan religious and ecclesiastical scene are abandoned. This scarcely does justice to an age in which the first distinctively Anglican generation came to maturity, formulating the main outlines of an appeal to Scripture, history, and reason on the integrity of which the Church of England has rested for four centuries.

Admittedly, it is difficult to evaluate the Queen's settlement of religion or to isolate the elements of permanent importance in the English Reformation experience that came to a critical point in the Elizabethan Church. We may, however, be led in the right direction by those whose lives and energies were devoted to the maintenance of the Establishment. Of such men, John Whitgift is clearly the leading figure. Archbishop of Canterbury from 1583 to 1604, he was entrusted for nearly half the reign of Queen Elizabeth with the defence of her ecclesiastical settlement against the attacks of its enemies. He, not Hooker, is the typical Elizabethan churchman.

Whitgift is not a man whom it is easy to know. We miss the intensely human touches by which Matthew Parker enlists our sympathy and affection; we cannot penetrate Whitgift's stern reserve to find ready acquaintance with his inner religious life. Yet his is the outlook of the generation that held tenaciously to the ground between the Puritans and the Romanists; his was the unshakeable courage and strong sense of duty on which more than once the success of the Queen's ecclesiastical policy appeared to depend.

The chapters in this book are the Hale Lectures for 1953, given at the invitation of the Dean and the Trustees of the Seabury-Western Theological Seminary. Inevitably they reflect the fashion in which the lecturer is straitened by the mode of presenting his material. He must have his auditory—as the Elizabethans would say

—constantly in mind, and the discipline of brevity demands suggestive rather than exhaustive treatment of many aspects of his subject. These lectures represent a stage in the preparation of a full-length biography of John Whitgift. They are printed here virtually as prepared for delivery, though quotations have been somewhat lengthened, and for the convenience of the reader, spelling and punctuation has been occasionally modernized. Ample documentation is provided for students; short title references in the footnotes are supplemented by a full bibliography.

It will be evident that my reliance upon the work of others is very great. Since my earlier research on Whitgift was done, a large number of Tudor studies have appeared, and a wealth of hitherto inaccessible ecclesiastical records and parish documents have been made available. Particularly, D. J. McGinn's *The Admonition Controversy* has reawakened interest in Whitgift's literary controversy with Thomas Cartwright; the writings of William Haller, M. M. Knappen, Leonard J. Trinterud and others have opened afresh the difficult subject of the origins and character of English Puritanism. The brilliant essay of A. L. Rowse in two chapters of his *England of Elizabeth* has sketched against the Elizabethan background a masterly picture of the English Church under Elizabeth I. The work of Professor J. E. Neale on the Parliaments of the Queen's reign has given the ecclesiastical historian an accurate and indispensable account of the formulation of the Elizabethan religious legislation. In resuming work upon Whitgift's life I have drawn freely upon the conclusions of these scholars and others, an indebtedness acknowledged at many points in the notes.

My thanks are also due Dean Alden D. Kelley and the Faculty, students, and friends of the Seabury-Western Theological Seminary for their hospitality in Evanston and their kindly reception of these lectures. It is not possible, however, to express so readily my gratitude to all those who have sustained and deepened my interest in the religious life of Tudor England. I owe much to a former teacher and friend at the Episcopal Theological School in Cambridge, Massachusetts, James Arthur Muller, remembered now for his admirable studies of the life and letters of Stephen Gardiner; to the late James Pounder Whitney, who supervised my studies some years ago in the University of Cambridge; to Canon Charles Smyth for his continued encouragement and helpful criticism; to my associate, Professor Robert S. Bosher, who has read the manuscript of these lectures and offered many valuable suggestions; and to Dr. Niels H. Sonne, Librarian of the General Theological Seminary, whose unfailing assistance has made the exacting task of proper documentation infinitely easier.

POWEL MILLS DAWLEY

September, 1954

THE GENERAL THEOLOGICAL SEMINARY
NEW YORK

JOHN WHITGIFT
AND THE ENGLISH REFORMATION

I

THE NATIONAL CHURCH

O N the 12th of February 1559 Sir Anthony Cooke, sometime tutor to Edward VI and ardent champion of the Protestant cause, now lately returned to London from his exile in Strasbourg during the reign of the Catholic Mary Tudor, scrawled a brief letter to his friend Peter Martyr. "We are busy in Parliament," he wrote, "about expelling the tyranny of the pope and restoring the royal authority."[1] Upon the accession of Elizabeth I, Cooke, like the other Marian exiles, had returned home in haste to claim a share in framing the fifth English ecclesiastical settlement since 1532. Already the first steps in the Elizabethan reconstruction of the Church had been taken when a bill "restoring to the Crown the ancient jurisdiction over the State Ecclesiastical and Spiritual" was laid before the House of Commons on February 9th. While three months of controversy over the precise form of the religious settlement ensued, one thing was plain at the outset. The national

[1] *Zurich Letters,* II, 13.

Church of Elizabeth Tudor would rest upon the constitutional foundations laid down in the reign of Henry VIII, "your most dear father of worthy memory," as Parliament described him to the Queen, in whose time

divers good laws and statutes were made and established as well for the utter extinguishment of all usurped and foreign powers and authorities, as also for the restoring and uniting to the imperial crown of this Realm the ancient jurisdictions to the same of right belonging.[2]

The Elizabethan settlement was supported by those same good laws and statutes enacted twenty-seven years before the Queen's first Parliament—in the years, in fact, of Whitgift's birth and early childhood. The life of John Whitgift exactly spans the critical period of the English Reformation. He was born on the eve of the decisive Henrician legislation; he lived through the successive reigns of Henry's children, for over twenty years himself the chief defender of the Tudor national Church, to witness its delivery into Stuart England. Properly, then, the story of John Whitgift and the English Reformation begins in the middle of the reign of Henry VIII.

In the early spring of 1532 there was great rejoicing in the home of a prosperous merchant and ship-owner of the flourishing port of Great Grimsby. Henry Whitgift's wife, Anne Dynewell, had presented her husband with the first of their several sons.[3] John, he was called, named for his

---

[2] 1 Eliz. c. 1. *Statutes of the Realm*, IV, i, 350-5.

[3] The date of Whitgift's birth is variously given between 1530 and 1533. Paule, *Whitgift*, p. 2; Strype, *Whitgift*, I, 6; *Athenae Cantab.*, II, 369. An entry in the Lincoln diocesan records suggests that 1532 is to be preferred. *Liber Cleri 1576*, fo. 1. See also Godwin, *Catalog of Bishops*, p. 179, and Harington, *Nugae Antiquae*, II, 21n.

grandfather, a shrewd Yorkshireman who had settled his family in Grimsby and linked their fortunes with the expanding commercial activity of that Lincolnshire town.

The Whitgifts belonged to that vigorous and increasing middle class before whose eyes the social and economic changes of the Tudor age opened new horizons of position and power. From these "new people," as well the substantial yeomanry and prosperous gentry of the countryside as the influential merchants and lawyers of the towns, the servants of the Tudor monarchy were drawn. Here were the people in whom national loyalty and personal ambition combined to identify both their prosperity and that of the nation with the monarchy of King Henry VIII. Here were the people whose sons in their maturity fashioned the glorious splendour of the Elizabethan age—Bacon, Cecil, Frobisher, Drake, Marlowe, Spenser, Shakespeare, Parker, Whitgift—names that call to mind the pageant of England's first greatness in the modern world.

How far the Whitgifts were affected by the challenge that was offered to some of the claims of the Church on the eve of the Reformation can only be conjectured. There is no evidence of their connection with the "known men" or the "secret multitude of professors" who maintained something of the Lollard tradition despite the vigilance of the ecclesiastical authorities. Yet they belonged to the class that supported Tyndale, Frith, and the other early English reformers. Henry Whitgift's ships may have had no part with those of the London merchants in flooding England with Lutheran literature, but he was surely aware of the activities of his colleagues in the south. Whether tinged with heresy or not, a sturdy anti-clericalism was characteristic of the "new people." Aroused by the Church's exorbitant financial exactions

and coercive jurisdiction, it was expressed in a deep resentment of the powers and privileges of the clerical order. The
restlessness of Richard Hunne and his friends in London
was undoubtedly reproduced on a suitable provincial scale
in all the eastern ports. It was the extent of this anti-clericalism, reinforced by a vigorous national self-consciousness,
that constituted the chief force on which Henry VIII relied
to carry the country with him in the first stages of the
Reformation. The Whitgifts may not have read *A Glasse of
the Truthe,* a tract widely circulated in the year of John's
birth, arguing England's need of a male heir in the Tudor
line and articulating the resentment of Englishmen against
a foreign papal interference in matters that pertained to the
security of the realm, but its sentiments were probably theirs.

The identification of the Whitgifts with the causes of
their King, however, moves out of the area of conjecture in
the figure of Robert Whitgift, the merchant's brother, since
1525 Abbot of the small but ancient house of Augustinian
Canons at Wellow-by-Grimsby. Enthusiastically devoted to
the new learning, Robert Whitgift's views seems to have
approached those of his more famous contemporary, Thomas
Cranmer. He had read over the Holy Scriptures again and
again, he said, and could find no warrant for the papal pretensions there.[4] Zealous in the cause of the national Church,
and not averse to reforms in matters of religion as well, the
Abbot of Wellow was to exert considerable influence upon
the mind of the child at whose birth he rejoices with his
kinsmen in the spring of this momentous year 1532.

Between 1529 and 1536 a long series of convocational
acts and parliamentary statutes extinguished papal authority
in England, and effectively asserted the ecclesiastical su-

[4] Paule, p. 3.

premacy of the Crown. In these six and a half years the most important Parliament in English history, its anti-clerical temper skillfully manipulated by Thomas Cromwell and the King, passed those "divers good laws and statutes" in which the constitutional doctrine of Tudor England respecting the Crown and the Church was embodied. In them also the English Reformation was launched upon its unique course, and the principles that undergirded the later Elizabethan establishment that Whitgift knew received enunciation. At almost any point the activity of the Reformation Parliament might be termed "decisive," yet in the year of Whitgift's birth there is a crisis in events that lays claim to peculiar importance. On the 15th of May 1532 the Convocation of the Clergy made its famous submission to the King. The next day Thomas More resigned his office, laying down the Great Seal. He saw the action of Convocation as a revolutionary step away from the unity of Christendom to the establishment of a national Church. However we may differ with More on some points of judgment, we can readily accept his conviction that the submission was of immense significance.

Few documents are as repetitive and confusing to students as the formidable mass of Henrician ecclesiastical legislation. But on close examination a pattern appears that is at once strikingly simple and audaciously revolutionary. So neatly are the successive steps in the formation of a national Church linked with the course of the King's suit for the annulment of his marriage, that historians have been unable to decide how far the pattern reflects a preconceived design, and how far opportunism, the pressure of events, and even unexpected success shaped the course of the movement once it had gathered momentum. In any case, the achievement of Henry's government was nothing less than the nationalization of the Catholic Church. Two bold strokes effected this radical constitutional change. The first, delivered in 1532, brought the Tudor monarchs a power over the Church that none of their medieval predecessors had enjoyed. Yielding to Henry's pressure, Convocation surrendered its legislative independence in the submission of the clergy. Henceforth, Convocation agreed, new canons would not be enacted without royal permission, nor promulgated without the assent of the Crown. Further, all existing ecclesiastical laws, some of which were described as "much prejudicial to your prerogative royal" and others as "onerous to your Highness' subjects," were to be submitted to the scrutiny and judgment of a royal commission. Only such were to be retained in force as "should stand with God's laws and the laws of your realm . . . your grace's most royal assent and authority once impetrate and fully given to the same."[5]

For over a year Henry had borne the title granted by the clergy when suing for pardon of a breach of *Praemunire* they had acknowledged him "their singular protector, only and supreme lord, and as far as the law of Christ allows, even Supreme Head."[6] The precise meaning of the new royal style was ambiguous, despite the King's explanatory letter to Cuthbert Tunstal, Bishop of Durham. One thing, however, is clear in Henry's references to the ancient ecclesiastical authority of Christian princes and his argument that the words "et cleri anglicani" interpreted the meaning of *ecclesia*

[5] Wilkins, *Concilia,* III, 754. These pledges of Convocation were given statutory form in 25 Henry VIII, c. 19.

[6] "Ecclesiae et cleri anglicani cuius singularem protectorem, unicum et supremum dominum, et quantum per Christi licet, etiam supremum caput." *Ibid.,* III, 742.

in the title. In the sixteenth century the notion of royal supremacy did not involve the subordination of a separate religious institution to the control of a secular government outside its life. The idea of separation of Church and State in this fashion is a modern one; in the Tudor period it was unknown to the overwhelming majority of men. Whatever further meaning was given to royal supremacy, it was at first the extension of the authority of the Crown over a class of persons—the clergy—hitherto privileged in their activities and partially exempt from the ordinary law, possessing a legislative independence subject only to the papal jurisdiction.[7] Tunstal, Gardiner, and others among Henry's conservative bishops could accept this extension of the Crown's power.

Whatever the implications of the titular supremacy, by the terms of the submission the authority of the Crown was more amply defined at the expense of the legislative and judicial independence of the Church. A long step was taken towards the realization of an undivided civil sovereignty that finally swept away the medieval principle of two separate powers, the *sacerdotium* and the *regnum,* on whose harmonious division of sovereignty the good order of a Christian commonwealth had hitherto been thought to rest. Thus it is said that the last independent action of the Henrician Convocation was the surrender of its legislative autonomy. In actual fact this autonomy was little enough in the subordination of the western Church to the papal system. There is a rough approach to truth in the familiar

[7] See the King's letter to Tunstal, known as "Henry VIII's Defense of his Supremacy." *Cabala, Sine Scrinia Sacra,* pp. 244-8. Reprinted in *Records of the Northern Convocation,* pp. 221-32. For Tunstal's inquiries see *Concilia,* III, 745.

comment that what happened was that a Church which for four hundred years had been subject to intermittent papal interference now embarked upon four centuries of intermittent royal and parliamentary interference. On the practical level it makes very little difference whether ecclesiastical authority is exerted by royal injunction or legatine decree. But on the constitutional level what happened in Convocation made an enormous difference.

The enforcement of this submission was the first of the two revolutionary acts, the decisive step between the grant of the ambiguous title "Supreme Head" and the *Act of Supremacy* by which Parliament declared

the King's Majesty justly and rightfully is and ought to be the supreme head of the Church of England, and so is recognized by the Clergy of this Realm in their Convocations; yet nevertheless for corroboration and confirmation thereof, and for increase of virtue in Christ's Religion within this Realm of England, and to repress and extirp all errors, heresies, and other enormities and abuses heretofore used in the same, Be it enacted by authority of this present Parliament that the King our sovereign Lord, his heirs and successors, Kings of this Realm, shall be taken, accepted, and reputed the only supreme head in earth of the Church of England . . .

Our said Sovereign Lord, his heirs and successors, Kings of this Realm, shall have full power and authority from time to time to visit, repress, redress, reform, order, correct, restrain and amend all such errors, heresies, abuses, offenses, contempts and enormities, what so ever they be, which by any manner spiritual authority or jurisdiction ought or may lawfully be reformed, repressed, ordered, redressed . . .[8]

[8] 25 Henry VIII, c. 1. *Statutes,* III, 492. The statute omitted the qualification "quantum per Christi licet."

The second revolutionary stroke, completing the pattern to be found in the Henrician legislation, was the successful extirpation of papal power in England. By it, as is evident in the statute quoted above, the largest measure of ecclesiastical jurisdiction hitherto belonging to the Pope was transferred to the supremacy of a monarch already master of the national Church. "We are, by the suffrance of God, King of England, and the Kings of England in time past never had any superior but God." So declaimed Henry VIII to an assemblage of bishops and nobles gathered to discuss the issues in the Standish case. Cited before Convocation for his defense of a statute that reduced the privileges of benefit of clergy, Standish of the Greyfriars had appealed to the King, supported by the temporal lords and judges. Upon a suggestion that the matter be referred to the Pope, Henry uttered his rebuke. "Know, therefore," he continued, "that we will maintain the rights of the crown in this matter like our progenitors."[9] That was in 1515. If then Henry's remarks sounded like the fulsome exaggerations of a youthful Renaissance prince, eighteen years later they accurately described the prerogatives of a Tudor monarch.

It is evident from a study of English constitutional history that what brought the Tudor monarchy a sharp increase in power was the successful nationalization of the Church under control of the Crown. The chief limitations upon royal power in the Middle Ages were imposed by the local jurisdictions of the feudal nobility and the independent sovereignty of the Church. For centuries these curbed the pretensions of the central monarchical power. During the

[9] Pickthorn, *Early Tudor Government Henry VIII*, p. 117. See also Maynard Smith, *Pre-Reformation England*, pp. 83-90.

fifteenth century, however, the remaining vestiges of the old aristocratic power largely disappeared, greatly strengthening the civil authority of the Crown. When under Henry VIII the citadel of ecclesiastical authority fell, the medieval division of powers gave way to the inclusion of all within the *regnum*. The regal authority of the Tudors came finally to differ in kind as well as in degree from that of those Plantagenet "progenitors" whom Henry was so fond of invoking. He and his children exercised a kind of sovereignty which no medieval prince had remotely claimed, at least since the general acceptance of Hildebrandine principles in Catholic Christendom. Despite all the reference to Henry II made in the years of the revolutionary legislation, the royal opponent of Thomas Becket never dreamed of wielding the ecclesiastical power with which Cromwell's statutes clothed his distant successor. The maintenance of the rights of "the Kings of England in time past," to use Henry's phrase, was displayed now in a claim to all sovereignty rather than a dispute over contested areas of a divided jurisdiction.

Yet it was precisely this constant reference to the past that became the significant element in the success of the Tudor constitutional revolution. Neither in the subjugation of the clergy nor in the denial of papal jurisdiction do we find any suggestion of a *new* authority appropriated to the Crown. On the contrary, royal supremacy was expressly affirmed to be a right and pre-eminence due unto the King by the laws of God, and recognized by the prelates and clergy of the realm in their synods. Such is the language of the legislation against the Pope. Only by the misguided suffrance of those same "progenitors" did the "foreign pretended power and usurped authority of the Bishop of Rome, by some called the Pope," unrightfully diminish the ancient prerogatives of the English "Imperial Crown."[10]

Nowhere is this appeal to the past more plainly enunciated than in the statute that for all practical purposes terminated the papal jurisdiction, the *Act in Restraint of Appeals* of 1533. The preamble of the statute affirmed that

by divers sundry old authentic histories and chronicles it is manifestly declared and expressed that this Realm of England is an Empire, and so hath been accepted in the world, governed by one Supreme Head and King having the dignity and royal estate of the Imperial Crown of the same, unto whom a body politic compact of all sorts and degrees of people, divided in terms and by names of Spirituality and Temporality, be bounden and owe to bear next to God a natural and humble obedience.[11]

The significant word is *empire*—or as we should say today, a nation-state, fully self-sufficient in its single sovereignty. In this nation-state the King, having the dignity of the "Imperial Crown," is furnished by the goodness of Almighty God with plenary and entire authority and jurisdiction. It is the responsibility of this monarch, therefore, to render justice to all manner of subjects within his realm, in all causes "without restraint or provocation to any foreign princes or potentates of the world."[12] Repeatedly, the act

---

[10] See the *Dispensations Act* of 1534. 25 Henry VIII. c. 21, and the *Act Against the Papal Authority* of 1536. 28 Henry VIII. c. 10. *Statutes*, III, 464; 663.

[11] 24 Henry VIII. c. 12. *Statutes*, III, 427-9.

[12] This appeal to the ancient "imperial" character of the realm was reflected in the attitude of some of the Henricians to the Canon Law. An Act of 1543 directed that all ecclesiastical laws "not being repugnant, contrariant, or derogatory to the laws or statutes of the Realm, nor to the prerogatives of the Regal Crown of the same" were to continue in force, being retained as

asserts, kings in the past have sought to defend the prerogatives of "the said Imperial Crown" and its "jurisdictions spiritual and temporal" from "the annoyance as well of the See of Rome as from the authority of other foreign potentates attempting the diminution or violation thereof."[13]

The statute then ordains that certain causes, hitherto appealed to the court of Rome, shall be

from henceforth heard, examined, discussed; clearly, finally, and definitively adjudged and determined within the King's jurisdiction and authority and not elsewhere, in such Courts Spiritual and Temporal of the same as the natures, conditions, and qualities of the causes . . . shall require.

As the causes enumerated were such as to abolish the Pope's juridical power, the breach with Rome was virtually complete.

The importance of the *Act in Restraint of Appeals* is hard to exaggerate. The singular thing is that it purported, in Pickthorn's phrase, "to make nothing, only to establish what once had been, what always should have been, and what alone properly was."[14] The constitutional revolution was not

---

"accustomed and used here in the Church of England." 35 Henry VIII. c. 16. *Statutes,* III, 976. The statutory phrases echo the theory of Standish and others that what was left of the *Corpus Juris Canonici,* having derived its original force from acceptance by Englishmen, was to be allowed because long observance in England had given it the authority of customary law. See *The Canon Law of the Church of England,* pp. 45-7. The question of the novelty of this theory is still argued despite the celebrated controversy of Maitland and Stubbs.

[13] The reference is to the 14th century anti-papal legislation, including the statutes of *Provisors* and *Praemunire.* See Tanner, *Tudor Constitutional Documents,* p. 42.

[14] *Early Tudor Government Henry VIII,* p. 202.

only over; it was reassuringly arrayed in the garments of ancient national tradition. In fact, it was no revolution at all, only the restoration to the Crown of those "great and inviolable grants of jurisdiction given by God immediately to Emperors, Kings, and Princes" which had been temporarily lost by the iniquitous papal usurpation.[15]

Such was the doctrine expressed in the statutes. To regard this as a tissue of historical self-deception only limits our understanding of the mind of the Tudor monarchs and their supporters. If men believed this interpretation of their history—and there seems no doubt that the vast majority did so—our search for the impelling reasons for that belief must be conducted not only amid their grievances with the papal system and the ecclesiastical institution, but also in the record of their history itself.

There is no longer any doubt that the medieval English Church was the faithful daughter of the Holy See. The question is rather one of that vantage point from which the temper of the medieval Church is to be gauged. The sturdy resistance offered by the Norman and Angevin kings to the extension of papal temporal sovereignty, and which again intermittently characterized relations with Rome in the fourteenth century, could easily be read in a new age as providing a basis for the assertion of the "imperial" character of the English Crown. Maitland's remark about those who liked to regard the Church of England as "Anglican" before the Reformation and "Catholic" afterwards is, however, meaningless unless there is some truth of which it is an exaggeration. The truth is that the old anti-papal legislation cited in the statute of 1533 bears witness to a peculiar temper or

[15] See the *First Succession Act* of 1534. 25 Henry VIII. c. 22. *Statutes,* III, 472.

spirit in medieval England. A growing national self-consciousness left its mark upon the ecclesiastical provinces that shared the insularity and territorial coherence of the island kingdom. The local peculiarity of the medieval English Church seems to have been the achievement of a singularly effective adjustment to the national life. Within that adjustment practical working arrangements were gradually devised to cover those areas where the conflict of spiritual and temporal authority might have been acute. The significant point is that in the long run the experience of these compromises and working arrangements shaped the minds of men more than the conflicting theoretic claims which they covered.

By the sixteenth century this adjustment of Church and nation was so deeply embedded in the English tradition that it carried the ecclesiastical institution virtually intact through the storms of the Reformation. Just as the English monarchy had succeeded, in the course of four centuries or more, in so relating its powers to the nation on all levels of political life that it exercised a control which enabled the Crown to nationalize the Church under a new constitutional doctrine, so also the Church was sufficiently involved in the national life that a reversal of its previous relation to the State could be effected without destroying the structure or continuity of its institutional life. Here one may well have uncovered the background against which all the unique elements of the Anglican Reformation appear in sharp outline.

In brief summary, the nationalization of the Catholic Church under the doctrine of royal supremacy was the achievement of the government of Henry VIII, and the principles secured in the legislation survived to form the foundations of the Elizabethan settlement. The scene of this revolution was the new political atmosphere of the Renaissance in which the modern civil state was born. The agent of the change was the only monarchy in Europe so firmly intrenched in the national life as to overturn the constitutional doctrine of centuries without civil war. The force of the revolution was derived from the combination of economic, political, and religious challenges that were simultaneously offered to the old order of Christian society. Finally, the overwhelming success of the Henrician revolution was inseparable from its appeal to history and the maintenance of the traditional faith and practice of Catholicism. Henry's uncompromising orthodoxy was as reassuring as the theory of the restoration of the powers of the Crown from papal usurpation.

The two factors that contributed decisively to the success of the Henrician achievement—an historical justification of the principle of royal supremacy and the continuity of the old patterns of faith and practice—require further exploration if we are to estimate correctly their hold upon men of Whitgift's generation. However modified by the religious changes in the reign of Edward VI or by the ecclesiastical policy of Queen Elizabeth, they continued to be the ground upon which the final success of the Tudor settlement rested. Ineed, in one form or another they have played a large part in Anglican apologetic for four centuries.

The appeal to the past in Henry's reign did not stop with the statutory references to England's national tradition. On the contrary, it was rapidly widened beyond those limits and given almost universal application by the episcopal defenders of the King's powers. Royal supremacy was maintained as both scriptural and anciently exercised by Christian princes. The kings of Israel were the Lord's Anointed; the

New Testament made it plain that God "doth garnish this world so that dominion and authority pertain only to princes"; and a long line of rulers in Byzantine Rome and Saxon England were accepted as God's vicars on earth.[16]

Stephen Gardiner, Bishop of Winchester and among the most staunchly conservative of Henry's bishops, wrote,

> Surely I see no cause why any man should be offended, that the king is called the head of the church of England, rather than the head of the realm of England . . . seeing the church of England consisteth of the same sorts of people at this day, that are comprised in this word realm of whom the king is called the head: shall he not, being called the head of the realm of England, be also the head of the same men when they are named the church of England?[17]

So runs the well-known quotation from *De vera obedientia,* the classic Tudor defense of the royal supremacy. Gardiner's argument is simple and direct. "The royal supremacy is no new thing. The kings of Israel exercised it; so did the Roman emperors; so did the ancient kings of England. To call the King Supreme Head in Earth of the Church of England is merely expressing an existing right in plain words."[18] Similar appeals to scripture and the history of the Christian Roman Empire characterized the *Oratio* of Richard Sampson of Chichester,[19] Richard Foxe's *De vera*

[16] See Henry's letter to James IV of Scotland rehearsing the papal usurpation of the prerogatives of Christian princes from the Merovingian Childeric to John of England. Strype, *Memorials,* I, ii, LXIII.

[17] *De vera obedientia* (Roane ed.), fos. xviii^v-xix.

[18] Muller, *Gardiner,* p. 61.

[19] *Oratio quae docet hortatur admonet omnes potissimum Anglos regiae dignitati cum primis ut obediant, etc.,* 1533.

differentia[20] and the exposition that Tunstal and John Stokesley composed for the benefit of Reginald Pole,[21] as well as the tracts of other defenders of England's constitutional revolution.

What were the dominating influences at work in the minds of these men? The question frequently exercises historians of the period, though often their judgment is shaped in part by the presuppositions with which they approach the problem. It is no longer possible seriously to maintain that in these writings there is a defense patched together in cowardly subservience to royal tyranny. Nor is it enough to trace their views entirely to the influence of political writings like the *Defensor Pacis* of Marsiglio of Padua, a fourteenth-century imperialist tract translated into English by order of Thomas Cromwell in 1533. Marsiglio's work played a large part in shaping Henrician opinion, but the circumstances of the sixteenth century imposed their own modifying conditions upon political doctrines enunciated two centuries earlier.[22]

More persuasive is the argument that in this defense of the supremacy there emerges a theory of the divine right of kings. Here, it is said, is that political doctrine of divine right, framed by the Reformation monarchies partly as a

[20] *Opus eximium de vera differentia regiae potestatis et ecclesiasticae, etc.,* 1534.

[21] 1537. Reprinted in Knight, *Erasmus,* App. lxvi. For Tunstal's correspondence with Pole see Sturge, *Tunstal,* pp. 205-10.

[22] The *Defensor Pacis* is discussed at length in the standard edition of Previte-Orton and the newer work of Alan Gewirth. See also Baumer, *Early Tudor Theory of Kingship,* pp. 44-6, 53. Roman Catholic historians are sometimes ready to deal uncritically with the influence of what Hughes calls "perhaps the most mischievous book of the whole Middle Ages." *Reformation in England,* I, 331 ff. Cf. Constant, *Reformation in England,* I, 127n, and Janelle, *Vielle du Schisme,* pp. 250 ff.

bulwark against the pretensions of theocracy, either papal or Reformed, and partly to place the civil authority of the king on unassailable ground. The only difficulty with this contention is that these early Tudor writings will not yield any doctrine of divine right in its developed and familiar form.[23] The proper historical background of the theory of divine right is the world of post-Tridentine Roman claims and Calvinist theocratic principles. Doubtless the seventeenth-century formulations of divine right include in their ancestry some reference to the views of Henry's apologists, but to call the monarch "the Lord's Anointed" is not to say with James I that he is "the living, breathing image of God on earth."[24]

The truth seems to be that two concepts dominated the minds of the Henricians, each clothing royal supremacy with significance. Both convictions were due in part to the exposure of these men to the humanism of the Erasmian tradition, and to the interest in legal studies that brought Constantinian and Byzantine notions of the powers of Christian princes and the claim of civil law before them with a new force. The first concept was that of the nature and function of the princely office in a Christian society. The monarch was less hedged with divine right than endowed with God-given responsibilities. The concern of the Henricians is with the sacred obligations of the Catholic prince, reigning by the authority of God in and over a state still assumed in a heritage from medieval thought to be essentially a religious society. Therein the prince exercises under God spiritual functions as well as temporal responsibilities. Indeed, these cannot be sundered. To his hands is com-

---

[23] See Figgis, *Divine Right Of Kings*, pp. 5-6.
[24] Whitney, "Erastianism and Divine Right," *H.L.Q.* (1939), ii, p. 396n. Whitney's article contains a number of illuminating suggestions on this point.

mitted the solemn duty of administering justice and maintaining truth in all causes, civil and ecclesiastical alike. He
guards the spiritual health as well as the temporal welfare
of his people. If the constitutional revolution terminated the
old divided sovereignty and brought all within the scope of
the *regnum,* it did not, in the minds of Tudor men, secularize
that power. Rather, it laid upon the Christian prince the total
obligation of governance.

Gardiner asserts the king to be the vicegerent of God, set
to reign by His authority. He is entrusted with the Lord's
vineyard, charged not only with human matters but also
those divine; he is so to minister unto the body of the people
that he may be ready to meet the reckoning that God will
one day demand of him.[25] While similar sentiments are
expressed by all the Henricians, the authoritative summary
of this view of the nature of the princely office and the
function of the monarch in a Christian society is given in
the *King's Book* of 1543. The exposition of the ninth article
of the Creed declares that

as all Christian people, as well spiritual and temporal, be bound
to believe, honour, and obey our Saviour Jesus Christ, the only
Head of the universal church, so likewise they be, by his com-
mandment, bound to honour and obey, next unto himself, Christian kings and princes, which be the head governors under him
in the particular churches, to whose office it appertaineth not
only to provide for the tranquillity and wealth of their subjects
in temporal and worldly things . . . but also to foresee that
within their dominions such ministers be ordained and appointed

---

[25] *De vera obedientia,* fos. xxix^v-xxx. Emphasis upon the responsibility of
the Christian monarch was present from the beginning of this literature. See
Tyndale, *Obedience of Christen man, etc.,* fos. lxxxiiii,^{v} clxiii.^{v} It continued
to be present throughout the Tudor period. See Elizabeth's "Golden Speech"
of 1601, D'Ewes, *Journals,* pp. 659-60.

in their churches as can and will truly and purely set out the true doctrine of Christ and teach the same, and see the commandments of God well observed and kept, to the wealth and salvation of their souls.[26]

This emphasis on the duty of the subject to honor the authority of God in His prince leads us to the second dominating conviction of the apologists for the royal supremacy, the inevitable concomitant of the first. There is a "true obedience," to use Gardiner's term, divinely-enjoined upon all men, a primary Christian duty. Disobedience to constituted authority is a disastrous, even, according to John Cheke, an unnatural crime. Thus Bishop Tunstal proclaims in a sermon that

By the word of God, all men ought to obey . . . princes of all sorts. St. Peter doth plainly teach us in the second chapter of his First Epistle, saying, Be ye subject to every human creature for God's sake, whether it be the king as chief head, or dukes, or governors, as sent from God . . . for so is the will of God.

And the Bishop reminds his hearers that kings "be ministers of God whose place in their governance they do represent, so that unto them all men must obey."[27]

A striking exposition of this "true obedience" is contained in Gardiner's letter to Martin Bucer. The theme of the tract is that contempt of human laws is the contempt of God Himself. Gardiner writes

It were too odious to place on a par things human and divine, and still more to give the first place to those which are human. Therefore it must be observed, that the contempt of human

---

[26] *A Necessary Doctrine and Erudition for any Christian Man,* f. iv.ᵛ "The King's Book" is reprinted in Lloyd, ed., *Formularies of Faith,* and Lacey, *The King's Book.*

[27] *A Sermon of Cuthbert Bysshop of Duresme, etc.,* 1539, p. 31.

laws implies injury offered to the majesty of God, in so far as he deemed it necessary that man should obey to men; and that every soul should be subjected to the higher powers; to such an extent that whoso despiseth a man endowed with power, despiseth not man, but God . . . I say that disobedience is the greatest and most infamous crime, which carries with it many other faults, and opens a door to all profligacy. Therefore the prince's first care must be, for the glory of God in whose place he stands, to maintain obedience.[28]

This claim of Law, embodying the will of the nation and consecrated by the sanction of the Christian monarch, is here recognized as a claim not only upon outward allegiance but upon Christian conscience as well. Indeed, the inward allegiance is the "true obedience." "The civil magistrate is ordained and allowed of God," declared Article 36 of the *Forty-Two Articles* of 1553, "wherefore we must obey him, not only for fear of punishment, but also for conscience sake."[29] Again and again this conviction finds expression in the half-century that follows the breach with Rome, and it is sometimes portrayed today as a degrading and soul-destroying allegiance precisely because the citadel of conscience itself is surrendered. Here, it is said, the will of God is subordinated to the whim of the king, the freedom of private judgment lost, the independent claim of truth rejected, and the autonomy of religion sacrificed. Such easy assumptions scarcely do justice to the Henricians. The historical context of the age must not be ignored nor the given theological background forgotten. There were implicit limits to the "true obedience." It was meaningless apart from the

---

[28] *Contemptum humanae legis, etc.,* Janelle, *Obedience in Church and State,* pp. 174 ff.

[29] Cardwell, *Synodalia,* I ,31. Cf. "An Exhortation to Obedience," *Certaine sermons appoynted, etc.* [The Book of Homilies, 1547].

framework of the Catholic faith and the concept of the
place of the Christian prince in a Christian society. Tunstal
made this significant point quite clear to Pole in 1536.

You suppose [wrote Tunstal] that the King's grace . . . in
taking upon him the title of Supreme Head . . . intendeth to
separate his church of England from the unity of the whole body
of Christendom . . . You do err too far. His full purpose and
intent is to see the laws of Almighty God purely and sincerely
kept and observed in his realm, and not to separate himself
or his realm any wise from the unity of Christ's Catholic
Church.[30]

Tunstal's phrases are echoed in the statutes and formularies. The *Act in Restraint of Appeals* required the clergy
to continue their spiritual ministrations "as Catholic and
Christian men owe to do." The *Act in Conditional Restraint
of Annates* proclaimed that "our said Sovereign Lord the
King, and all his natural subjects as well spiritual as temporal, be as obedient, devout, catholic, and humble children
of God and Holy Church as any people be within any
realm."[31] The *Dispensations Act* declared plainly that there
was no intent "to decline or vary from the congregation of
Christ's Church in any things concerning the very articles of
the Catholic Faith of Christendom."[32] Finally, the *King's
Book* reinforces the point. The unity of Catholic Christendom, it is declared, does not depend upon the authority of
the Bishop of Rome, but "is conserved and kept by the help

---

[30] Burnet, *Reformation*, VI, 178. The point that England had not broken
away from the true unity of Catholic Christendom was made by nearly all
the pamphleteers. See *De vera obedientia* and *Si sedes illa*, Janelle, *Obedience*,
pp. 36, 114.

[31] 23 Henry VIII. c. 20. *Statutes*, III, 386.

[32] 25 Henry VIII. c. 21. *Statutes*, III, 469.

and assistance of the Holy Spirit of God, in retaining and maintaining of such doctrine and profession of Christian faith, and the true obedience of the same, as is taught by the scripture and doctrine apostolic." The particular churches of Christendom are rightly called "Catholic" when they "profess and teach the faith and religion of Christ, according to the scripture and apostolic doctrine."[33]

There was the frame of reference for the "true obedience." There also were the implicit limits. For the Henricians the appeal to history and the continuity of the traditional faith and practice of Catholic Christendom were inseparably linked. The powers of the Christian prince and the duty of conscientious obedience to his laws were both set within the context of the profession of Catholic faith as taught by the scripture and the doctrine apostolic.[34]

Perhaps it will now be apparent that these Henrician ideas are to be strained at two points by the course of subsequent events, and at both of them the whole structure of Tudor politico-ecclesiastical theory will ultimately break down. The more remote collapse, and one beyond the scope of this present study, comes with the final disappearance of the idea of the state as essentially a religious society and the corresponding secularization of the *regnum*. Then Erastianism becomes first the intolerable doctrine of Hobbes' *Leviathan*, and finally a set of ideas quite irrelevant to the modern state.

The nearer strain, however, is imposed by the gradual modification of the religious framework surrounding the

---

[33] *A Necessary Doctrine and Erudition*, f. iii.

[34] *Contemptum humanae legis*, Janelle, *Obedience*, p. 176. See also *Certaine sermons appoynted*, T. l.ʳ It is clear in the homily on obedience that if the monarch's commands are contrary to the commandments of God the duty is not "true obedience" but non-resistance.

principles of "Christian principality" and "true obedience" by the doctrinal changes of the reformers. This is that point at which the political revolution and the religious changes, often presented as successive and disconnected stages in the English Reformation, reveal their essential link. The achievement of the one is inseparable from the extent of the other. What is the true Catholic faith, according to the "scripture and apostolic doctrine"? That was the question ultimately placed squarely before those who embraced the Henrician revolution. Can the Catholic faith be stretched to include the continental Protestant doctrines that influenced the Edwardian formularies? The only answer that Stephen Gardiner could give led to his imprisonment in the Tower. On the other hand, that he cannot part with the convictions of a lifetime and return to papal Catholicism is the bitter decision that takes Thomas Cranmer to death at the stake. In both men the strain is apparent at the point of the true doctrine of Christ and His Church under which the concepts of the supremacy of the Christian prince and the obedience of his subjects have their only claim upon conscience.

The institutional continuity of the English Church through the reigns of the earlier Tudor monarchs made these tensions the heritage of the Elizabethans. The task laid upon Whitgift and his contemporaries was that of maintaining, against Papalist and Puritan alike, the constitutional doctrine of Henry's national Catholicism within a religious framework that by 1559 had received considerable modification in the areas of faith and practice.

But at the moment the problems confronting Tudor Anglicanism in the reign of Elizabeth lie hidden in the future. Until he was fifteen years old John Whitgift lived under the influences of the Henrician settlement. He saw

his elders nod approvingly as they turned over the pages
of *A Litel Treatise ageynste the mutterynge of some papistes
in corners.*[35] He heard men spell out the proclamations on
the church doors. He listened to the preachers bid prayers
for "Our Sovereign Lord King Henry VIII, being immediately next under God the only and supreme Head of this
Catholic Church of England." In these early days, however,
what touched him with any lasting consequences seems to
have come through his uncle, the Abbot of Wellow.

When in 1536 Henry's hand fell upon the religious houses
of the land, the Reformation brought its first change into
the circumstances of the Whitgifts. Wellow Abbey, in consequence of the statute that suppressed all monastic houses
numbering fewer than twelve occupants and possessing less
than £200 of annual income, was surrendered before
Michaelmas of that year.[36] Robert Whitgift and his canons,
having sworn the oath of supremacy two years earlier, were
not disposed to resist the King's commissioners. They accepted a fate that could not have imposed any very severe
hardship. All received generous pensions, somewhat above
average, that of the Abbot being no less than £16 a year,
approximately £350 in our money today.[37] The possessions
of the Abbey having been granted to Sir Thomas Heneage,
a local Grimsby magnate and friend of the Whitgifts, Robert
Whitgift was allowed to remain in the monastic buildings
with the few small sons of prominent neighboring families
whose early education he had undertaken.

[35] Pocock, *Records,* II, 539 ff.
[36] 27 Henry VIII. c. 28. *Statutes,* III, 575. Wellow had eleven residents
and insufficient annual income. See the *Valor Ecclesiasticus* (ed. 1821), IV,
67.
[37] *VCH, Lincolnshire,* II, 161-2. Baskerville, *English Monks,* pp. 153, 256,
293 ff.

To this tutelage John Whitgift was entrusted as soon as he was old enough to learn. Reading and writing, the rudiments of Latin, a little music, and the sacred studies of the *Primer* were the limits of formal study at Wellow. But the former Abbot's keen interest in reform made it almost certain that some systematic knowledge of the scriptures was undertaken, undoubtedly in that "whole Bible of the largest volume" lately ordered by the King's *Injunctions* to be read "as that which is the very lively word of God, that every Christian man is bound to embrace, believe, and follow if he look to be saved."[38]

Prepared by the instruction of his uncle, in 1545 young Whitgift entered St. Anthony's School in London, an ancient foundation that had numbered Thomas More and John Colet among its pupils. He lodged in Paul's Yard with his father's sister Isabel, wife of one of the Cathedral vergers whose practice it was to board schoolboys. Twice daily John tramped the crowded streets halfway across the City to French Lane and back, bickering with the apprentices and brawling with the rival boys of St. Paul's School. Ten hours a day the shadow of the birch kept him at his lessons, learning slowly and laboriously at the dictation of the master. Books were comparatively few; memory was expanded to house the treasures of the mind. It was a primitive pedagogy, but one not without principle. "Children know not what they do, much less why they do it, till reason grow into ripeness in them, and therefore in their training they profit more by practice than by knowing why, till they feel the use of reason."[39] So later wrote Richard Mulcaster, a younger contemporary of Whitgift and High Master first at Merchant

[38] Frere and Kennedy, ed., *Visitation Articles and Injunctions,* II, 36.
[39] Oliphant, *Educational Writings of Richard Mulcaster,* p. 239.

Taylors' and then at St. Paul's—and Mulcaster was in many ways enlightened far beyond the ordinary schoolmaster of his age.[40]

In the Tudor schoolroom Latin was not only the keystone, but virtually the whole arch of learning. Its syntax disciplined the mind; its literature stretched the imagination; its histories provided an introduction to politics and government. One after another the classical authors were set before Whitgift. "I went to school, forsooth," said Robert Laneham, who was possibly in Whitgift's classes, "both at Paul's and also at Saint Anthony's. In the fifth form, past Esop Fables . . . read Terence . . . and began with my Virgil. I could conster and parse with the best of them . . ."[41] But Laneham was a bit of a braggart. He claimed four languages, considerable skill at music and grace in dancing— in fact, he admitted, "nothing comes amiss to me!" It is quite clear that as the boys were introduced to a long procession of ancient writers—Aesop, Terence, Virgil, Caesar or Sallust, Horace, Ovid—some of them acquired little more than the memorable tags that are known today as "quotable quotes." With the classics went a smattering of late Latin Christian authors, Erasmus, and the *Bucolica* of Baptista Mantuanus, Shakespeare's "good old Mantuan" of the scene in *Love's Labour's Lost* where the learning of Holofernes the schoolmaster is parodied. These completed the list, save for the famous grammar of William Lyly and the helps of John Stanbridge. Any time left was divided between the first principles of arithmetic, and religious instruction in the

---

[40] The imaginative and original suggestions of Mulcaster may be seen in his *Positions,* 1581, and his *Elementarie,* 1582. See Rowse, *England of Elizabeth,* pp. 503 ff.

[41] Nichols, *Progresses of Queen Elizabeth,* I, 483.

Bible, the articles of faith in the *King's Book,* and the new *King's Primer.*[42]

Our meagre knowledge of Whitgift's experiences in London is disappointing, the more so because his years at St. Anthony's were those of the confusion and change that marked the end of the reign of Henry VIII and the beginning of that of his young son Edward VI.[43] Whitgift might have heard the choir of St. Paul's sing the new English litany on St. Luke's day in 1545, or on the following Whitsunday he might have joined the long procession of civic dignitaries and townsmen who followed Bishop Bonner as he bore the Blessed Sacrament in the full panoply of Henrician Catholicism through the City from the Cathedral to Leadenhall Corner. Did he stand among the throng at Paul's Cross that summer to hear the former Bishop of Salisbury, Dr. Shaxton, acknowledge his heresy in respect to the Sacrament of the Altar and avow his return to the Catholic doctrine? Or when Henry VIII had been laid to rest at Windsor and the Duke of Somerset controlled Edward's Council, did Whitgift hear Bishop Barlow denouncing the images and the ancient ceremonies at that same Cross where fifteen months earlier Shaxton had recanted? And in the spring of 1548 did he receive the Sacrament in both kinds with the English devotions of the new *Order of the Communion?*

One thing at least we know. Touched by the spirit of revolt, the youthful Whitgift bluntly informed his Aunt Isabel that he would no longer attend daily Mass with her.

[42] *The Primer, in Englishe and Latyn, set foorth by the Kjnges majestie & his Clergie, etc.,* 1545. See C. 1ᵛ.

[43] See Wriothesley, *Chronicle,* I, 161, 164, 170; II, 1. *Greyfriar's Chronicle,* p. 55.

Isabel upbraided him angrily. The young saint had turned into a little heretic, and she would not endure him under her roof. Or, at least, that was the way Whitgift remembered it in later years as he sat by the fireside in Lambeth Palace recalling the days of his youth to George Paule, the admiring household officer who was to write the first biography of the archbishop. Did he forget that just at that time business reverses had cut his father's income sharply? Isabel Whitgift may have found heresy hard to endure, but it must have seemed much more difficult if she had to pay for its support. At all events, late in 1548 she packed him off to Grimsby and to continue his studies with the ex-Abbot of Wellow.

By the early summer of 1550 circumstances again made possible the continuance of Whitgift's formal education. Bidding farewell to his birthplace and family, he set out along the eastern road that led through the fens to Cambridge. His destination was the University whose fortunes were so closely linked with the Reformation and whose sons lighted the Tudor firmament like stars. It was a road that carried him to fame in the Master's Lodge of Trinity College, to the Elizabethan episcopate in Hartlebury Castle, and finally to Lambeth and the heavy responsibilities of the archbishopric of Canterbury.

Meanwhile in Cambridge, Roger Ascham, lately returned from Hatfield, had just written to his friend John Sturmius in Strasbourg.

The lady Elizabeth has accomplished her sixteenth year . . . [wrote Ascham] She has the most ardent love of true religion and of the best kind of literature. The constitution of her mind is exempt from female weakness, and she is endued with a masculine power of application. No apprehension can be quicker than her's, no memory more retentive. French and Italian she speaks like English; Latin with fluency . . . Greek, moderately well.[44]

The road that led Whitgift to Cambridge bore him also towards the distinguished pupil of Roger Ascham. In the end his life was linked for twenty years with that of Elizabeth Tudor. The time will come, when the Queen and her archbishop linger beyond their contemporaries in the sunset of the age bearing her name, that she will call him affectionately her "little black husband."[45]

[44] Ascham, *Works*, I, 181.
[45] Peachman, *Compleat Gentleman*, p. 165. *Notes and Queries*, 7th Series, vii, March 23, 1889.

II

THE ELIZABETHAN SETTLEMENT

THE reign of Edward VI is sometimes regarded as an isolated interlude of Protestant experiment in England. It is said that upon the death of Henry VIII, Cranmer, Ridley, Hooper, Latimer, and the other leaders of the reforming party, freed from the restraints of Henry's conservatism, carried the English Church rapidly towards continental Protestant doctrines and orders of worship. In the minority of the Supreme Head, those who hailed him as the "young Josiah" simultaneously dictated the changes made in his name. The authority of the royal supremacy and the "true obedience" it aroused, once meaningful within Catholic faith and practice, were now manipulated by the reforming divines and the members of the Council to the destruction of the ancient pattern of that religious framework itself. While Cranmer and the reformers may have been motivated by a sincere desire to establish the true religion of Christ and His Gospel as they saw it revealed in the Scriptures, no such earnest seeking for truth moved the Protectors and their friends who had seized the power of government. Completely disregarding the ecclesiastical statutes, they attacked and sought to destroy the strength of the Church as a national institution, appropriating to their own purposes its wealth and endowments. Thus, at least in the days of North-umberland's rule, the religious movement for reform was entirely subordinated to the secular aims of a body of men whose view of the relation of Church and State was that of Thomas Cromwell.

The difficulty is not that these generalizations are er-roneous. On the contrary, they contain a large measure of truth. But to marshall the facts in this way suggests that, except for such permanent modifications as were introduced into the liturgy and some areas of popular religious prac-tice in the English Church, the reign of Edward VI can be isolated from the whole stream of events of which it is a part. Furthermore, such treatment leaves us with no adequate understanding of the situations that produced these modi-fications. This, surely, is to impoverish our interpretation of the continuous movement of the Reformation in England.

The distinctive element in the Reformation experience of Englishmen was continuity in nearly all areas of church life. From the troublous days of Henry VIII through the storms of Edwardian controversy and Marian violence the structure of the English Church was preserved intact into the Eliza-bethan age. Convocations met as usual and debated the issues before them, bishops ruled their dioceses in the accus-tomed ways, the ecclesiastical courts still claimed and exer-cised competence in the same manifold areas of men's lives. The whole machinery of the Church's officialdom continued to work, perhaps falteringly at times but never ceasing, per-petuating even the administrative abuses of which the Catholic reformers had complained on the eve of the Refor-mation. And in the parishes, where continuity exercised its strongest influences on men, the patterns of church life re-mained much the same. The people worshipped in churches hallowed by the prayers of their ancestors and surrounded by churchyards where their grandfathers and grandsons alike were laid to rest. They were shepherded, or neglected, by the same clergy; they were themselves charged with the same familiar responsibilities towards the life of the parish. Underneath the liturgical alterations and the modifications in popular cult-practice the deeply embedded tradition of the relation of religion to life persisted. Finally, when what Mackie calls "the hoardings of demolition and the scaffolding of reconstruction" were removed, what was revealed was recognizably continuous with what had always been *Ecclesia Anglicana*.[1] This truth alone should remind us that the reigns of Edward VI and Mary I cannot be set apart from the whole story of Tudor Anglicanism.

By the Henrician constitutional revolution the royal supremacy of the "Imperial Crown" had brought the Church into its place in the fabric of the nation-state. But even before Henry VIII died the problem of the religious unity of Englishmen became the major issue confronting the government. Just as long as men assumed that the State was a Christian society in which a single civil allegiance was inseparable from a uniform religious loyalty, the touchstone of national unity was the problem of the religious framework around the "true obedience." What was the true and Catholic faith taught in the "scripture and apostolic doctrine?" The Henrician statutory assurances that England did not intend to decline or vary from "the very articles of the Catholic Faith of Christendom" were not sufficient to keep Englishmen in a common understanding of those articles—not with the open Bible, the rejection of papal authority, the investigations of the new learning, and the influences of continental reformers beguiling their minds. Hence the long procession of statutes, articles, and injunctions that marked the two

[1] *Earlier Tudors*, p. 569.

decades from 1538 to the accession of Elizabeth. In this
search for formularies that would submerge the religious
differences of men in a single allegiance, the changes in the
reigns of Edward and Mary find their proper place. Four
times an attempt was made to answer the primary question
on which the unity of the nation turned. Four times the
trial failed.

The first of these attempts was made in the *Act of the
Six Articles,* a statute "abolishing diversity in opinions."[2]
Following upon the failure of the *Ten Articles* of 1536 and
the *Bishops' Book* in the next year to achieve their avowed
purpose of ending the disputes on certain doctrinal matters,[3]
the repressive statute of 1539 rehearsed the perils of discord
and variance as contrasted with the benefits of unity and
concord. The *Six Articles Act* was expressly passed to secure
"uniform doctrine of Christ's religion." Yet even the severe
penalties attached to this "whip of six strings" could not
put an end to theological controversy and disorder. Henry
VIII rebuked his Parliament in 1545 in tones alternately
threatening and despairing. He declared to the bishops

I see and hear daily that you of the Clergy preach one against
another, teach one contrary to another, inveigh one against
another without charity or discretion. Some be too stiff in their
old mumpsimus, others be too busy and curious in their new
sumpsimus . . . How can the poor souls live in concord when
you preachers sow amongst them in your sermons debate and
discord? Amend these crimes, I exhort you . . . or else I whom

[2] 31 Henry VIII. c. 14. *Statutes,* III, 739-43. See also a statute of the following year ordering strict obedience to such decisions of the clergy in matters of religion that received royal confirmation. The act plainly expresses
the urgent necessity of finding peace and concord. *Ibid.,* III, 783-4.

[3] The *Ten Articles,* published "to stablish Christian quietness and unity"
are reprinted in the *Concilia,* III, 817-23. For the *Bishop's Book* see Lloyd,
ed. *Formularies of Faith,* pp. 21-211.

God hath appointed His Vicar . . . will see these divisions extinct.

Then, chiding the laity for railing, slandering, and taunting the clergy, the King reminded them that it was not their part to judge doctrine or reprove the teachers.

Although [he continued bitterly] you be permitted to read holy scripture, and to have the word of God in your mother tongue, you must understand that it is licensed you so to do, only to inform your conscience, and to instruct your children and family, and not to dispute . . . I am very sorry to know and hear how irreverently that most precious jewel the word of God is disputed, rhymed, sung and jangled in every ale-house and tavern.[4]

Even Henry could not manage to "see these divisions extinct" or halt the growing incoherence of the religious atmosphere. The Princess Mary and Stephen Gardiner might urge in the next reign that Henry's legislation had secured godly order and quietness; Cranmer and Somerset knew better. In July 1549 the Protector put the point forcibly to Mary when he told her that it was imperative that further action be taken to avoid the parties and divisions with which the realm was threatened by the uncertain situation left by Henry VIII.[5]

Twice in Edward's reign, after the repeal of the *Six Articles Act* and the withdrawal of parliamentary sanction from the *King's Book,* the authorities attempted a settlement that would quiet the doctrinal agitation, now increased by the tolerant policy of Somerset. The first attempt was in the form of the Prayer Book of 1549, established by the *First*

---

[4] *Hall's Chronicle,* pp. 865-6.
[5] Powicke, *Reformation,* p. 78. *Original Letters,* II, 468-73.

Act of Uniformity.[6] Unity was to be secured, not by the enforcement of legislation defining the true doctrine, but through the imposition of liturgical uniformity, reinforced by injunctions, proclamations, and orders in Council, and supported by the persuasions of the newly-authorized *Book of Homilies* and Udall's translation of Erasmus' *Paraphrases of the New Testament.* Plainly the government hoped that under a common experience of worship and the persuasive influence of homiletical instruction, less exacting upon conscience and more ambiguous in expression than statutory enactments defining orthodoxy and heresy, the theological controversy might gradually be controlled. If Cranmer relied on the essentially orthodox character of the Prayer Book and the force of "true obedience" to secure its acceptance by Henrician churchmen, he was not disappointed. Gardiner and the majority of conservative bishops were prepared, however reluctantly, to obey the act.[7] Supported by that much assent the government was prepared to deal firmly with refractory country clergy and the unruly peasants of Devon and Cornwall. The real difficulty was on the other side. The more Protestant-minded reformers, who could approve the settlement only as an *interim* concession, complained bitterly that the old doctrines and usages were perpetuated within the framework of the new service book.[8] Things were far from satisfactory to the continental divines

[6] 2 & 3 Edw. VI. c. 1. *Statutes,* IV, i, 37-9.

[7] Muller, *Gardiner,* p. 188. Constant, *Reformation in England,* II, 87. Day of Chichester refused obedience. Ellis, *Letters,* 3rd Series, III, 303.

[8] *O.L.,* I, 72. Bonner of London was among the chief offenders. See the Council's letters of rebuke. *Concilia,* IV, 34. Cardwell, *Doc. Annals,* I, 78 ff. The government prepared a special set of injunctions to stop these practices, but they appear to have been enforced only within the diocesan injunctions of reformers like Ridley and Hooper. *Visitation Articles,* II, 190-6, 241-5, 279 ff.

who had taken refuge in Edwardian England and where they exerted no little influence upon the course of reform. They found the settlement a "misshapen embryo," resting upon the ambiguities of a Prayer Book that "speaks very obscurely."[9]

Three years later the government tried again. This time the Protestant doctrines were given more central place. Although the first Prayer Book, according to the preamble of the *Second Act of Uniformity,* was "a very godly order . . . for common prayer and the administration of the sacraments . . . agreeable to the word of God and the primitive Church," it had failed to unify the disordered realm.[10] The second Prayer Book, therefore, not only made drastic concessions to reforming opinion, but was reinforced in 1553 by what approximated to a confessional statement in the *Forty-Two Articles.*[11] But the unpopular government of the Duke of Northumberland could not quiet the uproar, even had these formularies been capable of other than a divisive effect. Hooper's provocation of a vestiarian controversy, Ridley's unrestrained iconoclasm, and the fiercely Protestant influence of John Knox had created a breach among the reformers themselves. It was now Archbishop Cranmer's turn to protest. He was exasperated by the arbitrary manner in which the Council ignored Convocation and used Parliament to register the decrees of an unprincipled government in matters of religion. Reform had become simply a useful instrument to the Northumberland tyranny. Gardiner was not the only one to see more clearly the difficulties facing the national Church in a State where the single civil sov-

[9] *O.L.,* I, 351; II, 488. See also II, 481-4; 545-8.
[10] 5 & 6 Edw. VI. c. 1. *Statutes,* IV, i, 130-1.
[11] *Concilia,* IV, 73 ff.

ereignty might become rapidly secularized. There is little evidence that England as a whole was prepared to accept the attempted settlement of 1552-3. On the contrary, only the death of Edward VI a few months later saved the nation from an intensity of factional strife that might well have led to religious war.

One measure of the failure of the Edwardian attempts to secure peace and unity was the wave of popularity on which Mary Tudor was carried to the throne despite Northumberland's desperate effort to alter the lawful succession. It now became the task of the Catholic Queen to solve the problem that vexed the successors of Henry VIII. Mary, at once proclaiming her allegiance to the old faith and reminding men of the "dangers that have grown through diversity of opinion in matters of religion," charged her subjects to live together in charity, abandoning "those new-found devilish terms of papist and heretic," and applying themselves to maintain the tranquillity of the realm. The proclamation gave assurance that the Queen would compel no one to her way of thinking "until such time as further order, by common assent, may be taken."[12]

"Further order" appeared in Mary's *First Statute of Repeal,* dealing with the problem of "the unquietness and much discord," as the statute put it, "in very short time like to grow to extreme peril and utter confusion." By this act all the religious legislation of Edward VI was withdrawn, restoring the ecclesiastical situation of 1547, "the last year of the reign of our late Sovereign Lord King Henry the Eighth."[13] This attempt to put back the clock six years was only a preliminary step to Mary's cherished goal. Nothing

[12] *Concilia,* IV, 86.
[13] 1 Mary, St.2. c. 2. *Statutes,* IV, i, 202.

less than a complete return to the faith and allegiance of her girlhood could satisfy the daughter of Catherine of Aragon. In 1554, after her ill-advised and unpopular marriage with Philip of Spain, the medieval heresy laws were revived and the Church again endowed with its ancient coercive jurisdiction. Within the next year Cardinal Pole, clothed with legatine authority by the Pope, solemnly absolved the nation from the sin of schism, and Parliament passed the *Second Statute of Repeal,* sweeping away all the revolutionary legislation of Henry VIII.[14] England was thus launched upon the fourth unsuccessful attempt to find a settlement of the religious controversy.

The disturbed and uncertain years of Edward VI and Mary were those of John Whitgift's education at Cambridge. Entering Queens' College, he migrated almost at once to Pembroke Hall, matriculating there as a pensioner in the Michaelmas term of 1550. Apparently what took him to Pembroke was a grant of financial assistance in the form of a Bible-clerkship, arranged, according to Paule, by the saintly and earnest reformer John Bradford. Devoted wholeheartedly to the cause of Edwardian Protestantism and one of Foxe's best-loved heroes, Bradford was for a short time Whitgift's tutor. If it is difficult to evaluate the influence of Bradford's religious views upon his pupil, at least one may discern the effects of his high moral ideals and intense personal self-discipline. The severe austerity and self-less, unflagging devotion to duty that marked the whole course of Whitgift's life were beyond doubt fired by sparks caught from the spirit of John Bradford. Whitgift's bitterest enemies

[14] 1 & 2 Philip and Mary. c. 8. *Statutes,* IV, i, 246-54. The acts relating to the dissolution of the monasteries were excepted from the repeal. The statute confirmed the rights of the possessors of former ecclesiastical properties.

never accused him of laxity or successfully challenged the integrity of his moral character. Exemplary in those respects, even today the least sympathetic commentators will admit with Pierce that "he had no love of ease; he was no thrall to the comfort and luxury of his palaces. No folly, no human weakness, no sentimental yielding to the cry of intellectual or physical suffering, no perilous subjugation to woman's beauty or passion, hindered his progress . . . busy he was always; alert, tireless . . ."[15] The Puritans—not Whitgift—are Pierce's heroes, but even he cannot make a fault of the indefatigable and single-minded consecration to his tasks that came at least partly from close association with Bradford at an impressionable age.

Cambridge in the reign of Edward VI was in the throes of change reflecting the general incoherence on the wider English scene. When the Henrician visitation of 1535 altered the face of medieval Cambridge in the suppression of hostels and monastic houses, it changed the academic emphasis as well. The faculty of Canon Law was suppressed; the traditional theological curriculum was modified. With the abolition of the *Sentences* of the old school of commentators, public and private study of the scriptures was prescribed. Henry's professorships—Divinity, Hebrew, Greek, Medicine, Civil Law—reveal the new and more diversified emphasis under which the medieval institution began its transformation to a modern university. As A. L. Rowse has pointed out, here in the colleges may be seen the characteristic Tudor pattern of transition, an early flame of exciting promise and reform followed by the darker years of factional strife and depression in the middle Tudor period, and then the sudden and surprising brightness of the Elizabethan recovery.[16]

---

[15] *Introduction to the Marprelate Tracts*, pp. 111-2.
[16] *England of Elizabeth*, pp. 489 ff.

The decline was evident to some men during Whitgift's early years at Cambridge. The Edwardian commissioners had recently finished their effort, as Ridley described it, "to abolish statutes and ordinances which maintained Papistry, superstition, blindness, and ignorance," and "to establish God's word and good learning."[17] But the success of the visitation was not apparent to Martin Bucer, since 1549 Regius professor of divinity in the University. "By far the greater part of the fellows," he wrote Calvin in despair, "are either most bitter papists, or profligate epicureans, who, as far as they are able, draw over the young men to their way of thinking, and imbue them with an abhorrence of sound Christian doctrine and discipline."[18] The small group of ardent reformers led by Bucer, Bradford, and Grindal made little headway against the influence of Perne, Sedgwick, Young, and the other conservative Heads of colleges. The masters and fellows were deeply entrenched behind the bulwarks of university officialdom. Not readily dislodged, they controlled a large part of university and collegiate administration, exercising a quiet and steady pressure against the reformers. Between the two factions stood the greater number of fellows and scholars, some indifferent to the theological quarrels, others finding them only advantageous to the relaxation of academic standards and discipline.

University life does not change rapidly; Cambridge still moved in the well-worn grooves of the centuries. Whitgift embarked upon the studies of the familiar scheme: Latin, arithmetic and logic, and for bachelors, moral and natural philosophy, geometry and astronomy, music, and a little Greek. Theology and the Hebrew scriptures occupied the divinity men; civil law and medicine made new claims upon

[17] Burnet, *Reformation,* V, 347.
[18] *O. L.,* II, 546.

the minds of others. The gruelling schedules governing the students' day were still unaltered. Whitgift rose at five in the morning for a period of private devotion, followed by morning prayers in the college chapel. Breakfast, made edifying by scripture reading, concluded at six, and three hours of recitation followed. After lectures and public disputations, the college assembled in hall at eleven o'clock for the main meal of the day. Classes were then resumed until a break for relaxation came in the middle of the afternoon. Supper, prayers, and early retiring closed a daily round enjoined by ancient statute and injunction. Such, at least, was the ideal embodied in the regulations. Judging, however, from the time left for indolence, rioting, games, and the following of Bucer's "profligate epicureans," we may safely conclude that the regulations did not always bear heavily upon the students.

The dramatic interruption in Whitgift's undergraduate life came on July 5, 1553 when all Cambridge was aroused by the sudden appearance of the troops of the Duke of Northumberland in King's Parade. Edward VI had died, and the desperate Protector was marching to meet the swelling force of Mary Tudor's adherents. But the trumpet with which he had proclaimed the unhappy Lady Jane Grey gave an uncertain sound. England rallied to the daughter of Henry VIII, and a few days later Whitgift might have seen Northumberland yield. He proclaimed the rightful Queen on Market Hill and was taken into custody in King's College. The leaders among the reformers disappeared from Cambridge, Matthew Parker and William May into an obscurity from which Elizabeth brought them in 1559 to name them her archbishops; Richard Cox and Edmund Grindal with the stream of exiles to the cities of the Rhineland; and Nicholas Ridley and John Bradford to a prison that was the gateway to the fires of Smithfield and immortality in the pages of the *Book of Martyrs*.

Yet on the whole the accession of Mary brought surprisingly little change to the University. With the recision of the Edwardian statutes, Cambridge speedily reverted to the old ways. Stephen Gardiner, restored to the chancellorship, wisely refrained from subjecting the colleges to another visitation. He sought only to carry out quietly the commands Mary gave him to eliminate all innovations made "since the death of our Father of most worthy memory."[19] While Cambridge may not have welcomed the return of Henrician Catholicism with the same enthusiasm that was shown in some quarters,[20] the members of the University were prepared to give at least outward conformity to the Queen's laws.

Among the younger men, many of them disciples of the reformers, there was still some uncertainty and heart-searching that could be resolved either way. To those strongly drawn towards Protestantism the time of critical decision came when the Marian statutes finally restored England to formal papal obedience. For others, less set in their convictions, determination came through the influence of their seniors. Just at this crucial time Whitgift proceeded to his bachelor's degree, in company with the man destined to be his chief antagonist in the next half-century, Thomas Cartwright.[21] Cartwright, already distinguished for his learning in Clare and St. John's, had come under the compelling influence of Thomas Lever, the Protestant reformer who presided over St. John's College in the last years of Edward VI. Whitgift, on the other hand, had formed what was to be a

[19] Ellis, *Letters,* 2nd Series, II, 245-6.
[20] See *Robert Parkyn's Narrative, E.H.R.* (1947), lxii, p. 80.
[21] Whitgift was 20th and Cartwright 34th on the B.A. list, 1554. Baker MSS, Mm. I. 35, 119 (Cambridge University Library). Whitgift was made M.A. in 1557. *Ibid.,* 125.

life-long friendship with Andrew Perne, the new Master of
Peterhouse to whose conservatism and "good conformytie"
Stephen Gardiner testified.[22] The decisive thing was perhaps
a question of influence. Cartwright, after Lever's departure,
left the University for a space in 1556 and finally became
the most eminent Puritan opponent of the Anglican establishment.[23] Whitgift moved to a fellowship in Perne's College and in the end became the chief defender of the
Elizabethan Church.[24]

The more extreme reformers never forgot or forgave
Andrew Perne. At every turn the Puritans later excoriated
his conformity through the reigns of four Tudors, and
blamed him for his share in strengthening the heavy hand
that Whitgift laid upon them as archbishop. "Old Turner"
and "Judas Perne" were the least of the names called him
by the authors of the Martin Marprelate tracts. When they
turned to Whitgift, ordinarily describing him as "John of
Cant, the Pope of Lambeth," they could think of no more
scornful epithet than "Perne's boy."[25] Perne's experience
was only that of the vast majority of Tudor clergy, though
perhaps special circumstances drew greater attention to his
conformity. As vice-chancellor of Cambridge in 1551 it was
Perne's duty to lead the funeral procession of Martin Bucer
to Great St. Mary's Church where the body of the continental reformer was interred. Again holding office in 1557,
he was required to preach the official sermon of condemna-

[22] Gardiner, *Letters,* p. 468.

[23] Lever had gone to Geneva. See Garrett, *Marian Exiles,* p. 9. The tradition that Cartwright was among the Cambridge students who joined him
there is now rejected. Pearson, *Cartwright,* p. 7.

[24] In 1555 Bishop Thirlby of Ely admitted Whitgift to a perpetual fellowship as one of the Scholars of Ely. *Transc. Peterhouse Reg.,* p. 303, Baumgartner Papers Add. 10. 53(3) (Cambridge University Library).

[25] Cooper, *Admonition to the People,* p. 48.

tion when the bones of the condemned heretics, Bucer and Fagius, were exhumed and burned. It was surely the irony of fate that found him vice-chancellor for the third time in 1560, presiding over the memorial services that restored the reformers to honor![26]

Under this protection and patronage Whitgift remained secure during the last months of Mary's reign. Perne's bland assurances satisfied the commissioners of Cardinal Pole who, after Gardiner's death, turned a fierce scrutiny upon the colleges in their search for heresy. Whitgift was not molested in Peterhouse. Appointed a tutor at the age of twenty-four, he laid the foundations for the notable teaching career he later enjoyed in Trinity College.

The news for which England waited—the death of Queen Mary—came late in November 1558. The tragic attempt to return the nation to papal Catholicism was over. Mary's regime was scarcely more than a measure of the loyalty of Englishmen to the house of Tudor. There was always a faintly anachronistic air about it, a stage peopled with elderly figures of a past generation. Furthermore, it was never free from an international and somewhat foreign flavor, openly advertised by the Spanish marriage and more subtly conveyed by the aristocratic continentalism of a cardinal who had obviously repudiated the English heritage of his ancient royal blood. But in the end what burned the last vestiges of national loyalty to the papacy out of the hearts of Englishmen were the dreadful fires of persecution. Smithfield was the arena where Mary's battle was lost. Her effort to halt the progress of the Reformation was defeated by the heroic courage in which Cranmer, Latimer, Ridley, and a

[26] Perne held this office five times between 1551 and 1581. *Grace Book △*, p. 567.

long procession of her subjects faced the horrors of the stake rather than betray the truth to which they were convinced God had led them.

Elizabeth Tudor, in turn, was confronted by essentially the same problem that had vexed the government for two decades, the settlement of religion on a basis of such wide acceptance as would bring order and unity into England's national life. Yet in 1558 a new complexity was the accumulated legacy of the two preceding reigns. Political and social unrest now imposed a critical urgency upon the task of finding a successful solution. Financial depression and economic hardship at home were matched by the perilous uncertainty of England's position among the nations. Drawn into war with France by the maneuvres of Philip II, the country faced open or potential hostility on all sides. The marriage of the Romanist claimant to Elizabeth's throne, Mary of Scotland, to the French dauphin united England's hereditary enemies under the powerful Guise influence. Peace had to be made with France, while at the same time Scotland was detached from the French power and the threat removed from the northern border. Yet no step could be taken that would arouse the suspicions of the King of Spain or diminish his usefulness in restraining the enmity of the Pope. Into this precarious situation, the prestige and power so laboriously built up by her grandfather and enjoyed by her father almost gone, Elizabeth Tudor was thrust.

We are so accustomed to telescoping the forty-five years of Elizabeth's reign into a single glamorous picture of "good Queen Bess' glorious days" that we sometimes forget the tentative and perilous character of the early years. Our Elizabeth is the indomitable princess who parades her white charger at Tilbury while the sails of the ill-fated Armada lift themselves over Ushant. She is the irascible ruler who controls her Council and manipulates her Parliaments with consummate skill and no little temper, the vivacious old lady in a red wig whose palaces ring with laughter and music. She is *Gloriana,* at whose feet are laid the forests of the American shores and the plundered wealth of the Spanish Main, whose smile makes a man's fortune, whose disfavor is worse than outer darkness. But that was Elizabeth of Shakespeare's England, thirty years after an accession clouded with the threat of division and disloyalty at home, danger and disaster abroad. Amid the uncertainties of 1558 the settlement of religion was the paramount issue before the new Queen and her advisors. As long as the well-being of the State and the civic loyalties of its national life were thought to be safely grounded only in the religious unity of the people, the task of framing a settlement to which a common spiritual allegiance could be given was the primary responsibility of the government.

The increased complexity of the problem was only partly due to the tangled political situation. The religious experiences of the reigns of Edward VI and Mary had actually narrowed the limits within which a successful solution could be found. Maitland was probably guilty of over-simplification when he wrote that in 1558 "Henrician Anglo-Catholicism was dead and buried . . . the choice lay between Catholicism with its Pope and the creed for which Cranmer and Ridley died."[27] Any such clear-cut choice would command the loyalty only of small though powerful minorities. Papal Catholicism had collapsed with the Marian regime and its ruins were interred with Cardinal Pole. A restoration of the national Church under royal supremacy was the inevitable alternative to papal allegiance. Inseparable now from Tudor patriotism, only the power of the royal su-

[27] *Camb. Mod. Hist.,* II, 563.

premacy could fashion an acceptable settlement. On the other hand, if "the creed for which Cranmer and Ridley died" was the Protestantism of the second Edwardian settlement, it was by no means clear that without severe modification it would be any more acceptable to the vast majority of Englishmen in 1558 than it had been in 1552-3. Elizabeth recognized that her task was one of conciliating the Catholic mind of the greater part of the nation while still retaining those basic Reformation principles which had already found expression in the life of the English Church.

In these circumstances the unique and creative feature of the Elizabethan settlement proved to be its comprehensiveness. Hitherto the successive attempts to quiet and unify the realm had embodied rigid positions more or less explicitly defined on which it was thought all men could be made to agree. Now a settlement was brought out of the experience of the few years past, sufficiently coherent to be administered with firmness and vigor when necessary, yet broad and flexible enough to command the loyalty of virtually the whole nation. This meant a certain tolerance and forbearance within the requirement of outward uniformity, the maximum amount of liberty of opinion possible, and perhaps more than a little of the *politique* spirit. Tension might be expected between the more Catholic and conservative elements and those that were born of the Reformation, but this would find resolution partly in the Queen's steadfast refusal to "make a window into men's hearts," and partly on that deep level of unity in the faith and practice of a Church that knew no discontinuity with its own past. The first testimony to the extraordinary achievement of Elizabeth, Cecil, and Parker was the deeply rooted flowering of piety and learning that characterized Anglicanism a generation later in the age of Richard Hooker. The final testimony is that given by four centuries of Anglican church life.

The policy of comprehension was almost wrecked at the outset by the rough handling given it in Parliament. Only the inflexible determination of the Queen kept the settlement sufficiently conciliatory on the Catholic side to permit her plan to succeed. Even then, with the tensions more severe than Elizabeth had expected, she was forced to use her formularies and administrative system to widen the limits of the statutory settlement wherever possible.

Nothing reveals more clearly the narrow channel through which the plan of comprehension had to be steered than the controversy during the days when the form of the ecclesiastical legislation was hammered out between the Court and the Parliament house. For years there has been a baffling obscurity about the events of the first few months of 1559. While the various scraps of evidence shedding light upon the aims of the government and the character of its first legislative proposals have been known, the difficulty has been to arrange them into a pattern that utilizes every piece and does no violence to the meaning of any. Until recently no reconstruction has been entirely satisfactory.[28] Within the past few years, however, Professor J. E. Neale, biographer of Elizabeth and historian of her Parliaments, has brought his magisterial knowledge of Elizabethan parliamentary procedure to bear upon the obscurity of these crucial weeks.[29] We know now that Elizabeth's first approach

[28] See Dixon, *Church of England,* V, 20-94; Gee, *Elizabethan Prayer-Book,* ch. i-ii.

[29] "The Elizabethan Acts of Supremacy and Uniformity," *E.H.R.* (1950), lxv, 304-32. Within the brief space of this summary I have not done full justice to Neale's careful and convincing interpretation of all the evidence. Since the delivery of these Hale Lectures, Neale's reconstruction of the religious settlement has appeared in his *Elizabeth I and Her Parliaments 1559-1581,* pp. 51-84.

to the religious settlement was far more cautious and conservative than the statutes she was eventually forced to accept.

In February 1559 the government laid before Parliament a supremacy statute that suspended nearly all the ecclesiastical legislation intervening between the death of Henry VIII and the accession of Elizabeth. The purpose of the bill was to nullify Mary's *Second Statute of Repeal,* thus automatically restoring the Henrician legislation. With an eye to the allegiance of Marian Catholics and the conciliation of the conservative religious temper of the country, the Queen would return England to the Henrician Catholicism of 1547, re-establishing "religion as her father had left it," as she told the Spanish ambassador.[30] The legislation of the Edwardian settlement, still nullified by Mary's *First Act of Repeal,* was ignored—with one exception. The proposed statute made provision for the reception of the Sacrament in both kinds.[31] Clearly, the appearance of this provision governing a religious practice in a statute of royal supremacy meant that no act of uniformity or Prayer Book was intended by the government at this first parliamentary session. Moving cautiously, Elizabeth was seeking an *interim* program by which the loyalty of the vast majority of her subjects could be carried to a final settlement at a later date.

On all sides the establishment of an *interim* policy had been urged upon the Queen by the calmer spirits. "Succeed happily through a discreet beginning" was Throckmorton's

[30] *Spanish Cal. Eliz.* i, 37. See also i, 61-2.

[31] Reviving, therefore, 1 Edw. VI. c. 1. This inclusion remained firmly embedded in the bill throughout the later changes and survived into the final form of the legislation as Section v. See Prothero, *Select Statutes,* p. 4. An unnecessary accompaniment of legislation that established the Prayer Book of 1559, Neale makes this provision the starting-point of his discussion.

advice.[32] Armagil Waad's urging was in more picturesque language.

I pray God [he wrote] to grant us concord both in the agreement upon the cause and state of religion, and among ourselves for the account of Catholic and Protestant: so would I wish that you would proceed to the reformation having respect to quiet at home, the affairs you have in mind with foreign princes, the greatness of the Pope, and how dangerous it is to make alteration in religion, specially in the beginning of a prince's reign. Glasses with small necks, if you pour into them any liquor suddenly or violently, will not be so filled, but refuse to receive that same that you would pour into them. Howbeit, if you instil water into them by a little and little they are soon replenished.[33]

Where was the pattern for an *interim* program to be found? At this point Neale's suggestions are supported by the fact that Elizabeth found a course to follow, within the limits of England's recent experience, both conservatively comprehensive and sufficiently flexible in character. It was the pattern of events in the first years of Edward VI which led up to the Prayer Book of 1549. This formula Elizabeth proposed to repeat, and it appeared to promise success in 1559. Relying upon the force of "true obedience" to the supremacy to elicit loyalty to an *interim* program that did no violence to the Catholic faith, the government had distinctly reasonable hopes of the adherence of some of the

[32] Neale, "Sir Nicholas Throckmorton's Advice to Queen Elizabeth," *E.H.R.* (1950), lxv, 91-8. See also Richard Goodrich's "Divers Points of Religion," reprinted in Dixon, *Church of England,* V, 25-8. Even the famous "Device for the Alteration of Religion" raised the question of a suitable *interim* order. Gee, *Elizabethan Prayer-Book,* p. 201.

[33] *Ibid.,* p. 210.

bishops—perhaps not Mary's nominees, but at least Tunstal of Durham, Heath of York, Thirlby of Ely, and others remaining from Henry's reign.[34] Thus carrying along a segment of the old episcopate and the loyalty of conservatives, and having filled the vacant sees with men drawn from the ranks of the more moderate reformers, strict constitutional procedure could be followed. After the administration of the new oath of supremacy had winnowed out the intransigent papists, a Convocation composed of moderate men on both sides could produce a Prayer Book embodying the comprehensiveness the Queen desired. This, in turn, could be presented to Parliament for attachment to an act of uniformity. The *interim* period would then have been concluded in proper constitutional fashion by the discussion and determination of the final religious settlement in Convocation, not in Parliament.[35]

What threw the government's initial plan into confusion was not so much the hostility of Marian Catholics as the determined opposition offered in the House of Commons by Knollys, Cooke, and other Protestant leaders, returned from their exile in Germany and Switzerland, and backed by an influential group of reforming divines—Jewel, Grindal, Cox, Sampson, Scory, Aylmer, and others.[36] The Commons were

---

[34] These well-known hopes remained alive through the summer of 1559. The first commission for the consecration of Matthew Parker named three of the "old learning" and three of "the other sort." Thompson, *Consecration of Archbishop Parker,* p. 2. Elizabeth seems to have felt that the extent to which she had succeeded in modifying the Edwardian settlement might overcome the opposition with which Tunstal and others regarded the second Edwardian Prayer Book.

[35] During her entire reign Elizabeth resisted repeated Puritan attempts to initiate and frame legislation for further reform in Parliament. The course of action forced upon her by the early events of 1559 proved a later embarrassment when the Puritains persisted in regarding the settlement as a parliamentary one.

[36] *Z. L.,* I, 10-11.

determined to permit the re-establishment of "the religion used in King Edward's last year." When this unexpectedly severe pressure was strengthened by the news that peace had been concluded with the French at Câteau-Cambrésis and caution was no longer dictated by the foreign situation, the *interim* plan collapsed. The government was forced to yield to the clamor for an immediate act of uniformity. Any possibility of the eventual restoration of the Prayer Book of 1549 vanished amid the implacable hostility of the returned exiles to the more conservative Edwardian service book. Indeed, there appears to have been a momentary threat of possible further modification of even the 1552 liturgy along continental lines.[37] In the face of this opposition Elizabeth surrendered her original design, salvaging what she could. During the Easter parliamentary recess the Westminster Disputation was permitted, a poor substitute for the initial plan of later convocational debate and decision. When Parliament reassembled, the statutes were passed that revived the Edwardian settlement. The Prayer Book of 1552 was prescribed with the few significant alterations that represented Elizabeth's determination to leave as much room as possible for the operation of her principle of comprehensiveness.

The Elizabethan settlement came finally to rest upon the two statutes of 1559, the *Act of Supremacy* that restored to the national Church the constitutional doctrine of Henry VIII, and the *Act of Uniformity* within the framework of which the religious character of the Elizabethan Church developed. Both reflected the continuity of the Church with the experiences of Englishmen since 1529; both re-

[37] See the "Supplication to the Parliament" in *The Seconde Parte of a Register*, II, 84.

vealed the extent to which the government had been able to modify the earlier and more rigid settlements.

The *Act of Supremacy,* "restoring to the Crown the ancient jurisdiction over the State Ecclesiastical and Spiritual," repealed the Marian legislation by which England had again been brought under a "usurped foreign power and authority," and revived the significant portions of the Henrician ecclesiastical laws.[38] The notable exception was Henry's supremacy act. The Elizabethan statute dealt with the supremacy anew. While for all practical purposes the ecclesiastical authority of the Crown remained the same, yet nowhere did the odious term "supreme head" appear. "The Queen's Highness is the only supreme governor of this Realm . . . as well in all spiritual and ecclesiastical things or causes as temporal." In this way the phrases of the corporal oath required by section ix of the act softened the earlier abrupt assertions that the monarch was "the only Supreme Head in earth of the Church of England."[39] It was a forbearance that not only made the allegiance of Marian Catholics easier, but perhaps also soothed the consciences of those Protestant reformers who had been attracted by the consistorial theocracy of Geneva.[40]

Everywhere the royal authority was explained. The *Injunctions* of 1559, the chief instrument whereby the settlement was initially enforced, required the clergy to bid prayers for the Queen only as "supreme governor of this realm, as well in causes ecclesiastical as temporal," and at the same time turned earlier phrases concerning the "Bishop of Rome" into vague generalizations about the abolition

[38] 1 Eliz. c. 1. *Statutes,* IV, i, 350-5.
[39] See Tanner, p. 47; see also Cardwell, *Synodalia,* I, 31.
[40] *Z. L.,* I, 1-2.

of "all usurped and foreign power having no establishment or ground by the law of God."[41] Moreover, appended to the *Injunctions* was Cecil's carefully-worded "Admonition to simple men deceived by the malicious." It ran

The Queen's majesty, being informed that . . . sundry of her native subjects, being called to ecclesiastical ministry in the Church, be by sinister persuasion and perverse construction induced to find some scruple in the form of an oath . . . required of divers persons for the recognition of their allegiance to her majesty . . . forbiddeth . . . her subjects to give ear or credit to such perverse and malicious persons, which most sinisterly . . . labour . . . how by the words of the said oath it may be collected, that the kings and queens of this realm . . . may challenge authority and power of ministry of divine offices in the church . . . Certainly her majesty neither doth, nor ever will, challenge any other authority than that was challenged and lately used by . . . King Henry the Eighth and King Edward the Sixth, which is, and was of ancient time due to the imperial crown of this realm; that is, under God to have the sovereignty and rule over all manner of persons born within her realms . . . of what estate, either ecclesiastical or temporal . . . so as no other foreign power shall or ought to have any superiority over them.[42]

The points of this restrained statement were echoed in the *Thirty-Nine Articles* of 1563 where it is explained that

When we attribute to the Queen's Majesty the chief government . . . we give not to our princes the ministering either of God's word or of Sacraments, the which thing the Injunctions also lately set forth by Elizabeth our Queen doth most plainly

[41] *Visitation Articles,* III, 9, 28; see also II, 115.
[42] *S.P.Dom. Eliz.* xv. 27. See Cardwell, *Doc. Annals,* I, 232-3. ["challenge" = claim.]

testify: But that only prerogative which we see to have been given always to all godly princes in Holy Scripture by God himself, that is, that they should rule all estates and degrees committed to their charge by God, whether they be ecclesiastical or no . . .[43]

Finally, Elizabeth further softened the impact of her supremacy by entrusting its exercise to the statutory Ecclesiastical Commission, and relying upon her episcopate to exercise an authority with which she seldom interfered. One result of this consistent policy was that in time even Archbishop Parker could express the opinion to Cecil that the Queen's ecclesiastical prerogative, while more than the "head papists" would admit, yet was something "not so great as your pen hath given it her in the Injunction."[44]

The kind of authority that Elizabeth made of the royal supremacy is plainly set forth in the famous *Declaration of the Queen's Proceedings,* a document prepared at the time of the Northern Rebellion. In phrases already familiar to us, the Queen's power is affirmed to be that inherent in the office of a Christian prince.

We know no other authority, either given or used by us, as Queen and Governour of this Realm, than hath been by the Law of God and this Realm always due to our Progenitors . . . Kings of the same . . .

Our Realm hath of long time past received the Christian Faith . . . we are by this authority bound to direct all estates, being subject to us, to live in the Faith and Obedience of Christian Religion, and to see that the Laws of God and Man, which are ordained to that end, to be duly observed . . . and consequently to provide that the Church may be governed and

---

[43] Cardwell, *Synodalia,* I, 71.
[44] *Parker Correspondence,* p. 479.

taught by Archbishops, Bishops and Ministers according to the ecclesiastical ancient Policy of the Realm . . . an office and charge, as we think, properly due to all Christian monarchs and princes sovereign, whereby they only differ from pagan princes, that only take care of their subjects bodies . . .[45]

The new reassurance of the *Declaration* is the explicit denial that by the Queen's powers

we do either challenge or take to us (as malicious persons do untruly surmise) any superiority to ourself to define, decide or determine any article or point of the Christian Faith or Religion, or to change any ancient Ceremony of the Church from the form before received and observed by the Catholic and Apostolic Church . . .[46]

Here is Elizabeth's supremacy, tempered as far as possible. It is sometimes argued, and it was argued in 1559, that the distinction between "supreme head" and "supreme governor" made small difference in practice. On the contrary, it made small difference in theory. Elizabeth's practice was so restrained as not only to win wide acceptance on the ground of "true obedience," but also to endow the national Church in the end with a surprising measure of freedom.

The moderating policy that was applied to the interpretation and exercise of royal supremacy was similarly apparent in the widening of the religious settlement in the interests of comprehension. The *Act of Uniformity* imposed the Edwardian Prayer Book of 1552 with three changes: an alteration in the lectionary, the omission of a portion of the Litany,

---

[45] *Burghley State Papers*, pp. 589-93. There is a copy containing corrections and additions in Elizabeth's own hand. *S.P.Dom. Eliz.* lxvi. 54. The *Declaration* is reprinted by Collins in *Queen Elizabeth's Defense of Her Proceedings*, pp. 35-47, and more recently in Rice, *The Public Speaking of Queen Elizabeth*, pp. 125-33.

[46] *Burghley State Papers*, p. 591.

and the provision for the use of communion sentences combined from both Edwardian service books.[47] Two of these changes were of considerable importance to Elizabeth. She could scarcely hope to reconcile Marian Catholics as long as the Litany required them to pray for deliverance from "the tyranny of the bishop of Rome and all his detestable enormities." This petition, therefore, disappeared. Furthermore, the use of the communion sentence from the Prayer Book of 1549—"The body of our Lord Jesus Christ, which was given for thee"—at one stroke restored to the Holy Communion a doctrine of the presence of Christ in the Sacrament that some of the reformers felt had been decisively rejected in the words of 1552—"Take and eat this, in remembrance that Christ died for thee." No single action was more important in ensuring a wide acceptance of the religious settlement.

The first enthusiasm with which the returned exiles informed their friends on the Continent that "religion is again placed on the same footing on which it stood in King Edward's time" proved, however, to be premature.[48] Jewel, Grindal, Parkhurst, Cox and their friends did not know what Elizabeth could do with the settlement. When the Prayer Book of 1559 appeared, for example, it contained more than the three changes prescribed by the statute. The famous "Black Rubric" interpolated into the second Edwardian liturgy by Edward's Council was omitted, removing another barrier to conscientious Catholic conformity.[49] The orna-

---

[47] 1 Eliz. c. 2. *Statutes,* IV, i, 355-8.

[48] *Z. L.,* I, 33. See also I, 23; 28-9; II, 19.

[49] The rubric declared that in kneeling to receive the Sacrament "it is not meant thereby that any adoration is done, or ought to be done, either unto the sacramental bread and wine there bodily received, or to any real and essential presence there being of Christ's natural flesh and blood." Ketley, ed. *The Two Liturgies,* p. 283.

ments rubric, reworded to give force to section xiii of the
Act of Uniformity, now prescribed that

the minister at the time of the communion and at all other times
in his ministration, shall use such ornaments in the church as
were in use by the authority of parliament in the second year
of the reign of king Edward VI, according to the act of parliament set in the beginning of this book.[50]

Only by the immediate assumption that the ornaments requirements would not be enforced could the reformers quiet
their growing uneasiness with the formularies of the settlement.[51] Furthermore, in 1560 came the *Liber Precum Publicarum,* the Latin Prayer Book of Walter Haddon for use
in the universities and colleges, full of what the Puritans
termed "the dregs of popery." Showing remarkable affinities
with Aless' Latin translation of the Prayer Book of 1549,
the *Liber Precum Publicarum* made provision for the reserva-
tion of the Sacrament for the sick, and for a celebration of
the Holy Communion at funerals.[52] Other examples might
be enumerated from the precise requirements of the *Injunctions* of 1559, the tone of the first Elizabethan *Primer,* which
on the whole approximated the religious orientation of the
first *Primer* of Edward VI rather than the second, and the
new *Calendar* providing for the observance of numerous
saints' days.

[50] Clay, ed. *Liturgies of Queen Elizabeth,* p. 53. Section xiii of the *Act of
Uniformity* required that "such ornaments of the Church and of the ministers
thereof shall be retained and be in use, as was in the Church of England, by
the authority of Parliament, in the second year of the reign of King Edward
the sixth, until such other order shall be therein taken by the authority of
the Queen's Majesty . . ." *Statutes,* IV, i, 358.

[51] *Parker Correspondence,* p. 65.

[52] *Liturgies of Queen Elizabeth,* pp. 404, 433. In 1571 Haddon's *Liber*
was replaced by a more exact translation of the Elizabethan Prayer Book.
See Pullan, *History of the Book of Common Prayer,* pp. 124-5.

Clearly Elizabeth made full use of her power to widen the limits of the settlement to secure maximum acceptance.[53] Behind the formularies the theological tradition was broadly assumed to be that of the old faith, now purged of superstitious errors and papal corruptions. By the *Act of Supremacy* nothing was to be accounted heresy except as had been so adjudged "by the authority of the Canonical Scriptures, or by the first four General Councils . . . or such as hereafter shall be ordered, judged, and determined to be heresy by the High Court of Parliament of this Realm, with the assent of the Clergy in their Convocation."[54] In the *Canons of 1571* the clergy were enjoined to teach nothing "which they would have the people religiously to observe, and believe, but that which is agreeable to the doctrine of the Old Testament, and the New, and that which the Catholic fathers and ancient Bishops have gathered out of that doctrine."[55] Such was the settlement as it emerged under Elizabeth's hand, coherent enough to be administered with firmness and vigor, yet sufficiently flexible to take further impress from the years of her reign.

Within the limits of her comprehensive policy the Queen demanded only the outward conformity that expressed the loyalty of her subjects and formed the matrix in which their unity might grow. The extent of her forbearance was clearly shown in the *Declaration*.

We know not, nor have any meaning to allow, that any of our subjects should be molested either by examination, or inquisi-

[53] It is evident that Elizabeth took full advantage of the clause in the *Act of Uniformity* permitting the Queen to "ordain and publish such further ceremonies or rites as may be most for the advancement of God's glory, the edifying of his Church and the due reverence of Christ's holy mysteries and sacraments." *Statutes*, IV, i, 358.

[54] *Ibid.*, IV, i, 354.

[55] Cardwell, *Synodalia*, I, 126-7.

tion, in any matter, either of faith, as long as they shall profess the Christian Faith, not gainsaying the authority of the holy Scriptures, and of the articles of our Faith, contained in the Creeds Apostolic and Catholic; or for matters of ceremonies, or any other external matters appertaining to Christian Religion, as long as they shall in their outward conversation show themselves quiet and comfortable . . .[56]

Elizabeth would force no man's conscience, nor "make windows into men's hearts and secret thoughts." But with this tolerance she stood fast. The settlement must succeed. The Queen was quite aware of the truth of Norfolk's warning that England could bear no more changes in religion.[57]

To this settlement John Whitgift cheerfully gave his loyalty. On July 7, 1560 he was ordained deacon in Ely Cathedral by the newly-consecrated bishop of that diocese, Richard Cox. Ordered priest a few months later, to the duties of his fellowship at Peterhouse were added those of the living at Teversham, a small village three miles northeast of Cambridge from which the towers of the University were clearly visible across the meadows. Willingly subscribing the oath required upon admission to a cure, he affirmed "with freedom of mind and conscience, from the bottom of my heart," that "the book of common prayer and administration of the holy sacraments . . . is agreeable to the scriptures, and that it is catholic, apostolic, and most for the

[56] *Burghley State Papers,* pp. 591-2. See also "Elizabeth's Declaration in the Star Chamber" where it is declared that "her majesty would have all her loving subjects to understand, that, as long as they shall openly continue in the observation of her laws . . . her majesty's meaning is, not to have any of them molested by any inquisition or examination of their consciences in causes of religion . . ." Strype, *Annals,* I, ii, 371-2. Note Elizabeth's significant veto of an act passed by Parliament in 1571 requiring everyone to receive Holy Communion at least once a year. Neale, *Elizabeth I and Her Parliaments,* pp. 192, 240, 304.

[57] HMC, *Bath MSS,* II, 18.

advancing of God's glory, and the edifying of God's people."[58]

The freedom of Whitgift's mind and conscience was not shared by everyone, though Elizabeth's policy was already vindicated by the conformity of the overwhelming majority of Catholic clergy. Deprivations among Marian priests amounted to few more than two hundred, and these, as one might expect, were chiefly drawn from the ranks of Cathedral clergy, administrators, and other members of the official-dom of Mary's Church. But on the other side could be heard the first mutterings of what was presently to become a storm of Puritan opposition to the settlement. The Queen had disappointed the reformers of the extremer sort by dis-regarding Rudolph Gualter's advice against putting new wine into old bottles, and showing no sign of agreement with his conviction that God had raised her up to complete "what the most godly king your brother had piously and successfully begun." Already some reformers feared that the settlement was betraying the truth of Gualter's warning that "a form of religion which is an unhappy compound of popery and the gospel . . . may at length be an easy passage to the ancient superstition."[59] Parker might so ex-plain the position of the Church of England to the French Ambassador and the Bishop of Constance that they were delighted at its moderation, though it took some effort to do so; that same moderation seemed to Jewel less a golden mean than a "leaden mediocrity."[60] Anthony Cooke had long since lost the enthusiasm with which he first described the activity of Parliament to Peter Martyr. His schemes had been washed away by the "deliberation, and prudence, and wari-

---

[58] *Concilia*, IV, 195-6.
[59] *Z. L.*, II, 5.
[60] *Parker Correspondence*, p. 215. *Z. L.*, I, 23.

ness, and circumspection" that he saw attending the settlement.[61]

Jewel's letters to Martyr give us the first hints of the forth-
coming vestiarian phase of the Puritan controversy. Full of
regret at what he scornfully labels "the scenic apparatus of
divine worship," he deplores the "little silver cross of ill-
omened origin" that kept its place on the altar in the Queen's
chapel.[62] Thomas Sampson was less restrained. His high
hopes were dashed when in January 1560 he informed Peter
Martyr that "three of our lately appointed bishops are to
officiate at the table of the Lord, one as priest, another as
deacon, and a third as subdeacon, before the image of the
crucifix, or at least not far from it, with candles, and habited
in the golden vestments of the papacy, and are thus to
celebrate the Lord's supper"—the crowning iniquity of all—
"without any sermon . . . Lord have mercy upon us!"[63]

At the end of his letter Sampson raised the crucial question of obedience. "Should we not," he asks, "rather quit
the ministry of the word and sacraments, than that these
relics of the Amorites be admitted?" This glimpse into the
conscience of the Puritan returns us to Cambridge. There
the forces are first marshalled for the Puritan challenge to
the Elizabethan establishment; there John Whitgift first
bends his bow in defense of the Queen's settlement of
religion.

[61] *Ibid.*, I, 17.
[62] *Ibid.*, I, 55. See also I, 17-9; 23-5; 52-4; 67-9.
[63] *Ibid.*, I, 63-4.

III

CAMBRIDGE AND CONTROVERSY

ON the 4th of August 1564 Sir William Cecil, travelling by coach to ease "the unhappy grief" of gout, arrived at St. John's College in Cambridge. He was the harbinger of the Queen's visit to her favoured university. On the next afternoon Elizabeth, met at Newnham by the mayor and other civic officials and escorted by her courtiers, rode through Queens' College to the west portal of King's Chapel. There the principal reception took place with all Cambridge crowding the courts and lanes around King's. The Queen listened gravely to a Latin oration, charmingly commended the orator, gave her hand graciously to the doctors, and under a canopy borne aloft by the vice-chancellor and other University dignitaries entered the chapel for Evensong and a solemn *Te Deum*.

The following day, being Sunday, King's Chapel was filled to overflowing with the members of the University as Dr. Perne preached before the Queen, a sermon so pleasing to Elizabeth that she declared "she thought she should never hear a better."[1] During the service, ranked in the stalls of the long choir, sat the Heads of colleges, doctors and professors—John Whitgift proudly among them. His lectures

[1] *Desiderata Curiosa,* p. 266.

as Lady Margaret's professor of divinity in the University had already attracted the favorable attention of his elders.[2]

Elizabeth's visit to Cambridge was a triumphant success. Making a progress of the colleges, she alternately praised the dons' loyal addresses and criticized their shabby academical dress, all the while collecting innumerable gifts of gloves, books, and comfits. The courtiers heard solemnly the disputations arranged for their edification and watched delightedly the plays performed for their amusement. Perhaps the moments of chief interest for us were those of the debate in Great St. Mary's where Elizabeth, enthroned on a high stage erected in the chancel, heard the disputants expound, attack, and defend the thesis *Monarchia est optimus status reipublicae.* Among those prominent in the disputation was Thomas Cartwright, bachelor in Whitgift's year, who had fled Marian Cambridge with the exodus from St. John's. Returning after the accession of Elizabeth, he had been elected to a fellowship at Trinity in 1562. A brilliant and skillful controversialist, Cartwright distinguished himself in the role assigned him by a devastating attack upon the thesis.[3] Possibly his natural abilities were considerably stimulated by the task imposed upon him. To challenge the virtues of monarchy in the Tudor pattern even as a forensic exercise was perhaps not altogether uncongenial to the man who was soon to offer in deadly earnest a challenge to the whole structure of the Elizabethan Church.

If the royal visit brought a pleasant and gratifying interlude to the routine of Whitgift's university life, the next interruption was of a far different character. In 1565 a

[2] Whitgift MSS, I, 9; II, 36 (Cambridge University Library). Whitgift was made B.D. and Lady Margaret's professor in 1563. Baker MSS, Mm. I, 35, 136-7. He received the D.D. four years later. *Ibid.,* 147.

[3] Pearson, *Cartwright,* pp. 13-4.

noisy disturbance threatened to imperil the whole discipline of the academic community. On October 12th some three hundred undergraduates of the troublesome St. John's College, largely under the influence of impatient Puritan-minded dons, appeared in chapel, in defiance of the regulations, without that "rag of popery," the prescribed surplice. Similar outbreaks of nonconformity occurred at Trinity and at King's, and when the good order of the University seemed to have vanished in tumult the Heads of colleges and the divinity professors implored Cecil to halt the recent attempt to enforce the use of the surplice.[4] The vestiarian controversy that marked the first phase of the Puritan assault upon the Elizabethan settlement had thrust itself into the University.

The immediate occasion of the trouble in 1565 was the increased pressure with which Archbishop Parker applied the regulations touching the vestments of ministers and the ornaments of the Church. At the very outset the conciliatory aim of Elizabeth's retention of some of the traditional externals of the Church's worship had been seriously impaired by the refusal of the "Precisians," as Parker called them, to comply with the ornaments requirements.[5] Deeply affected by their contacts with continental Protestant Churches during the years of their Marian exile, many of these men were earnestly and impatiently eager to carry the reformation of their own Church to the conclusions reached in Geneva or the Rhineland cities. They were convinced that the formularies of the Elizabethan settlement represented that "unhappy compound of popery and the Gospel" against which Gualter had warned. Their protest was foreseen by the author

<hr>

[4] Strype, *Annals*, I, ii, 154-60; *Parker*, III, 125-6.
[5] *Parker Correspondence*, pp. 279, 438.

of the famous "Device for the Alteration of Religion" when he wrote

> Many such as would gladly have the alteration from the Church of Rome, when they shall see peradventure that some old ceremonies shall be left still, or that their doctrine which they embrace is not allowed and commanded only and all other abolished and disproved, shall be discontented, and call the alteration a cloaked papistry or a mingle-mangle.[6]

The prophecy indeed proved to be correct. In the first months of 1559 the unregulated iconoclasm of the reaction against Marian Catholicism swept away many of the traditional ornaments and devastated the chancels of the churches despite the Queen's attempts to halt this destructive activity.[7] The commissioners carrying out the initial visitation sometimes had less difficulty extirpating popery than inducing the "precise men" to conform to the rubrics and injunctions. By the time that the Elizabethan bishops entered upon their authority the situation was beyond easy repair in many places. Observance of the regulations that prescribed the ornaments and vestments of 1549 was impossible to enforce.

Elizabeth's initial settlement was unquestionably regarded as both tentative and transitory. Its formularies were viewed by many, not as those of an enduring ecclesiastical structure, but as temporary measures regrettably given conservative expression by the dictates of a conciliatory policy made necessary by reasons of state. It is difficult to see how the reformers of the more extreme sort could have thought otherwise. Experience placed before them only the clear-cut alternatives of Marian Catholicism or Protestantism of the continental

[6] Gee, *Elizabethan Prayer-Book*, p. 197.
[7] *Parker Correspondence*, pp. 132-3.

Reformed type. On the principles enunciated in Jewel's *Apologia* they had rejected the one; the forces at work in the Anglican settlement had not yet revealed the deepest grounds for refusing the other. Conformity therefore became a matter of the extent of conscientious scruple. Were the externals of apparel and usages things in themselves "indifferent," prescribed by constituted authority and hence to be endured until religion could be separated from state policy and the Word of God given free course to cleanse men's minds from devotion to these "relics of the Amorites"? Or were they so associated with superstitious beliefs and idolatrous practices that they must be resisted even to the point—not of resisting the constituted authority by which they were enjoined: that will come later—but of abandoning the ministry if no deviation be allowed from the letter of the law? Bishop Cooper of Winchester in 1589 accurately described the attitudes of those who precipitated the vestiarian controversy. In his *Admonition to the, People of England* he declared

At the beginning some learned and godly preachers, for private respects in themselves, made strange to wear the surplice, cap, or tippet: but yet so that they declare themselves to think the thing indifferent, and not to judge evil of such as did use them. Shortly after rose up other defending that they were not things indifferent, but disdained with Antichristian idolatry, and therefore not to be suffered in the Church.[8]

The problem of obedience to the orders of constituted authority was complicated by the inconsistencies in the formularies. The Queen's *Injunctions,* for example, required the use of wafer-bread at the Holy Communion "of the same fineness and fashion as the singing cakes which served

[8] P. 158.

for the use of the private Mass," but the Prayer Book rubric directed the use of "bread such as is usual to be eaten."[9] Similarly, while the ornaments rubric ordered the continuance of the traditional Catholic vestments, the *Injunctions* spoke obscurely of "such seemly habits, garments, and such square caps, as were most commonly and orderly received in the latter year of King Edward VI," and the bishops' "Interpretations" allowed a cope to be used at the Holy Communion and a surplice at all other services.[10] Even the well-intentioned conformist might plead some confusion; the determined Precision had almost limitless scope for contentious argument.

In the Convocation of 1563 an effort to secure clarification of the existing requirements had been made. Proposals were offered for the modification of the rubrics and the simplification of the rites and ceremonies of the Church. When moderated from their initial form these demanded the abrogation of the observance of saints' days, the removal of organs, the omission of the baptismal sign of the cross, distinct reading of prayers by the officiant facing the people, and made kneeling for the reception of the Sacrament optional at the discretion of the ordinary. During the sessions original proposals that would have eliminated all the ancient vestments, as well as the distinctive clerical outdoor garb, were altered to require the surplice alone for all services, with the additional proviso that no minister officiate save in "a comely garment or habit"—a point so obscurely phrased as to leave room for the black gown.[11] Hotly contested in acrimonious debate, when the scrutiny was made the members of the

---

[9] *Liturgies of Queen Elizabeth*, p. 198. *Visitation Articles*, III, 28.
[10] *Ibid.*, III, 20, 61.
[11] *Concilia*, IV, 237-40.

Lower House rejected the proposals by the narrow margin of fifty-nine to fifty-eight votes.

It is sometimes said that the dissidents at this Convocation, heartened by the extent of sympathy with their proposals, continued the vestiarian controversy with redoubled vigor, confident that success would attend the next attempt to modify the requirements of the formularies. There are, however, some difficulties with this assumption. The scene of future Puritan agitation was chiefly the Parliament, not the Convocation. It is entirely probable that the surprise in Convocation in 1563 was not the amount of support given to the Precisians but the unexpected extent of loyalty to the existing regulations. Convocation was a body less representative of the English Church as a whole than of ecclesiastical officialdom. Among its members, therefore, due to the appointment of so many returned exiles to fill the offices vacated by Marian officials, was the greatest concentration of Puritan opinion. If the dissatisfied reformers were unable to control the Convocation of 1563, they were unlikely to gain that control in the future. But continue the disturbances they did, to the point of utter chaos in some centers of disaffection. A report to Cecil on the lack of uniformity described prayers as said variously in the chancel, the pulpit, or the body of the church. Some clergy kept strictly to the Prayer Book order; others interpolated metrical psalms. The holy tables stood in nearly every conceivable position; the Sacraments were administered with all manner of vestments or none at all. Common cups alternated with chalices, wafer-bread with the ordinary loaf, and the Holy Communion was received kneeling, sitting, and standing.[12]

By the end of 1564 Elizabeth's patience was tried to the breaking point. The uniformity she cherished as the expres-

[12] Strype, *Parker*, I, 302.

sion of the unity of her people had not been achieved—
indeed, the framework of the settlement itself was being
narrowed, its comprehensive nature imperiled. On the 25th
of January 1565 her imperious temper flared up and she
gave vent to it in a letter to Archbishop Parker.

In sundry places of our realm of late [she wrote], for lack of
regard given thereto in due time, by such superior and principal
officers as you are, being the primate and other the bishops of
your province, with sufferance of sundry varieties and novelties,
not only in opinions but in external rites and ceremonies, there
is crept and brought into the church by some few persons,
abounding more in their own senses than wisdom would, and
delighting with singularities and changes, an open and manifest
disorder and offense . . .

And then, reproving the archbishop for not stopping what
for five years he had striven earnestly to end by gentle
persuasions, the Queen continued in no uncertain tone:

And therefore, We do by these our present letters require,
enjoin, and straitly charge you, being the metropolitan, according to the power and authority which you have under us over
the province of Canterbury, (as the like we will order for the
province of York), to confer with the bishops your brethren . . .
And thereupon, as the several cases shall appear to require
reformation, so to proceed by order, injunction, or censure . . .
so as uniformity of order may be kept in every church, and
without variety and contention.
And for the time to come, we will and straitly charge you
to provide and enjoin in our name, in all and every places of
your province, as well in places exempt as otherwise, that none
be hereafter admitted or allowed to any office, room, cure, or
place ecclesiastical, either having cure of souls, or without cure,
but such as shall be found disposed and well and advisedly

given to common order . . . and shall also . . . promise . . . to observe, keep, and maintain such order and uniformity in all the external rites and ceremonies . . .

The sharp rebuke ended with a threatening note that must have filled the harassed primate with despair.

We require you [concluded the Queen] to use all expedition that, to such a cause as this is, shall seem necessary, that hereafter we be not occasioned, for lack of your diligence, to provide such further remedy, by some other sharp proceedings, as shall percase not be easy to be borne by such as shall be disordered: and therewith also we shall impute to you the cause thereof.[13]

Parker had reason to despair. Many of the bishops, themselves former exiles who regarded the externals as at best things "indifferent" and had considerable sympathy with their brethren of more tender consciences, turned a deaf ear to the archbishop's entreaties for firmer discipline. Grindal's reluctance to enforce conformity in London is well-known. Even at the end of the controversy he was willing to conform himself only "for order's sake and obedience to the prince."[14] Sandys of Worcester had been the first to interpret the ornaments requirements as of no force and to affirm his hope that even the minimum demands would soon be abandoned.[15] Jewel of Salisbury regretted the continued use of the surplice as late as 1566.[16] The Bishop of Durham, Pilkington, encouraged by his non-conforming dean, William Whittingham, who had lately returned from Geneva, flatly refused to enforce the regulations. Instead, he sought to

[13] *Parker Correspondence*, pp. 223-7.
[14] Grindal, *Remains*, p. 211.
[15] *Parker Correspondence*, p. 65. Z. L., I, 74.
[16] *Ibid.*, I, 149.

make Parker's task more difficult by enlisting the support of Robert Dudley, newly created Earl of Leicester and the Queen's favorite.[17] Bishop Parkhurst of Norwich was one of the worst offenders in the cause of the Precisians. As early as 1561 Cecil reported to the archbishop that Parkhurst was remiss in ordering his clergy. "He winketh at schismatics and anabaptists," wrote Cecil. "Surely I see great variety in administration. A surplice may not be borne here."[18] Parkhurst's petty triumphs in the vestiarian controversy are not particularly attractive. In 1564 he rejoiced at the funeral of the Duchess of Norfolk which he arranged, as he wrote Simler, with "no ceremonies . . . wax candles or torches. Except the sun nothing shone, which sadly annoyed the papists." And he continued gleefully, "Nothing of the kind has ever been seen in England, especially at the funeral of a peer or peeress."[19]

Outside the ranks of the bishops there was a large number of other sympathetic dignitaries, protected in their offices from Archbishop Parker's direct authority. Dean Nowell of St. Paul's, who received a rude rebuke from Elizabeth in the midst of a sermon against images, had taken an active part in presenting the Puritan proposals to the Convocation in 1563. Dean Turner of Wells, a constant thorn in the side of Bishop Berkeley, proclaimed his scorn for the prescribed apparel by setting a convicted adulterer to do his open penance in the square cap of the priest. At Oxford both the Dean of Christ Church, Thomas Sampson, and the President of Magdalen, Laurence Humphrey, were unyielding in their refusal to conform.

Parker, convinced that the only effective remedy for the

---

[17] *Parker Correspondence,* p. 237.
[18] *Ibid.,* p. 149.
[19] *Z. L.,* I, 137. Strype, *Annals,* I, i, 45.

disorder was the promulgation of a set of articles of conformity which would be unmistakable in their meaning, drew up a series of injunctions, beseeching Cecil to use his influence to secure royal authorization.[20] Elizabeth refused her consent, partly, as Parker later surmised, because of the inclusion of some doctrinal articles and partly because of her consistent reluctance to modify the existing requirements.[21] The archbishop, fearful lest the statutes be invoked against him if he promulgated constitutions without the Queen's license, set his articles aside. The only recourse was to enforce the laws as they stood. A number of clergy were suspended or deprived, and it was under this pressure that the tumult invaded Cambridge with the disturbance in St. John's College.

In November 1565 Whitgift joined Hutton, the Regius professor, and some of the Heads of colleges in their request for moderation and liberty to tender consciences in the matters of vestiarian dispute.[22] Cecil, however, reminded by Archbishop Parker that his authority as chancellor of the University was sufficient to the occasion, returned a sharp rebuke. Whereupon Beaumont, the vice-chancellor, hastened to make it plain that the University officials were not lacking in obedience, but rather uncertain concerning their authority to suspend or deprive recalcitrant Precisians.[23] They sought only some speedy means of restoring order in Cambridge. What disturbed them most was not the excessive zeal of the few sincere non-conformists, but the joyous rioting of undergraduates for whom any pretext served as an excuse to disobey the university regulations. The young man in King's

[20] *Parker Correspondence*, p. 234.

[21] *Ibid.*, p. 272.

[22] Strype, *Annals,* I, ii, 160. See also Cooper, *Annals of Cambridge,* II, 217.

[23] *S.P.Dom. Eliz.* xxxix, 14.

College, for example, whose pious scruples about the surplice were found to exist only after he had pawned that garment to pay for a dinner party was perhaps more typical of those with whom they had to deal.[24] Yet the request of these Heads and professors was remembered against them. Two years later Whitgift was forced to assure Cecil of his loyalty and obedience in the face of reports circulating about him.

For God's sake [he wrote], let it be judged what I am by my doings, and not by the report of those, who do not unto me as they would be done unto. As touching my non-conformity . . . I never encouraged any to withstand the queens majesty's laws in that behalf; but I both have, and do by all means I can, seek to persuade men to conform themselves. For it grieveth me that any man should cease from preaching, for the use of these things, being of themselves indifferent.[25]

The vestiarian controversy was finally brought to an end in the summer of 1566 by the publication and enforcement of Archbishop Parker's *Advertisements*.[26] Elizabeth had at last agreed that Parker might have a free hand to secure uniformity in his own way. Signed by the episcopal members of the Ecclesiastical Commission, the articles of the *Advertisements* were issued under a reference to the Queen's sharp letter to the archbishop in the previous year—"by virtue of the Queens Majesties Letters commanding the same, the 25th day of January, in the seventh year of the Reign of our Sovereign Lady Elizabeth."[27] Based upon the "Interpretations" which the bishops had compiled early in the

[24] Strype, *Annals,* II, ii, 161-2.
[25] Whitgift, *Works,* III, 597. Strype, *Whitgift,* III, 8-9.
[26] *Visitation Articles,* III, 171-80.
[27] Sparrow, *Collection,* p. 121.

reign, Parker's articles were in effect a compromise between the requirements of the ornaments rubric and the practices of the Puritan clergy. They represented the maximum amount of conformity that could be secured in the circumstances. The *Advertisements* required the wearing of the surplice at all ministrations and the use of the prescribed outdoor garb. In cathedrals and collegiate churches the cope was ordered for celebrations of the Holy Communion. Holy tables were to be decently covered and reverently used; communicants were to receive kneeling. All preaching licenses were ordered renewed and unlicensed ministers were enjoined to use the homilies without gloss or addition. Finally, a new pledge of conformity was exacted from those admitted to any ecclesiastical cure or office.

Imposed without deviation in all the dioceses, the *Advertisements* provoked a momentary uproar, but their simplicity and clarity left little room for tendentious debate. Parker's hand grew firmer as he felt the support of the Queen, and the bishops had no alternative save to obey orders that were backed by royal authority. Though a few remained stubbornly obdurate, temporary suspensions and threats of deprivation brought the majority of non-conforming clergy into obedience.[28] The shower of letters that rained upon the continental divines, appealing for their support of the Precisians, served little purpose.[29] The word that came from Zurich was disappointing. Bullinger supported the side of authority and the bishops lost no time publishing his sentiments.[30] In the end a surprising measure of conformity resulted, due as much to Archbishop Parker's generous and

[28] *Z. L.,* II, 119. *Parker Correspondence,* pp. 267-70, 275-9, 285.
[29] *Z. L.,* I, 151-5; II, 121-4.
[30] *Ibid.,* I, 345-55; I, 168.

patient forbearance as to the firmness with which the regulations were imposed.

Yet an ominous cloud remained upon the horizon of the settlement. Despite the lull in the controversy, the storm was not over. The more earnest Puritans perceived that there was more involved in this struggle than "merely disputing about a cap or a surplice," as Humphrey and Sampson put it.[31] Was their Church, after all, truly reformed? Was not their quarrel really with a settlement in which godly discipline was entirely wanting, and in its place an authority constituted without reference to the Word of God? Here and there little signs of dispute on a new level appeared. A tract of 1566 raised the question of whether in the scriptural plan for the Church the magistrate was not subordinate to the Church.[32] The hearing that resulted in the deprivation of the Puritan minister Brokesley in 1565 sounded an equally ominous note. Refusing the vestments as "stinking and abominable rags," Brokesley declared that "in time of ministration he was above the Queene."[33] It is plain that a critical doubt had arisen in the minds of an increasing number of Puritans. Was the settlement one in which true obedience could be given to the Word of God and to a Church constituted under royal supremacy at the same time?[34] But it was as yet a little cloud, and the trouble brewing was unnoticed at Cambridge.

Early in January 1567 Bishop Horne of Winchester suggested Whitgift's name for preferment to the vacant deanery of Canterbury, describing him to Cecil as "honest and verye

[31] *Ibid.*, I, 163. See also II, 358-62.

[32] *A Briefe Discourse against the Outwarde Apparell, etc.* See McGinn, *Admonition Controversy*, pp. 17 ff.

[33] *Seconde Parte*, I, 52.

[34] *Ibid.*, I, 58, 188.

well learned."[35] Cecil would not be hurried. After a careful investigation of Whitgift's career he summoned him in the spring to preach before the Queen. Elizabeth was delighted by Whitgift's vigorous discourse on the duty of conformity. Here was a cleric after her own heart, and almost at once advancement came from all sides. By summer Whitgift found himself a royal chaplain, Regius professor of divinity, and Master of Trinity College.[36] In the next year these offices were augmented by the gift of a prebend in Ely Cathedral.

The "Royal and Ancient Foundation of Trinity College," into the Master's lodge of which Whitgift shortly moved, was in 1567 a rambling collection of medieval halls and hotels seized by Henry VIII for its foundation some twenty years earlier. Whitgift never knew the spacious courts that were rebuilt during Neville's mastership at the end of the century and which have made Trinity the most beautiful and impressive collegiate foundation in England. Yet the lavish patronage of Henry's children, tangibly advertised by Elizabeth's completion of Mary Tudor's chapel, had already raised the new college to a position of importance in the University. A decade of Whitgift's able administration left Trinity College with that repute it has since enjoyed. The college became his at once. His spare figure policed the courts; his watchful eye roved warningly over the hall. Disorder would not interrupt the pursuit of learning in his college. He would not have his boys caught by the proctors bull-baiting at Chesterton or sneaking off for a swim in the river. The statutes, laws, and customs of the college would be scrupulously observed. Fellows, suddenly made aware

---

[35] *S.P.Dom.Eliz.* xlii. 7.

[36] He had been elected Master of Pembroke in April 1567, but within three months Elizabeth appointed him to fill the vacancy at Trinity left by Beaumont's death. Baumgartner Papers, Add. 10. 53(5). Strype, *Whitgift,* I, 19.

that their pledges of loyalty and obedience to the Master were serious commitments, longed for the lax days of Beaumont's rule, while readers protested a tyranny that made them lecture during the summer term. The whole college chafed uneasily but unavailingly under the adjustment to a new discipline in which Whitgift grimly insisted upon exact obedience to every statute. He willingly abolished obsolete regulations—undertaking, in fact, a revision of the entire set of Trinity statutes—but until such changes were ordered by proper authority, conformity would be a salutory disciplinary exercise.

Whitgift's stern rule of the college was nearly always presented in the worst possible light by his enemies. For example, the charges of Giles Wiggington, later one of the most stubborn Puritans, concerning Whitgift's "hard dealinge" with him when he was a scholar and Junior Fellow of Trinity are hardly unbiased. They reveal at least as much of Wiggington's contentiousness as they do of Whitgift's severity. The Master, he complained, made diligent inquiry "after such scholars and boys as durst be bold to reprove sin and call for reformation." Them, Whitgift termed "saucy boys, busy bodies, and meddlers," and Wiggington is pleased to be able to say that he was found "as happy it was, to be of that number." He appends to his complaints a list of breaches of discipline for which Whitgift made his life miserable in Trinity. Apparently Wiggington, free with his criticisms of "prelacie," abandoned the surplice and square cap when he could, was generally thought to be unsociable, and was reproached for lack of personal cleanliness.[37] Puritanism was not at its most attractive level in Giles Wiggington.

But pupils like Bacon, Coke, and Essex were young men

[37] *Seconde Parte,* II, 241.

of another stamp. They responded to the high state of order and intellectual activity to which Whitgift carried Trinity College. If his methods were unpopular and his austerity aroused little affection, his integrity and willingness to assume himself the burdens he laid upon others won the respect of the best men in all faculties and colleges. His purpose never faltered.

I may not suffer [he wrote] those with whom I have to do to disquiet the university or college with false doctrine and schismatical opinions: I may not suffer them openly to break and contemn those laws and statutes which they are sworn to observe, and I to execute: I may not suffer any man, against the express words of his oath, against all honesty and conscience, to live under me, lest I be partaker of his perjury. These be the things I have done, and these be the things that I intend to do; whereby as hitherto I have kept the place where I am in some quiet and good order, so do I trust to continue it, both to the glory of God, the honour of the prince, the great increase of learning, the edifying of Christ's church, and the commendation both of the college and the whole university.[38]

We should not be far wrong to see in Whitgift the Elizabethan prototype of the Anglican schoolmaster-bishop so prominent in the nineteenth century, and whose contributions to both the learning and the good order of the Church have been far from negligible.

Fresh from the tumults of the vestiarian controversy, the Heads of the colleges looked upon Whitgift as a deliverer. If he could bring order into Trinity College, why not into the whole University? Consequently, they supported whole-

[38] Whitgift, *Works*, III, 395-6.

heartedly his project to reform the general statutes of Cambridge. The disorders of the recent dispute had convinced Whitgift that such changes must be made as would prevent another collapse of discipline. With the opportunity and support at hand he turned to the task with resolute determination, rapidly assuming a place of vigorous and undisputed leadership in University affairs.[39]

The new project was scarcely under way, however, when the thunder of a fresh Puritan storm echoed over Cambridge. Thomas Cartwright, absent from the University during the vestiarian troubles, returned to his fellowship at Trinity College, and at once his Puritan influence spread through Cambridge. A powerful and persuasive preacher, Cartwright soon attracted a large and loyal following. The inevitable crisis came late in 1569. When Whitgift resigned the Regius professorship in order to devote all his energies to administrative responsibilities, Laurence Chaderton was moved to that chair from the Lady Margaret professorship and Cartwright took that place. At once, lecturing on the book of *Acts,* the Puritan leader launched an attack upon the church order of the establishment and a provocative exposition of the presbyterianism of primitive Christianity. The Heads of colleges were aroused by the overt assault upon the ecclesiastical settlement and alarmed by his deliberate encouragement of dissension in the University. William Chaderton of Queens' wrote Cecil in June 1570 that Cambridge would soon be "all in a hurly-burly and shameful broil" over "such doctrine as is pernicious and not tolerable for a Christian commonwealth." It was Cartwright's intent, he declared, "to overthrow all ecclesiastical and civil

[39] Corpus Christi College MSS, 118.40; 106.300; 119.86. Whitgift was vice-chancellor twice: 1570-1; 1573-4. *Grace Book* △, p. 570.

governance that now is, and to ordain and institute a new-found policy."[40]

The letter was but one of many that poured in upon Cecil from all sides. Whitgift, Perne, and John May of St. Catherine's continued the complaints of the Heads, while even Grindal raised his voice against Cartwright's "busy head . . . stuffed full of singularities."[41] Despite the memorials drawn up by Cartwright's supporters, the university authorities acted decisively. Having refused the Puritan lecturer admission to the doctorate, the Heads suspended his lectures and stopped his salary, informing Cecil in August that they "thought it very convenient and necessary to stay Mr. Cartwright from reading."[42] Whitgift, after a painful interview with him, prepared to dispatch to the court a list of Cartwright's acknowledged propositions for further reformation of the Church which contained in summary form the chief points of the new Puritan attack upon the constitution of the establishment:

I. The names and functions of archbishops and archdeacons ought to be suppressed.

II. The names of lawful ministers in the Church, such as bishops and deacons, when abstracted from the office described in Holy Scripture, are likewise to be rejected, and the whole brought back to apostolical institution. And thus the bishops' functions ought to be limited to praying and preaching, and the deacons' to taking care of the poor.

III. The government of the Church ought not to be entrusted with bishops' chancellors, or archdeacons' officials, but lodged in the hands of the minister and elders of the same Church.

[40] *S.P.Dom.Eliz.* lxxi. 11.
[41] *Ibid.*, lxxi. 23, 58.
[42] *Ibid.*, lxxiii. 11.

IV. That the ministry ought not to go loose and at large; but that everyone ought to be tied to a particular congregation.

V. That nobody ought to solicit for the function of a minister, nor stand candidate, as it were, for that employment.

VI. That ministers ought not to be ordained by the sole authority of the bishop, much less are they to receive orders in a study, or such private place; but this office ought to be conferred by a public choice of the congregation.[43]

Meanwhile, during the uproar Whitgift had worked feverishly upon the new university statutes, and in September they were granted by the Queen. It became evident at once that the new regulations would make far-reaching changes in the structure and life of Cambridge. The curriculum was reorganized, residence requirements were stiffened, and the conditions governing admission to degrees made more stringent. Administrative changes were equally drastic. The power of the proctors and the independence of the collegiate fellows were seriously curtailed, while governance over nearly every area of university life was securely vested in the hands of the small group of Heads of colleges.[44] In effect the new statutes, which remained in force nearly two and a half centuries, completed the transformation of medieval Cambridge into the University familiar until recent times. They were in many ways the greatest monument to Whitgift's work in the University. Furthermore, their appearance was nicely timed to secure control of Cambridge to the supporters of the Elizabethan settlement, driving the Puritan influence out into the Church at large.

[43] *Ibid.*, lxxiii. 26; lxxiv. 29. Whitgift, *Works*, III, 598-600. See also a broadside on Cartwright's view of church government. Lambeth MSS, 30.6. 24(5).

[44] Peacock, *Observations on the Statutes*, pp. 45 ff. For the statutes see Heywood and Wright, *Cambridge University Transactions*, pp. 1-45 or *Statutes of the University*, ed. Heywood, pp. 360 ff.

On November 7, 1570 the Heads of the colleges thanked
Cecil for his aid in procuring the statutes, informing him
also of their intention to deprive Cartwright of his professorship.[45] Cartwright refused to recant, and under the
inflexible leadership of Whitgift, now serving his first term
as vice-chancellor, the Heads declared the Lady Margaret
chair vacant. Cartwright departed for Geneva, there to study
the godly reformation of the Church at first hand, and Cambridge subsided into quiet once more. "With Mr. Cartwright's presence here," Whitgift described Trinity College
as "marvellous troublesome and contentious"; with Cartwright gone, it became "as quiet a college as any was in all
Cambridge."[46]

Whitgift's defense of the established ecclesiastical order
and his administrative leadership at Cambridge were amply
rewarded by the government. In June 1571 he was named
Dean of Lincoln, an office richly endowed and requiring
little onerous duty.[47] With characteristic thoroughness he
shifted his interests to Lincoln, resigning his preferment in
Ely for similar positions in the diocese to the north. The
Ely canonry was exchanged for the prebend of Nassington
in Lincoln Cathedral; the Teversham living for the parish
of Laceby.[48] Installed on August 2nd, Whitgift thereafter
spent some months each year in the Old Deanery among
the canons' residences encircling the hill above the ancient
city of Lincoln. Here he could indulge a display of state
appropriate to his office and dignity, basking in the inherited
grandeur of the Deans of Lincoln whose trains were ceremoniously borne across the Minster Yard. Here, too, he

[45] *S.P.Dom.Eliz.* lxxiv. 29.

[46] Petyt MSS, 538. xxxiii. f. 61.

[47] *Chapter Act Records,* Lincoln, A. 3.8. f. 48.

[48] *Athenae Cantab.,* II, 369-70. *Bishop Cooper's Act Book,* Lincoln Reg-
istry, f. 2. *Lincoln Episcopal Records,* pp. 1, 312.

cherished the tradition of learning from the days of St. Hugh and Robert Grosseteste, spent long hours in the magnificent library, and began a friendship with Bishop Cooper that was to last for twenty years. Though one of the wealthiest pluralists in the Elizabethan Church during the decade of the 'seventies, Whitgift was given neither to waste nor to self-indulgence. His meticulous accounts reveal a careful stewardship of his monies.[49]

The effects of the dispersal of the Cartwright faction from Cambridge were not long in appearing. If the Puritan lecturer's opinions had caused alarm in 1570, the disturbance was mild compared with the outbreak of controversy that came little more than a year later. Between the spring of 1571 and the summer of 1572 the sessions of Parliament were the scenes of a determined effort to modify the ecclesiastical formularies and legalize the practices of the Precisians. The attempt was well-timed, for from the appearance of Mary Stuart in England in 1568 through the crisis of the Northern Rebellion in the following year to the publication of the papal bull deposing Elizabeth in 1570, the nation was in the grip of passionate anti-Catholic feeling. Fear of Rome and Protestant patriotism ran high. Consequently, the Puritan hopes seemed well founded, and the more so because in this decade appear the first clear signs of that growing alliance between the revolutionary challenge which Puritanism offered to the religious settlement and the encroachments of parliamentary Erastianism upon the ecclesiastical prerogatives of the Crown.

Twice Elizabeth was forced to prevent the passage in the House of Commons of religious legislation that would alter

---

[49] Lambeth MSS, 807. The income from Whitgift's benefices amounted to about £6000 in our money. Few Elizabethan pluralists surpassed that. HMC, *Salis*. MSS, XIII, 34.

the settlement of 1559. Strickland, the author of a proposal to reform the Prayer Book, was briefly suspended "for exhibiting a bill into the House against the prerogative of the Queen."[50] In the following spring Elizabeth again intervened, suppressing debate upon measures that in their most extreme form would have restricted the application of the *Act of Uniformity* to those "who shall use any manner of superstitious or papistical service," while allowing Puritan ministers to abridge or alter the prescribed forms of worship at will.[51] The Queen's action was sharp and decisive. She impounded the bills and the Speaker informed Commons that "her Highness' pleasure is that from henceforth no bills concerning religion shall be preferred or received into this House, unless the same should be first considered and liked by the clergy."[52]

Meanwhile the Puritan agitation had made itself felt in another fashion. Convocation, assembling for business after hearing a vigorous sermon by Whitgift against the enemies of the Church, made the final small changes in the *Thirty-Nine Articles* drawn up by that body in 1563.[53] A bill thereupon appeared in Parliament requiring subscription, but only of those selected articles to which there were no Puritan objections.[54] The other articles were to be omitted. Elizabeth promptly refused her consent to a measure that would mutilate the formularies in this fashion.[55] Pressure was con-

[50] D'Ewes, *Journals,* p. 175. Strickland was evidently the spokesman for a group of determined Puritans. Neale, *Elizabeth I and Her Parliaments,* p. 195.

[51] *Puritan Manifestoes,* pp. 149-51.

[52] D'Ewes, *Journals,* p. 213.

[53] Cardwell, *Synodalia,* I, 34-107. The changes are discussed by Bicknell, *Thirty-Nine Articles,* pp. 19 ff.

[54] Neale, "Parliament and the Articles of Religion, 1571" *E.H.R.* (Oct., 1952), lxvii, p. 515. See the references to this measure in Wentworth's speech in 1587. D'Ewes, *Journals,* p. 239.

[55] *Ibid.,* p. 180.

tinued, however, and the final form of legislation to which she reluctantly gave the royal assent was a statute that confirmed all the articles, but limited the required subscription to those "which only concern the Confession of a true Christian faith and the doctrine of the sacraments."[56] All ordained by forms other than those of Edward VI and Elizabeth—a clause aimed at Marian clergy—and all who in future were admitted to benefices were to subscribe. The statutory limitation led the Puritans to suppose that the articles on the Church and its ministry might be evaded, but unfortunately for these hopes, the *Canons of 1571,* approved by Convocation, made it plain that preachers would subscribe the entire set of articles.[57] Though despite Parker's request these canons never received the Queen's formal assent, the archbishop was certain of Elizabeth's support. He assured Grindal that "there would be no fear of praemunire-matter," and the *Canons of 1571,* like the *Advertisements,* were regarded as authoritative and so acted upon by the Ecclesiastical Commission. Parker and his supporters, thus armed, proceeded against the Puritans with a firm hand, strengthened by the Queen's command that "none should be suffered to decline either on the left or on the right hand from the direct line limited by the authority of our said laws and Injunctions."[58]

Disappointed in both Parliament and Convocation, the fury of the Puritans was unbounded, and a few days before Parliament rose in June 1572 the authorities were shocked by the appearance of a brief, anonymous tract entitled *An*

[56] 13 Eliz. c. 12. *Statutes,* IV, i, 546.
[57] Cardwell, *Synodalia,* I, 112, 127. The intricate story of the Puritan attempts to modify the ecclesiastical settlement in the parliamentary sessions of 1571-2 is clearly detailed by Neale, *Elizabeth I and Her Parliaments,* pp. 177-217; 291-304.
[58] *Parker Correspondence,* p. 386.

Admonition to the Parliament.[59] Launching a bitter and un-restrained attack upon the alleged abuses remaining in the English Church, it presented the Puritan demands for reformation in crisp and inflammatory language.

We in England [complained the authors] are so far off from having a church rightly reformed, according to the prescript of God's word, that as yet we are not come to the outward face of the same.[60]

The *Admonition* opened its challenge with an attack upon the clergy, for

either must we have a right ministry of God, and a right gov-ernment of his church, according to the scriptures set up (both which we lack) or else there can be no right religion.

The existing ministry was declared ignorant, neither properly qualified nor rightly ordained, abounding with "King Henry's priests, King Edward's priests, Queen Mary's priests." The authority of bishops to ordain men without cure and to force ministers upon congregations, the regula-tions concerning clerical vestments, the exercise of civil authority by the clergy, the

prescript order of service, and book of common prayer, in which a great number of things contrary to God's word are contained . . . patched out of the Pope's portuis,

homilies, articles, injunctions—all these must be removed or "God's church in this realm shall never be builded."

As for the Sacraments, their right ministration was abused

[59] Reprinted in *Puritan Manifestoes,* pp. 8-19.
[60] Quotations are from a copy of the 1st edition (*S.T.C.* 10847).

by practices borrowed from the papists—wafer-bread, fragments of epistles and gospels, kneeling for reception of communion, interrogatories at the font, "singing, piping, surplice and cope wearing . . . crossing and such like pieces of popery," and all other things lacking "the express warrant of God's word."

Defects of polity in the Queen's Church occupied the largest part of the *Admonition*. A return was demanded to what was conceived to be the order of the primitive Church.

Instead of an Archbishop or Lord bishop, you must make equality of ministers . . . plant in every congregation a lawful and godly seignorie . . . and to these three jointly, that is, the Ministers, Seniors, and Deacons, is the whole regiment of the church to be committed.

The exhortation that followed revealed that the pattern of the primitive Church was a Geneva model.

Is a reformation good for France, and can it be evil for England? Is discipline meet for Scotland, and is it unprofitable for this Realm? Surely God hath set these examples before your eyes to encourage you to go forward to a thorough and a speedy reformation . . . altogether remove whole Antichrist, both head, body, and branch, and perfectly plant that purity of the word, that simplicity of sacraments, and severity of discipline, which Christ hath commanded, and commended to his church.

The effect of the *Admonition* is easily imagined. It caused a stir such as had not been felt in England since Elizabeth's accession. Although the authors, John Field and Thomas Wilcox, were speedily apprehended and imprisoned, the bishops were unable to locate the hidden press and halt the publication. The authorities had little doubt that Thomas

Cartwright, now back from Geneva, was the chief instigator of the tumult, but they had no evidence with which to proceed against him. Whitgift alone could take steps to curb his influence, and in 1572 Cartwright was deprived of his fellowship at Trinity on the undeniable ground that he had broken both the statutes of the college and his personal oath of loyalty to its Master.[61] Cartwright's protest was only a formality; his sphere of activity was now far wider than the courts of a Cambridge college.

With the appearance of the *Admonition* Elizabethan Puritanism entered its mature phase. Though often given lengthier or more precise expression, Puritan demands thereafter changed but little from their summary by the authors of this tract.[62] Moreover, the dissidents called into question not merely the rites and usages, but also the very foundations of the established Church. When two decades later Bishop Cooper had finished describing the discontent of the early Precisians, he continued,

Not long after there came forth another sort affirming that those matters touching apparel were but trifles, and not worthy contention in the Church, but that there were greater things far of more weight and importance, and indeed touching faith and religion, and therefore meet to be altered in a Church rightly reformed: as the book of Common Prayer, the administration of the Sacraments, the government of the Church, the election of ministers, and a number of other like.[63]

If further evidence of the new Puritanism was needed, it was supplied in no uncertain terms by the violent diatribe

[61] Pearson, *Cartwright,* pp. 428-9. Whitgift, *Works,* I, 123, 507; III, 324, 395.

[62] See the Puritan complaints assembled in 1593 in *A Parte of a Register,* pp. 401 ff., and *Tracts Ascribed to Richard Bancroft,* pp. 22 ff.

[63] Cooper, *Admonition to the People,* p. 158.

attached to the *Admonition to the Parliament,* entitled *A view of popishe abuses yet remaining in the Englishe Church for the which Godly Ministers have refused to subscribe.* While not much more than a catalog of Puritan objections to the three-fold subscription that Parker and the bishops enforced—that is, to the Prayer Book, the *Thirty-Nine Articles,* and the orders for clerical apparel—the treatise contains a significant admission of the real point at issue. "Neither is the controversy betwixt them and us . . . as for a cap, a tippet, or a surplice, but for great matters concerning a true ministry and regiment of the church."[64]

The *Admonition* left the bishops aghast at the temerity of their opponents, and those most shocked were men who had formerly been sympathetic with the scruples of the Precisians. Their letters to Bullinger and other continental divines betray their bewilderment and opposition to the revolutionary turn of the Puritan attack. Bishop Cox complained to Gualter,

It is not enough to have the papists our enemies, without stirring up men . . . who are labouring to bring about a revolution in the church.[65]

He described the Puritans to Bullinger as

factious and heady men, who in their writings and sermons . . . pull in pieces the whole economy of our church . . . Their object is to revive the ancient presbytery . . .[66]

A few months later Cox's wrath was almost uncontrollable.

---

[64] *Puritan Manifestoes,* p. 36n.
[65] *Z. L.,* I, 281.
[66] *Ibid.,* I, 284-5.

These unruly men [he wrote Gualter] have burst by their reckless attacks the barriers of law and religion . . . zealously endeavouring to overthrow the entire order of our Anglican Church.[67]

Sandys, so lenient with the earlier malcontents, was scarcely less restrained than Cox. Perhaps it was because the diocese of London to which he had been translated from Worcester was the center of the worst Puritan disaffection. He poured out his feelings to Bullinger:

New orators are rising up from among us, foolish young men, who while they despise authority, and admit of no superior, are seeking the complete overthrow and rooting up of our whole ecclesiastical polity, so piously constituted and confirmed . . .

He then summarized the Puritan opinions which he believed would make for the confusion and ruin of the Church:

1. The civil magistrate has no authority in ecclesiastical matters. He is only a member of the church, the government of which ought to be committed to the clergy.

2. The church of Christ admits of no other government than that by presbyteries; viz. by the minister, elders, and deacon.

3. The names and authority of archbishops, archdeacons, deans, chancellors, commissaries, and other titles and dignities of the like kind, should be altogether removed from the church of Christ.

4. Each parish should have its own presbytery.

5. The choice of ministers of necessity belongs to the people.

6. The goods, possessions, lands, revenues, titles, honours, authorities, and all other things relating either to bishops or cathedrals, and which now of right belong to them, should be taken away forthwith and for ever.

[67] *Ibid.,* I, 298.

7. No one should be allowed to preach who is not a pastor of some congregation; and he ought to preach to his own flock exclusively, and no where else.

8. The infants of papists are not to be baptized.

9. The judicial laws of Moses are binding upon christian princes, and they ought not in the slightest degree to depart from them.[68]

Even the mild Grindal complained of the virulent pamphlets in which the presbyterian system was advocated. Ever trying to think the best of the Puritans, however, he wrote,

They are young men who disseminate these opinions, and they have their supporters, especially from among those who are gaping for ecclesiastical property: but yet I am glad to say that Humphrey, and Sampson, and some others, who heretofore moved the question about ceremonies, are entirely opposed to this party.[69]

It was hardest, perhaps, for Bishop Pilkington of Durham, whose previous leniency with the Precisians had led to considerable disorder. He admitted that he had misplaced his sympathy, and was constrained to write Gualter,

Your prudence has heard, I well know, and that often enough to weary you, of that unhappy dispute among some of our friends respecting the affair of the habits and dress of the clergy . . . it has now so broken out afresh, nay more, that which heretofore lurked in dissimulation has now so openly discovered itself, that not only the habits, but our whole ecclesiastical polity, discipline, the revenues of bishops, ceremonies or public forms of worship, liturgies, vocation of ministers, or

[68] *Ibid.,* I, 295-6.
[69] *Ibid.,* I, 292.

the ministration of the sacraments—all these things are now openly attacked from the press, and it is contended with the greatest bitterness, that they are not to be endured in the church of Christ.[70]

The *Admonition to the Parliament* had not been long in circulation before the bishops determined that an answer should be made, and the Master of Trinity was selected to defend the principles of the establishment. Whitgift needed little urging from Archbishop Parker to undertake a task so much to his liking. Hard work during the summer of 1572 brought the first draft of his answer near completion by September.

I have finished the confutation of the Admonition [he wrote Parker], and the first part of it I have written out fair, which I mind to send to your grace very shortly, after I have let my Lord of Ely and Dr. Perne, or some other peruse it . . .[71]

Assurances of the approval of Cox and Perne were in the archbishop's hands by early October, and steps were taken for speedy publication. But just at that moment there appeared from the Puritan press *A Second Admonition to the Parliament*, widely but erroneously attributed to Thomas Cartwright.[72] The *Second Admonition* was a confused exposition of the courts, synods, and consistories of the presbyterian system, showing the evident influence of the polity of the French Reformed Church and Scottish presbyterianism. Lacking the fiery freshness of the original *Admonition*,

---

[70] *Ibid.,* I, 287.
[71] Petyt MSS. 538. xxxviii. f. 61.
[72] *Puritan Manifestoes,* pp. 80-133. The evidence against Cartwright's authorship is entirely convincing. Pearson, *Cartwright,* pp. 74 ff. Whitgift ascribed only its instigation to Cartwright. *Works,* I, 46, 54, 93.

the chief significance of the second tract is in its guidance to presbyterian practice. It is not mere coincidence that in the month of its publication the Puritans formed their first presbytery at Wandsworth in Surrey.[73]

The bishops urged Whitgift not to delay his refutation in order to deal with the *Second Admonition*. It was an open secret that he was preparing to confound the Puritans, and the importunate episcopal zeal sprang from the fear that their opponents would have an answer ready as soon as Whitgift's volume left the press. This humiliation was spared them. In February 1573 Whitgift's book appeared, *An answere to a certen Libel intituled, An admonition to the Parliament.* It was a masterpiece in the usual Tudor pattern of controversial writing. The text of the *Admonition* was reproduced page by page, and paragraph after paragraph was refuted in detail. At once the authorities strove to ensure that there would be no Puritan reply. Censorship was rigidly enforced; the countryside was scoured in an attempt to locate the hidden Puritan press.[74] These efforts, however, were of no avail for in April the rejoinder was printed in the form of Thomas Cartwright's *A Replye to an answere made of M. Doctor Whitgifte Agaynste the Admonition to the Parliament.*

The summer of 1573 saw the Puritan disturbances at their height. While Whitgift's *Answer* had only one reprinting, both the original *Admonition* and Cartwright's *Reply* ran through edition after edition. Elizabeth's proclamation of June 11th had not the slightest effect upon the circulation of the Puritan books. In diocese after diocese, the followers of Cartwright, inflamed by the controversial literature, plunged the bishops into despair. Edmund Scambler, Bishop of Peter-

[73] Knappen, *Tudor Puritanism*, p. 304.
[74] *Acts of the Privy Council*, VIII, 93.

borough, found his see completely out of hand. He wrote pathetically to Cecil, now Lord Burghley,

My very good Lord, I most entirely, in the name of Christ Jesus, beseech you . . . to aid me with your counsel for the better discharge of my office, and the peace of the country. I am, without God's assistance and yours, very weak and unable to execute and discharge the same in these troubles, now moved and procured by those whom men do call Puritans . . . They are grown apparently to neglect, if they do not abhor the divine service set out by public authority. So that in the town of Over-ston . . . there is no divine service upon most Sundays and holy days, according to the book of Common Prayer, but instead thereof two sermons be preached . . . by . . . men for their opinions not licensed by me to preach at this day. When they are determined to receive the communion they repair to Whiston . . . there to receive the sacraments with preachers and ministers to their own liking, and contrary to the form prescribed by the public order of the Realm . . ."[75]

Archbishop Parker confided to Burghley his fears that the Puritans not only "cut down the ecclesiastical state, but also gave a great push at the civil policy."[76] It was a threat already made plain to the Queen's chief minister by the brash statements of a leading Puritan of London, Edward Dering. Dering, whose common boast was that Parker might be the last Archbishop of Canterbury, was difficult to silence. The leniency shown him by Bishop Sandys was rewarded with the warning that if the bishop dared take disciplinary action he might find himself unhorsed in Cheapside by some "disordered fellows."[77]

[75] Ellis, *Letters,* 2nd Series, III, 33-6.
[76] *Parker Correspondence,* p. 434.
[77] Strype, *Parker,* II, 270.

Sandys' authority was openly flouted in London. He could not trust even those he invited to preach at Paul's Cross. They surprised the bishop with an unexpected attack upon the Church, and then fled before his officers could catch them. "There is a conventicle, or rather conspiracy breeding in London," he wrote Burghley and Leicester. "The city will never be quiet until these authors of sedition, who are now esteemed as gods, as Field, Wilcox, Cartwright, and other, be removed."[78] Sandys wasted his time complaining to Leicester. He, with Walsingham and Knollys, was largely responsible for that "comfort these Puritans have," as Parker put it, from some members of the Council.[79]

Yet in the autumn of the same year the tide began to turn. Forcing the Council to uphold the bishops, Elizabeth published "A Proclamation against the Despisers and Breakers of the Orders prescribed in the Book of Common-prayer."[80] Warrants were immediately issued and arrests were numerous. Thoroughly alarmed by the attempt of an unbalanced Puritan fanatic to assassinate Sir Christopher Hatton, reputedly the staunchest opponent of Puritanism on the Council, the authorities showed no leniency. A score of deprivations and prison sentences scattered the Puritan leaders. Dering was silenced, and when Stroud the printer was seized the unlicensed press ceased to function. In December, under the threat of a special order issued for his apprehension, Cartwright fled abroad. By the following summer the controversy had died down, and the bishops somewhat optimistically informed their friends on the Continent that

---

[78] Strype, *Whitgift*, III, 32-5.
[79] *Parker Correspondence*, p. 418. See also *Seconde Parte*, I, 187.
[80] Sparrow, *Collection*, pp. 169-70. See *Acts of the Privy Council*, VIII, 140.

this new fabric of new discipline will shortly fall in pieces by its own weight, since it appears that many of our countrymen who formerly admired it, are now grown weary of it.[81]

Bishop Cox wrote Gualter that finally

these noisy disturbers now give us scarcely any trouble, except that they continue to carp at our rites, like ghosts in the dark; they have for sometime past been restrained by a rather severe correction, and are now vanquished by a most learned confutation.[82]

But the Bishop of Ely, who regarded Whitgift as "the most vehement enemy of the schismatics, and the chief instrument against them," nevertheless exaggerated the effects of his answer to the *Admonition*. The Puritans moved in the dark, but not like ghosts. On the contrary, they were busily occupied with the underground organization and development of the Genevan system of polity and discipline.

Meanwhile, John Whitgift was only remotely touched by these alarms that disturbed the Church. During the months of 1573, his attention riveted on Cartwright's *Reply,* he labored to prepare a rebuttal that would silence his antagonist. In June he informed Parker that his new work should provide the final word, warning the archbishop modestly that "the book will be something big."[83] This, indeed, was no exaggeration for Whitgift's *Defense of the Answere to the Admonition against the Replie of T. C.,* published in February 1574, was a fat folio of some eight hundred pages, reproducing within the framework of its argument nearly all

---

[81] *Z. L.,* I, 311. See also I, 320.
[82] *Ibid.,* I, 306.
[83] Strype, *Parker,* II, 254.

the material of the earlier books of the controversy. In the end the *Defense* proved simply a summary of the whole debate.[84]

Whitgift dispatched a copy to Lord Burghley at once. He wrote,

I am bold to offer unto you my book of Defense, against the last Replye of T.C. . . . And although I know that your leisure will not serve you to peruse it through, yet if it shall please your Lordship sometimes to read of it . . . you will soon perceive how little cause there is so grievously to accuse this Church of England, and so bitterly to inveigh against such lawful, godly orders, and kind of government, as is used in the same . . .

If I have not answered every point of the Replye to the satisfying of every man's opinion . . . there be divers learned men in England, to which I am in all respects far inferior, that are able to supply my want, and to satisfy to the full that which lacketh in me. And in my opinion it were not amiss if they were moved to do so. For so common a cause ought not to be ventured upon by one man's labours . . .

It becometh me not, neither is it needful, to move your Lordship to be zealous in the cause . . . Only this I am well assured of, that if they should be suffered to proceed as they have begun, nothing else in the end can be looked for, than confusion both of the Church and of the State. But convenient discipline, joined with doctrine, being duly executed will soon remedy all. For sects and schisms can by no means abide these two: neither will they long continue, where they are not by some in authority cherished and maintained. This, experience and the stories of all ages teach

[84] Cartwright, somewhat half-heartedly, continued the controversy from abroad. *The Second replie of T. C. against Maister Doctor Whitgiftes second answer* appeared in 1575, and *The rest of the second replie of T. Cartvurihght* two years later.

us to be true. The Lord give peace unto his Church: the Lord preserve your Lordship and govern you with his Holy Spirit . . .

From Trinity College in Cambridge, the 5th day of February 1573[4]. To your Lordship most bound, and forever to command,

John Whitgift.[85]

[85] Strype, *Whitgift,* III, 35-6.

IV

WHITGIFT AT WORCESTER

THE Elizabethan government was seldom slow to increase the responsibilities of the staunch upholders of the established ecclesiastical order. In the spring of 1575 Archbishop Parker named Whitgift among those who might be preferred to the vacant see of Norwich. It was one of Parker's last acts. Two months later he was dead, and before the end of the year Elizabeth yielded to Burghley's suggestion that Edmund Grindal be translated from York to Canterbury. Though Freke had been chosen for the Norwich vacancy and Piers replaced him at Rochester, in 1576 the death of the Bishop of Worcester, Nicholas Bullingham, turned the Queen's mind again to John Whitgift. Assailed by doubts of her wisdom in placing Grindal at Lambeth, Elizabeth could ill afford not to count among her bishops the most vigorous champion of the establishment. Already she was at loggerheads with her new archbishop over the "exercises" or "prophesyings" sponsored by the Puritan clergy, Grindal defending them as "set down in holy scriptures," and serving "to the great profit of the church," the Queen convinced that those who took part in them were "schismatically divided among themselves into variety of dangerous opinions . . . and manifestly thereby encouraged to the violation of our laws, and to the breach of common order."[1]

On March 24, 1577 the royal *congé d'élire* went to the Dean and Chapter of Worcester and eleven days later Whitgift was elected to the bishopric. Consecrated in Lambeth Chapel on the 21st of April, he took formal possession of the see by proxy enthronement on May 12th.[2] Meanwhile, resigning his offices and livings, he prepared to leave Cambridge. If the break with Lincoln and Bishop Cooper was not easy, the severance of his associations with the University was hard in the extreme. For more than twenty-five years Cambridge had been his life. Yet duty could not be denied, and early in June, Whitgift preached in Trinity College for the last time. The chapel was crowded to the doors with his friends and supporters. "Finally, brethren, fare you well: Be perfect," he pleaded, "be of good comfort, be of one mind, live in peace, and the God of love and peace shall be with you."[3] A few days later, amid tumultuous demonstrations, he was ceremoniously escorted out of Cambridge on his way to Worcester and a new quarter-century of labor in the Elizabethan episcopate.

Few historians of the English Church have resisted the temptation to make sweeping generalizations about the corrupt character of the Elizabethan bishops. Cranky old John Scory of Hereford, for example, has long provided the favorite illustration of episcopal venality and maladministration.[4] Sometime a Dominican friar, Edwardian Bishop of Chichester and one of Parker's consecrators, Scory was nom-

[1] Cardwell, *Doc. Annals,* I, 430-2.
[2] *Reg. Whitgift* (Worcester), 32, II, f. 13b. His consecrators were Edmund Grindal of Canterbury, John Aylmer of London, Richard Curteis of Chichester, and Robert Horne of Winchester. *Reg. Grindal,* f. 34.
[3] Paule, p. 26.
[4] Even Sir John Harington suggested that if he were in the line of apostolic succession it was as successor to Judas. *Nugae Antiquae,* II, 178.

inated to Hereford in 1559. It was not a happy appointment. Loathing Hereford with a detestation cordially returned by the clergy and gentry of the diocese, the bishop was forced to fend for himself. He stripped the episcopal estates of much valuable timber, a practice all too common among Elizabethan bishops, and showed remarkable skill at diverting ecclesiastical revenues to his own use. Mrs. Scory actually held three sinecure collegiate prebends, and strong suspicions of simony and extortion were aroused by the bishop's administration of patronage.[5] But it was the weakness of desperation rather than calculated wickedness that drove Scory to his sharp practices. Despite his protests, upon his appointment to Hereford Elizabeth ruthlessly stripped the see of a number of valuable manors, diminishing the total revenue of the bishopric by more than half.[6] A man of stronger character than Scory would have found such impoverishment a ground of temptation.

Generalizing from examples like this has created the impression that except for Parker, Jewel, Whitgift, and perhaps one or two others of attested ability and integrity, Elizabeth's bishops were a poor lot. At best inefficient administrators, possessed of a misplaced zeal that often resulted in the destruction of many of England's ecclesiastical monuments, at worst they were ambitious and avaricious place-seekers, ready to despoil their sees and alienate the possessions of the Church for their own security and advancement.

If we sift the sands of this denigration carefully there are, of course, some grains of truth to be found. Place-seekers there were, as Burghley complained. Howland, for example, was eager to exchange Peterborough for a richer see lest

[5] *S.P.Dom.Eliz.* xcviii. 35. See also cvii. 34; cxxxvii. 72.
[6] *Ibid.* xvii. 32.

poverty force him, as he picturesquely put it, "to let fall my sail and withdraw myself under the hatches."[7] Freke of Norwich, whose episcopal household was unpleasantly dominated by "Mrs. Bushopp," more than once indicated his readiness to move to a less turbulent diocese. Fletcher, incompetent and avaricious, propelled himself rapidly through a number of lesser offices to the successive sees of Bristol, Worcester, and London. His undoing was a second marriage to a rich and attractive young lady, a step that brought the royal wrath down upon Bishops Cox and Godwin also. DeMaisse's observation that "the Queen takes no pleasure in the sight of a married bishop" was an absurdly restrained comment upon Elizabeth's strong dislike of married clergy.[8] As for their second marriage, the Queen's fury could convert it into a disaster.

There were also, no doubt, lax and inefficient administrators on the Elizabethan bench of bishops. Lichfield suffered for many years under Bentham and Overton; Bullingham, Sandys, Grindal, and Parkhurst all lacked administrative ability. Perhaps the Welsh dioceses had the longest run of incompetent rulers, though this was scarcely a novelty in Wales. Meyrick despoiled Bangor for his own gain, Hughes of St. Asaph at one time held no less than fifteen benefices, and Middleton at St. David's was thought guilty of fraud and embezzlement. But with them the record of incompetence or rascality is almost complete. When we add Richard Curteis of Chichester, commonly held to be dishonest and a drunkard, and John Bullingham of Gloucester, that rarity among Elizabethan bishops, an ignorant man, the catalog of unfitness is virtually concluded. Here are a dozen or so fail-

---

[7] q. White, *Lives*, p. 290.

[8] *Journal*, p. 21. Parker's comments are stronger. *Correspondence*, pp. 146-61, 379. See also Harington, *Nugae Antiquae*, II, 21, 151.

ures out of nearly eighty bishops appointed during Elizabeth's reign.[9]

On the other side, the testimony of character, ability, and surprising accomplishment amid very difficult circumstances is far more impressive. Parker, Jewel, and Whitgift were not the only bishops who left upon the Elizabethan Church a mark of work well done. Alley ruled Exeter with commendable diligence, while Horne, Best, Berkeley, and Westphaling would be reckoned good bishops in any generation. Few churchmen had greater learning than Guest or Cooper; few have been better loved than Bickley. Wickham, Young, and Pilkington made valiant efforts to halt the forced alienation of episcopal manors and the spoilation of sees by the rapacious lords and gentry. Hugh Jones impoverished himself to provide preachers for the people of Llandaff, and not a few others were reduced to heavy indebtedness to the Crown by Elizabeth's constant financial exactions. Richard Cheney's sensitive and kindly nature may not have endeared him to the passionate Puritan or Romanist partisans in Gloucester, but he reflected a spirit more permanent in Anglicanism than their intolerant bigotry. Finally, towards the end of the reign and chiefly as a consequence of Whitgift's long influence at Lambeth, the episcopal bench was filled with men like Bancroft, Bilson, Still, Watson, Cotton, Vaughan, and others possessing the distinction we associate with the early Jacobean episcopate.

Elizabeth's average bishop was a conscientious prelate, beset with problems that defied easy solution. Surrounded by changing social and political patterns that he scarcely understood, he was uncertain of the extent of his episcopal authority and the precise nature of his administrative func-

---

[9] Rowse's glance at a "clutch" of bishops conveys an accurate impression of the Elizabethan episcopate. *England of Elizabeth,* pp. 408-16.

tions in a national Church that had not yet reached its maturity. The Elizabethan bishops were pioneers, bringing the traditional Catholic episcopate into an ecclesiastical settlement at once broadened by the religious reformation and constricted by the association with the Crown. Past experience contributed little to the solution of their problems. Like all pioneers, they were forced to decisions and actions out of which, at least in part, the future would be shaped. Theirs was the immediate responsibility of steering the Elizabethan Church through the narrow straits between the Scylla of Rome and the Charybdis of Puritanism. It was an uncharted course between the rock of Peter and the ever-widening whirlpool that spread out from Geneva. They not only had to find the channel, but to mark its path in their writings—Parker's *De Antiquitate,* Jewel's *Apologia,* Whitgift's *Defense of the Answer,* and Cooper's *Admonition to the People.* Here were the buoys, so to speak, along the way to the safer waters of Hooker's *Laws of Ecclesiastical Polity.*

This was sufficient labor for the ablest of men, yet there was also laid upon the Elizabethan bishops the task of maintaining the principles of the Tudor Church amid far-reaching changes of thought that were destined ultimately to make its ideal quite irrelevant to the emerging secular State. Already the shifting character of the episcopal office itself was a weathercock of those profound changes by which eventually men abandoned the concept of the State as essentially a religious society. Elizabeth's bishops were churchmen in the modern sense, not statesmen, and in that respect the transition from the medieval to the modern world was far advanced. The days of Morton, Wolsey, and Gardiner were over. With their passing, ecclesiastics disappeared from the chief positions of civil government, bringing to an end an episcopal activity which had testified for a thousand years

to the centrality of the Church in England's national life.
Servants of the royal supremacy, the Elizabethan bishops
were administrators of the Crown's authority in ecclesiastical
matters. As the long reign of the Queen wore on and the
scope of episcopal functions was increasingly restricted to
things specifically religious or narrowly ecclesiastical, it became evident that the day was not far distant when the
activities of the ecclesiastic would be welcomed or suffered
only as long as they were confined to the enunciation of
moral principles and the encouragement of personal religion.

Perhaps here some light is shed upon the tragedy of Archbishop Laud. However much he was opposed in religious
matters by the fanatical Puritans, it was not Laud's church-
manship in the narrow sense that aroused the implacable
hostility which brought the old man to the scaffold; what
led him there was his attempt to implement an anachronistic concept of the State as essentially a Christian order, a
religious society in which statesmen and churchmen could
not be sharply distinguished in their service to the realm
under God and His anointed Prince. Familiar as these ideas
might have been to Gardiner, Tunstal, and the other Henricians, between them and that January day in 1645 when
Laud went to his death the long Elizabethan Age had intervened and the forces that destroyed political Laudianism
had taken shape.

When John Whitgift was enthroned at Worcester in 1577,
however, few of these profound changes were discernible.
They were partly obscured by the continuity of so much that
had long been familiar in the institutional life of the Church.
The medieval ecclesiastical machinery with its complex
system of courts, its Avignonese army of officials, its fees and
dispensations, fines, taxes, penances and excommunications,
was virtually untouched by the sixteenth-century Reforma-

tion.[10] Indeed, when one contemplates this aspect of the Elizabethan Church it is not difficult to feel a certain sympathy with Puritan impatience, and it is easy to see why the Puritan often appeared to be more zealously concerned with the things of the spirit than the clergy of the establishment. Continuity in the life of the Church of England was all too clear when the abuses and inequities that had aroused John Colet survived to confront Bishop Blomfield three centuries later.

Few things made the administrative task of Elizabeth's bishops so toilsome as the burden of maintaining the ancient and expensive ecclesiastical machinery on greatly reduced and insufficient episcopal incomes. The Church's revenues and properties, already plundered by the commissioners of Edward VI beyond any significant repair by Mary Tudor, were still the object of continuous and thinly disguised robbery and extortion. In this the Crown was the worst offender. Elizabeth systematically bled the very Church she supported so firmly. Though she seldom kept sees vacant very long in order to administer their revenues—Ely was a notable exception—she translated her bishops frequently in order to enjoy a steady income of first-fruits and taxes.[11] Both translations and new appointments were often accompanied by royal appropriation of episcopal manors, in some instances drastically reducing the income of the bishoprics. Long leases of property, palaces, and estates on highly advantageous terms were forced upon the bishops by the Crown and the gentry; annuities out of ecclesiastical revenues were frequently extorted.[12] Despite this constant plundering, the bishops were expected to maintain their estates, administer

[10] Even DeMaisse comments on this. *Journal,* p. 20.
[11] See *Hutton Correspondence,* p. 87.
[12] *Desiderata Curiosa,* p. 167.

the dioceses, provide lavish hospitality, pay necessary pensions and benevolences, and be ready to meet special charges by the government and make extraordinary gifts to the Queen. It is little wonder that the endowments of some sees fell to the point where the bishop could maintain the charges upon his office only by holding benefices *in commendam,* or that more than one Elizabethan prelate struggled hopelessly against poverty.[13]

Clothed with the Queen's favor and equipped with unusual administrative ability, John Whitgift was more fortunate than many of his colleagues. Though the see of Worcester had suffered some impoverishment in the days of Northumberland's rule, careful husbanding of the resources of the bishopric allowed Whitgift to maintain himself in considerable state. On more than one occasion the display of his troop of retainers in their tawny coats aroused mixed feelings in his brother bishops.[14] The protection and patronage of Queen Elizabeth were powerful assets. Not only did Whitgift successfully resist the machinations of the royal "concealers"—commissioners seeking to condemn lands as forfeit to the Crown on the grounds of invalid title or original grant to the Church for "superstitious uses"; he vigorously defended the rights of the Church before the Queen herself.[15] Moreover, his recovery of estates alienated

[13] Ellis, *Letters,* 3rd Series, IV, 17, 20. See the discussion in Usher, *Reconstruction,* I, 222-5. Also White, *Lives,* pp. 109, 134, 177-8, 188, 276. Not all Elizabethan bishops, however, died poor. *Ibid.,* pp. 167, 294. See Bishop Cooper's will. *Lincoln Episcopal Records,* pp. 339-43.

[14] Harington, *Nugae Antiquae,* II, 22-3. "Tawny coats" were evidently characteristic episcopal livery. See the references to the retinue of the Bishop of Winchester in Shakespeare's *Henry VI* (Part I), I, iii.

[15] Strype, *Whitgift,* I, 171-5. Some instructive notes on the "concealers" or "greedy cormorants" are contained in the *Journal of the Chester and North Wales Architectural Archeological and Historic Society* (1951), xxxviii, 90-4. Whitgift saved the episcopal residence at Hartlebury Castle from the fate that overtook Cox's Ely House in London.

earlier from the see of Worcester, the "princely and extraordinary bounty" in which Elizabeth forgave him the charges of first-fruits, and her grant of the right to dispose the prebends in the Cathedral Church, previously patronage in the Queen's gift, were all signs of remarkable royal favor.[16]

Whitgift ruled the diocese of Worcester as all Elizabethan bishops discharged their administrative functions, chiefly by visitations in person or by his archdeacons. Searching articles of inquiry were followed by the imposition of injunctions based upon the replies. Consequent ecclesiastical discipline was executed in the courts of the archdeacon or the bishop. At the highest level of the system the statutory Ecclesiastical Commission, armed with unlimited discretion as to procedure and ever-widening powers, sustained the whole administrative machinery. In Whitgift's judgment the Commission was the only effective instrument for the reinforcement of episcopal authority and the extension of the government's control over matters outside the bishops' jurisdiction.[17] At the lowest level the parochial churchwardens bore the major responsibility for the efficient working of the system.

Episcopal injunctions were drawn from the legislation and official articles that constituted the basis for visitatorial inquiry. After the statutes of *Supremacy* and *Uniformity*, the most important among these were Elizabeth's *Injunctions* of 1559 and the subsequent royal orders.[18] Supplementing them were the "Interpretations of the Bishops," drawn up in 1561,[19] and a "Declaration of Certain Principle Articles

[16] Paule, pp. 26-7. Upon his translation to Canterbury Whitgift succeeded in securing a reduction of £100 in first-fruits, and recovered from the Crown a valuable Kentish manor of a thousand acres. *Ibid.*, p. 38.

[17] Strype, *Whitgift*, I, 266-7.

[18] For royal orders see Cardwell, *Doc. Annals*, I, 289-92, 294-7; *Visitation Articles*, III, 108-10.

[19] *Ibid.*, III, 59-73.

of Religion," originally made in 1559 and confirmed by the bishops two years later.[20] Though in time superseded by Archbishop Parker's *Advertisements* and the *Thirty-Nine Articles*, these supplementary documents resting upon episcopal authority alone continued to influence later visitation articles. Finally, the *Canons of 1571* and the articles devised by Convocation in 1576 for the improvement of clerical education and discipline became part of the official collection before Whitgift was made Bishop of Worcester.[21] Among the whole mass of regulations, the Queen's *Injunctions* provided the bulk of material that went into diocesan orders, while the *Advertisements* of 1566 set the standard of practice to which conformity was normally expected.

Conscientious bishops gave special attention to their Cathedral Churches.[22] Whitgift's inquiries and injunctions for Worcester Cathedral, for example, showed meticulous concern for the fabric of the church and its maintenance in good order, the condition of the grammar school, the faithful observance of all ecclesiastical laws and regulations, the orderliness of divine service, and the diligence of Cathedral clergy and other officials. Precise preaching schedules were arranged for the dean and the prebendaries in order to secure a weekly succession of "sufficient preachers." In this latter responsibility Whitgift himself was indefatigable. He regularly preached on Sundays, usually riding off to a nearby parish church in the morning and occupying the Cathedral pulpit in the afternoon. Such untiring efforts to enforce the ecclesiastical regulations inevitably had their permanent ef-

[20] Cardwell, *Doc. Annals,* I, 263-7. See *Visitation Articles,* III, 95.

[21] Joyce, *Convocation of the Clergy,* pp. 580-3.

[22] See the injunctions for Cathedrals in *Visitation Articles,* III, and Kennedy, *Eliz. Epis. Ad.,* II and III. An interesting account of Chester Cathedral is contained in Burne, "Chester Cathedral," *J.C. & N.W.A.A. & H. Soc.* (1951), xxxviii, 54-85.

fects at the parish level. In the long run, of course, it is what happened to the religious life of Englishmen in their parishes that mattered most.

The impression created by the majority of parish churches in the 'seventies and 'eighties must have been one of a simplicity approaching austerity. Signs of neglect and decay, frequently met in the first years of the Queen's reign, were still occasionally encountered, even to the point of ruinous chancels, breached walls, and unmended roofs. But such extensive disrepair was not common after 1570. The vigilance of the bishops and their officers in this matter is attested by the numerous episcopal articles and injunctions; the conscientiousness with which the churchwardens discharged their responsibilities is revealed in the contemporary parish accounts.[23] The fact is that when the early iconoclastic activity was terminated, the fabric of the churches was maintained in better condition than is sometimes supposed. Neglect in the care of the churches, Whitgift maintained, was "to the disgrace of religion, and great offense to many well-disposed, and occasion to such as are enemies to our profession to think that we are but profanely minded and without devotion."[24]

Nevertheless, changes were extensive.[25] Most of the warmth and color familiar in the churches of Whitgift's boyhood disappeared with the removal of chapels, altars, images and pictorial representations of "feigned and false miracles."

---

[23] See Whitgift's *Articles for Worcester* in Kennedy, *Eliz. Epis. Ad.*, II, 53-61. Typical churchwardens' accounts are *Elizabethan Churchwardens' Accounts* (Bedfordshire Historical Record Society, xxxiii), *Durham Parish Books* (Surtees Society, lxxxiv), and Beresford, "Churchwardens' Accounts," *J.C. & N.W.A.A. & H. Soc.*, xxxviii.

[24] *The State of the Church*, p. 220.

[25] The account books of Holy Trinity parish, Chester, contain a revealing set of entries by which the changes from 1532 onwards for a century may be seen in detail. Beresford, "Churchwardens' Accounts," pp. 106 ff.

Despite the Queen's proclamation of 1560 against the destruction of monuments erected "only to show a memory . . . and not to nourish any kind of superstition," tombs were defaced, brasses stripped from the floors, and much that made the parish church a treasure-house of remembrance vanished. For the most part the stained glass windows were spared, though instances of their removal or wanton destruction are recorded. But the light of the windows fell now upon the bare stone and whitewashed areas, illuminating the somewhat incongruous but edifying Scripture texts that had begun to be placed upon the walls.[26]

The most striking alteration in the aspect of the churches was the destruction of the old roodlofts where the great rood with its attendant figures had once compelled the attention of the worshippers at mass. Though the tympanum—a boarding that had filled the chancel arch above the crucifixion figures—was still occasionally found in place, its paintings were whitewashed over and the royal arms or the table of the Ten Commandments might catch the eye there. More often, however, the tympanum had also disappeared with the roodloft, and the Commandments, in accordance with the requirements of the *Advertisements,* were set on the east wall of the chancel.[27] The screen separating the nave from the chancel was left in place—indeed, the Royal Order of 1561 required a "comely partition" to be retained or re-erected—and the plaque of the royal arms was generally affixed to its beam.

Within the chancel the stone altar had been replaced by the wooden holy table, ordered by the *Injunctions* of 1559

[26] *Ibid.,* p. 124.

[27] *Visitation Articles,* III, 108-9, 175. For instances of the gradual removal of roodlofts and the tympanum see *Elizabethan Churchwardens' Accounts,* pp. xviii, 7, 71; Beresford, "Churchwardens' Accounts," p. 127; *Tudor Parish Documents,* p. 32.

to be set altarwise against the east wall except during "Communion time." Then it was moved into the body of the chancel for the convenience of those gathered there for the ministration of the Sacrament.[28] Heavy and cumbersome to move, in time the holy tables came to remain permanently in the lower part of the chancel, if not, as was nearly always the case when the chancels were small, outside the screen at the head of the nave.[29] For the celebration of the Holy Communion the table was covered with a fair linen cloth, sometimes fashioned out of the disused albs of the parish. At all other times it was concealed by the silk or buckram carpet, a "decent covering" not infrequently made from former vestments.[30] Ornaments were few. Candles were used only for illumination, and repeated injunctions laid down the brief list of appointments: a Prayer Book, a copy of "the English Bible in the largest volume," an extra Psalter or two, a silver Communion cup and paten, "two comely pots of pewter" or other suitable vessels for the wine, a "clean and decent surplice with large sleeves"—these sufficed for the services. In addition, each parish was expected to own a parish register, Parker's "Table of the Prohibited Degrees" within which marriage was forbidden, both books of *Homilies,* the *Paraphrases* of Erasmus, and Bishop Jewel's *Apologie, or answere in defence of the Church of Englande.*[31]

[28] *Visitation Articles,* III, 27-8.

[29] *Injunctions of Bishop Barnes,* p. 119. See Addleshaw, *The Architectural Setting of Anglican Worship,* p. 109.

[30] Bishop Cooper evidently found funeral palls used in this fashion. *Visitation Articles,* III, 371.

[31] The entries in parish accounts of the purchase of "my Lord of Salsburyes his boke" refer to the translation of Jewel's *Apologia Ecclesiae Anglicanae* made in 1564 by Lady Anne Bacon, daughter of Sir Anthony Cooke and mother of Francis Bacon. *Parker Correspondence,* pp. 219-20. With Jewel's approval and Parker's commendation, it was ordered placed in every church.

Not every parish church possessed even this sparse collection, as the visitation records and lists of presentments show. We meet with "an old chyste" used as a holy table, decayed and tattered coverings, no proper "communion cuppe" or one of base materials—tin, pewter, or glass— surplices soiled, uncomely, or even missing altogether, Erasmus' "paraphraseis torne and rente," Bibles "partlie torned," one or more of the "tomes of the Homylies" lacking, and churches where the only Prayer Book was "a Communion Boke of King Edward."[32] But presentments and records from the act books of ecclesiastical courts inevitably bring the worst features of the Elizabethan Church into high relief. They list only the instances of irregularity, laxity, and disobedience. Behind them is the much more common but less colorful record of reasonable care, reverence, and orderliness that characterized the majority of parish churches. A careful study of churchwardens' accounts reveals regular payments for cleaning the churches, washing and mending the linen, providing surplices, replacing lost or damaged books, and generally endeavoring to keep the appointments in decent order.[33]

Sunday services were normally conducted from the new reading desk or "convenient seat" erected for the minister at the head of the nave near the pulpit, or in some commanding place in the body of the church.[34] Here the offices were said and the lessons read. A "modest and distinct song" might be used, with organ accompaniment if the incumbent

---

[32] *Tudor Parish Documents,* pp. 29-34, 63-5, 158-9. See also *Bishop Redman's Visitation,* pp. 10-3 and *Visitation Articles,* III, 275.

[33] Beresford, "Churchwardens' Accounts," pp. 124-31; *Durham Parish Books,* pp. 11-2, 20, 27, 120, 270; *Elizabethan Churchwardens' Accounts,* pp. 9, 19, 22, 73, 76, 85, 92.

[34] *Visitation Articles,* III, 208-9. Nearly all parish accounts mention the construction of this new "seat for the minister."

did not entertain a Puritan prejudice against that instrument. Pews, settles, and forms for the congregation were variously placed, their position often determined only by the demand of proximity to the minister and sometimes resulting in a confusion of benches that later outraged the sense of order of the Laudian bishops.

Three times a year the people of the parish were required to receive the Holy Communion. The Sacrament was usually provided once a quarter with Easter, Whitsunday, Michaelmas, and Christmas being the normal sequence. Parishes sometimes observed Hallowtide and Midsummer in this fashion, and at a few places there were celebrations more often, but it is evident from the records that their frequency depended largely upon the individual minister. The regularity of purchases of bread and wine in the churchwardens' accounts indicates that some clergy shared Bishop Barnes' concern that "the Blessed Sacrament of the Body and Blood of our Saviour Jesus Christ be reverently ministered and received in every parish church at least once every month," but on the whole monthly "Communion days" were uncommon.[35] Opportunity was given for a large number of people to communicate by providing several celebrations of the Holy Communion, usually on successive days, at the quarterly observances.[36]

The ecclesiastical authorities strove to secure sermons in each parish at least four times a year, but the want of sufficient learning in some clergy and the suspicion of popery or Puritanism that attached to others drastically reduced the number of men licensed to preach. One of the homilies was ordered to be read every month, and in many places the

[35] Kennedy, *Eliz. Epis. Ad.,* II, 70. See the Shillington and Northill records in *Elizabethan Churchwardens' Accounts.*
[36] *Ibid.,* 67-8; *Durham Parish Books,* p. 24.

people heard either this or no sermon at all. There is no doubt that the problem of providing educated and loyal preachers was a constant vexation to the bishops. Throughout his entire episcopate Whitgift devoted an immense amount of time to the education of the clergy.[37] In these circumstances catechizing provided at least some of the religious instruction that might have been received in more frequent sermons. The incumbent was expected to catechize the youth of the parish every second Sunday, usually before Evensong, but if the people were given all the instruction enjoined by the bishops there must have been other times as well.[38]

If the parish priest were scrupulously obedient to the regulations, each quarter the people heard the Queen's *Injunctions*. This prescription was often ignored, but we need not suppose that all the ministers who disobeyed the order regarded the *Injunctions* with Puritan distaste. There may have been a number of other reasons. Injunction 29, for example, could not have been a favorite with the increasing numbers of married clergy, for it almost inevitably stimulated parish gossip about the vicarage family. By it the people were reminded that although the Word of God did not prohibit a parson from having "an honest and sober wife, for the avoiding of fornication," yet

because there hath grown offense, and some slander to the Church by lack of discreet and sober behavior in many ministers of the Church . . . in choosing of their wives . . . it is thought therefore very necessary that no manner of priest or deacon shall hereafter take to his wife any manner of woman without the

---

[37] See below, pp. 196-205.
[38] Kennedy, *Eliz. Epis. Ad.*, II, 71. See Whitgift's *Articles for Worcester, ibid.*, II, 59.

advice and allowance first had upon good examination by the bishop . . . and two justices of the peace . . .[39]

Every aspect of the Elizabethan parish, from the white-washed walls of the churches to the scenes of continuous catechizing, testified to the tremendous upheaval wrought by the Reformation. What was happening was no less than the religious reorientation of virtually an entire nation. From a piety narrowly centered upon the sacrifice of the mass Englishmen were turned towards far wider spiritual horizons. It is sometimes said that in the Elizabethan Church, sermon took first place over sacrament, and the edifying devotions of the offices were substituted for the sacrificial worship of the mass. This is a simplification that fails to convey the whole truth. The new spiritual orientation was not towards the sermon or the offices—these were rather its means; it was to the Scriptures. The new Anglican piety was thoroughly Biblical. In this context offices, sacrament, and sermon all embodied the living Word of God. The unique feature of the English Reformation at this point, moreover, is that Bible and Church were not set one against the other. The appeal was to both Scripture and history—"the Word of God and the primitive Church"—or, as the *Canons of 1571* put it, "to observe and believe that which is agreeable to the doctrine of the Old Testament and the New, and that which the Catholic fathers and ancient Bishops have gathered out of that doctrine." This firm grasp upon the centrality of the Scriptures within the life of the Church brought to Anglicanism its precious freedom from the restraints of sixteenth-century confessional dogma, bound its integrity inseparably with sound learning, and made it possible for later generations to perceive truth in both the sacramentalism of

[39] *Visitation Articles,* III, 18-9.

Archbishop Laud and the moralism of Archbishop Tillotson.

However much these distinctive characteristics of later
Anglicanism are rooted in the life of the Elizabethan Church,
they do not take full and coherent shape rapidly in the
Queen's reign. The religious orientation of a people changes
slowly, and Elizabethan folk clung tenaciously to the older
patterns of their piety. In the articles of the bishops and the
presentment lists we catch a glimpse of a people who kept
holy water stocks in their cottages, treasured ancient primers
for their family prayers, and hoarded the old vessels, images,
and vestments when the parish authorities disposed of them.
Some perhaps had an eye to the day of the restoration of
Romanism, like the man who sold a Tyndale New Testament for ten shillings, to be paid "when mass shall be said
with this realm."[40] But for most it was simply an ingrained
reverence for objects with sacred associations. People stole
into the churches at night to pray, occasionally burning a
candle stub on the feasts of Our Lady and the saints; they
paused before the ruined churchyard crosses to utter the
familiar intercessions. During the services they fingered their
beads and could not keep their hands from the sign of the
cross or penitent "knockings" upon the breast. Through
many a darkened village on the eve of All Souls' the bells
of the parish tolled the forbidden remembrances of the departed, and by the time the churchwardens arrived at the
church they found either the belfry ropes stilled, or a group
gathered there too formidable to restrain.

These things were less the mark of a rebellious people
than that of the persistent character of pious custom. The
"Ave" or "Ora pro nobis" that "slipped out" was not necessarily the sign of intransigent Romanism, any more than

[40] *Tudor Parish Documents*, p. 150.

absence from the services indicated a conscientious disobedience of the ecclesiastical laws. The ordinary human elements must not be forgotten. Many a man found it convenient to stay away from church lest he be served with a process for debt; many another preferred to snare rabbits at a time when he was least likely to be caught poaching. Those who stretched themselves quietly on the grass of the churchyard during the sermon were not always stubborn Puritans or obdurate papists; more often they sought a relief from tedium that had taken their ancestors to that same grassy plot.

Not infrequently the clergy abetted their parishioners in the continuance of the old devotional practices. There were some who treated the holy table with the same reverence paid the former altar, who elevated the Host at the Sacrament, rang the passing bell more often than allowed, turned a blind eye upon those who knelt in the old Lady Chapel, absolved folk whose consciences could not be quieted by the new general confession they were taught to say, and remembered the dead to whom they had ministered in life. Such parsons were neither enemies of the establishment nor deliberately disobedient to the ecclesiastical laws. They simply carried on some of their spiritual and pastoral responsibilities in ways too firmly fixed to be easily altered.

There was, of course, a rebellious Catholic minority. Whitgift's appointment to Worcester took him into a countryside where Romanist opposition to the Elizabethan Church was far stronger than Puritan discontent, and where lay the chief pockets of "recusancy"—a term speedily applied to Catholic nonconformity.[41] From the west of England northwards into Cheshire, Lancashire, and parts of Yorkshire,

---

[41] "Recusant" was occasionally applied to the Puritan nonconformist. See *Seconde Parte*, I, 210.

resistance was sufficiently stubborn to ensure the survival of a small minority of English Roman Catholics, largely in those areas. The inaccessible reaches of the western and northern counties, where remote manor houses provided sanctuary for priests and centers of recusant activity, made it difficult for the government to deal effectively with Romanist hostility there. While the lax administration of Bishop Downham of Chester was partly responsible for the increased disaffection in the 'seventies, it is evident from the correspondence between the Council and William Chaderton, his more vigorous successor, that the total suppression of northern recusancy was a task beyond the powers of the local authorities.[42]

Elizabeth's initial policy of Catholic conciliation in the interests of political loyalty and ecclesiastical comprehension was reflected in the remarkably tolerant attitude of the government towards Romanists in the early years of the reign. The government could afford to be lenient with all but the most obstinate and open papists, for time worked on the side of the establishment. Only a relatively small group of Marian priests had joined their bishops in refusing the oath, and the ablest of these—those drawn from the ranks of Mary's university clergy and officials—had fled abroad. That left, for the most part, an ever-dwindling company of ignorant "massing priests," precariously passed along from house to house and despairingly fighting a losing battle against the strength of the Elizabethan Church. The famous "Uncle James" was a typical figure among these hunted clergy. Ordained by Bishop Tunstal in the last years of Henry VIII, he was over seventy years old when apprehended and brought before the Earl of Derby. He had no interest in high matters of state—only a duty to say mass

[42] *Desiderata Curiosa*, pp. 85 ff.

"as often as the opportunity of time, place and company have given leave."[43] His old mass book, tin chalice, single set of worn and threadbare vestments, little boxes of chrism and "singing cakes" were not alarming to the government, only the pathetic signs of a vanishing past. In time such men would disappear from the scene, and the former religious loyalties could not survive without their ministrations.

What drastically altered the nature of the Roman Catholic problem, sustained the resistance of the recusants, and drove the government to a more severe and repressive policy was a series of events during the years 1566 to 1570. The conclusion of the Council of Trent and the promulgation of its decrees launched Rome upon a relentless spiritual war against Protestantism. The tide of counter-reformation everywhere swelled alarmingly after 1566 when the stern and uncompromising Pope Pius V directed the fierce Catholic onslaught. The word from Rome to the English recusants was one of embarrassing severity: no compromise with the Queen's Church, no attendance at "the schismatical service or damnable communion now used." Half-hearted Romanists, who had at least openly conformed, were winnowed out by the demand for recusancy without the concealment of church attendance, and the passions of fanaticism began to blaze among those who chose loyalty to the Pope's commands.

At the same time Englishmen were gravely alarmed by the turn in continental events. The Netherlands seethed with revolt; France was again plunged into religious strife. Both the cruel atrocities of the Duke of Alva and the murderous ferocity of the French wars of religion were inseparably linked in the English mind with the activities of Tridentine Rome. In 1568 the flight of Mary of Scotland into England

[43] Leatherbarrow, *Lancashire Elizabethan Recusants,* p. 91.

provided a rallying point for Catholic disaffection and a
tangible object for Romanist plots, the placing of the rightful
and Catholic heir and descendant of Henry VII upon the
throne usurped by the bastard daughter of Anne Boleyn.
That such conspiracies were more than imaginary was sharply
brought home by the Northern Rebellion of 1569. Whatever
were the ultimate economic and social forces behind the
rising, its religious aims were unmistakably displayed when
in Durham Cathedral on November 14th the English Bible
and Prayer Book were torn into shreds, the holy table broken
down, and the old mass once more said. Hard on the heels
of this brief insurrection in the north came the final blow,
the papal sentence of Elizabeth's deposition. Too late to
support the rebels, the Bull *Regnans in excelsis* nonetheless
confirmed the English in their conviction that the most dangerous enemies to the peace and security of the Elizabethan
State were the adherents of the Pope's religion. Pius V
reckoned among the ungodly "Elizabeth, the pretended
Queen of England, the servant of wickedness. . . ."

This very woman [declared the Bull] having seized on the
Kingdom, and monstrously usurped the place of Supreme Head
of the Church in all England, and the chief authority and
jurisdiction thereof, hath again reduced the said Kingdom into
a miserable and ruinous condition, which was so lately reclaimed
to the Catholic Faith . . .
For having by strong hand prohibited the exercise of the true
religion . . . she hath . . . abolished the Sacrifice of the Mass
. . . and the Catholic rites and ceremonies; commanded books
to be read throughout the whole Realm containing manifest
heresy, and appointed impious titles and institutions, by herself
entertained and observed according to the prescript of Calvin,
to be likewise observed by her subjects . . .
We do, out of the fulness of our apostolic power, declare the

aforesaid Elizabeth . . . to have incurred the sentence of ex-
communication, and to be cut off from the unity of the Body of
Christ. And, moreover, we do declare her to be deprived of her
pretended title to the Kingdom . . . and also the nobility, subjects and people of the said Kingdom and all others who have in
any sort sworn unto her, to be forever absolved from any such
oath, and all manner of duty of dominion, allegiance and obedience.

We do command and charge . . . that they presume not to
obey her, or her orders, mandates and laws; and those which
shall do the contrary, we do include them in like sentence of
anathema.[44]

The Bull forced a sharp conflict between the patriotism
and the religion of those who remained steadfast adherents
of the papacy. Treason became virtually the religious duty
of the true Romanist when the Pope demanded resistance to
the Queen's civil laws, and after 1570 Romanism could no
longer be regarded as a matter of religious dissent alone.
When his religious allegiance made every papist at least a
potential traitor, Roman Catholicism constituted a serious
political threat.

The immediate parliamentary reply to the Pope's attack
was made in two statutes passed in 1571.[45] By a new *Treasons
Act* it became high treason to attempt to harm the Queen, to
deny her lawful right to the Crown, or to affirm her to be
schismatic, heretic, or a usurper.[46] Another statute brought
the penalties of treason upon those who obtained or pub-

[44] Camden, *Elizabeth*, pp. 146-7.

[45] The act of 1563 in which the ecclesiastical jurisdiction of the Crown
was reaffirmed and by which those maintaining the authority of the Bishop
of Rome in England were threatened with the penalties of *praemunire* was
considered insufficient protection against the political dangers in the new
Roman hostility.

[46] 13 Eliz. c. 1. *Statutes*, IV, i, 526-8.

lished bulls from Rome, and provided severe punishment for any who concealed knowledge of such actions or who imported for the use of Englishmen crosses, pictures, beads, and "suchlike vain and superstitious things from the Bishop or the See of Rome," or pardons and absolutions granted by him or that See.[47] Not all English Catholics, of course, were conspirators against the Queen and her government. The bulk of them remained genuinely loyal, caught in a tragic dilemma. Allegiance to their sovereign was disobedience to their Church, and nothing could free them from the sufferings of that position. But in the active minority of fanatical papalists there was a real danger to the State. Elizabeth and her councillors were aware that the significant factor after 1570 was the link between English Romanism and the international Catholic power. "Uncle James" had been thoroughly English, the representative of some Englishmen's dissent from their own established Church; the new Romanist was captured by a foreign allegiance, and inevitably involved with the menace Catholic States offered to England's national security.

What is truly remarkable is the refusal of the Queen and her government to adopt the inquisitorial procedures that were familiar in sixteenth-century conflicts. All that was demanded was the recognition of the Queen's sovereignty, the assurance of the political loyalty of the Catholic and his willingness to obey the laws. No man's conscience would be sifted, nor would Elizabeth search out what affection the obedient and conformable Englishman might have to the old religion.[48] Even this measure of tolerance, admittedly

---

[47] The *Act against the bringing in and putting in execution of Bulls, etc.,* 13 Eliz. c. 2. *Statutes,* IV, i, 528 ff. See Prothero, pp. 60-3.

[48] See the Queen's *Declaration* above, p. 60. Also Walsingham's letter to the French state secretary, *Cabala,* p. 372; and the observations of Francis Bacon, *Works,* III, 470-1; V, 428-9.

hard to apply, availed but little. The majority of Romanists writhed painfully in a situation that was not materially altered when Gregory XIII declared that the Bull of 1570 need not prevent Catholics from recognizing Elizabeth as a *de facto* sovereign. At best, they hoped to make their loyalty to the Queen plain enough to spare them the ordeal of examination. The minority of zealous papists, on the other hand, strengthened by the support from overseas, were prepared to welcome the shadow of martyrdom cast by the statutes.

For nearly twenty years this conflict was waged just behind the scenes in Elizabethan England, now and then occupying the center of the stage with the execution of men like Cuthbert Mayne and Edmund Campion, but more often momentarily revealed in a glimpse of the intrigues of Robert Parsons. Tension mounted slowly but surely. The fears aroused by the Ridolphi Plot were heightened by the discovery of a succession of conspiracies, culminating in the schemes of Throckmorton, and the plans of Parry and Babington for the murder of Elizabeth. Horrified by the Massacre of St. Bartholomew's Eve and the assassination of William the Silent, Englishmen were prepared to believe their Queen to be in mortal danger from her Catholic enemies. The web of each intrigue held a throne for Mary Stuart, while behind its thin veil loomed the menacing power of Spain. The government could counter the threatening dangers only by stiffer penal legislation against the Romanists. In 1581 the penalties of treason were laid upon those who sought to withdraw men from "their natural obedience of her Majesty, to obey . . . the usurped authority of Rome," or to withdraw them *for that intent* from adherence to the established Church. Fines for persistent recusancy were raised to the crippling sum of £20 a month; the saying and hearing of mass was made punishable by a heavy fine and a year's imprisonment.[49]

With this parliamentary action went renewed efforts to hunt down the Romanist clergy and expose intransigent recusancy. Here the Council depended largely upon the vigilance of the bishops. The fact that recusants were detected, at least in the first instance, by their disobedience to the ecclesiastical laws made the bishops the chief security officers in the realm. Returns on cases of recusancy were demanded from all the dioceses, and they poured in to arm the government for more repressive measures against the Catholics.[50] Vigorous action was made the more necessary by the appearance of scores of courageous and highly disciplined seminary priests from William Allen's college at Douai, dedicating themselves to the recovery of England to the Roman allegiance, and followed by a band of papal missionaries in the Jesuit order, equally reckless in their zeal. Jesuit priests, complained Knollys, went from house to house "to withdraw men from the obedience to her majesty";[51] seminary priests slipped through the countryside in disguise, sheltered by the recusants, performing marriages, giving absolution, rebaptizing children, celebrating mass, and holding the Romanists fast in their loyalty to the Pope.

By 1585 further protective legislation was believed necessary, and the *Act against Jesuits, seminary Priests, etc.* ordered their departure from England on the pains of high treason, making it a felony to give them aid or maintenance.

---

[49] The *Act to retain the Queen's Majesty's Subjects in their due Obedience,* 23 Eliz. c. 1. *Statutes,* IV, 657 ff. See Prothero, pp. 74-6. Neale's discussion of the drafting of this bill emphasizes the significance of the qualification "for that intent." Room was left for the government to distinguish between political disloyalty and religious dissent. *Elizabeth I and Her Parliaments,* p. 391.

[50] *S. P. Dom. Eliz.* cxvi. 15. The returns are found in vols. cxvii-cxviii.

[51] Ellis, *Letters,* 3rd Series, IV, 36.

All persons who had gone "beyond the seas" to be "brought up in any college of Jesuits or seminary" were recalled to subscribe the oath of supremacy under the penalty of being adjudged traitors.[52] Parliament in the same sessions passed a statute giving legal status to an association of nobles and gentry that had been formed to protect Elizabeth's life, and excluding from the succession to the Crown any person who plotted her death.[53] It was the only possible answer to the encouragement of the Queen's murder that came from Rome. In 1580 the papal Secretary of State had written the nuncio in Spain:

There can be no doubt that so long as that guilty woman of England holds the two noble Christian kingdoms she has usurped, and so long as she remains the cause of such great harm to the Catholic faith and of the damnation of so many millions of souls, whosoever removes her from this life, with the intention of doing God service, not only would not sin, but would actually be doing a meritorious deed, especially since the sentence which Pius V of holy memory passed against her still stands.[54]

If the nuncio was thereupon enabled to set his mind at rest concerning the encouragement he had given to Humphrey Ely and his circle of conspirators, the worst fears of Englishmen were confirmed by the blessing that high Roman ecclesiastics appeared to give to murder.[55] Little more, perhaps, need be said. The irreconcilable conflict was not of Queen Elizabeth's making, nor did the government

[52] 27 Eliz. c. 2. *Statutes,* IV, ii, 706 ff. See Prothero, pp. 83-6.

[53] *Harleian Misc.,* I, 3-9.

[54] See Hughes, *Rome and the Counter-Reformation in England,* pp. 212 ff.

[55] Hughes' discussion points to the contention that the morality of the Roman action turned on the question of the acceptance of Elizabeth as Queen by the majority of her subjects. On that matter the Roman ecclesiastics were, he maintains, badly informed. *Ibid.,* 220-221.

fail to moderate its action when the strictly religious issue could be isolated from political disloyalty. Roman Catholicism survived the reign, under heavy penalties and civic disabilities that were to last over two hundred years, but it did survive, tenaciously maintained by a small minority whose capacity for sacrifice and earnest Christian devotion was a regrettable loss to the national Church.[56] Its survival, however, was more than would have been accorded the Queen had success attended the Romanist endeavors. When all is said and done, one incontrovertible fact remains. Reconciliation of England to the papal allegiance could have meant only deposition or death for Elizabeth Tudor.

Whitgift, like all the bishops, was constantly occupied with the search for Romanist clergy and stubborn recusants. His articles asked pointed questions in respect to the willingness of the clergy to pray for the Queen as "in all causes spiritual and temporal, and over all persons supreme head and governor under Christ in these her Kingdoms and dominions," and concerning suspicions that might be entertained of people attending secret masses. His returns of recusancy went promptly to the Council; his spies and informers prowled through the diocese—certainly the least attractive part of the task—and often with little result.[57] It was not easy to lay hands on priests so well concealed by

[56] The penal legislation against Roman Catholics culminated in the *Act against Popish Recusants* in 1593. 35 Eliz. c. 2. *Statutes,* IV, ii, 843 ff. By it obstinate and convicted recusants could be registered with the parochial authorities and restricted to an area within five miles of their homes, except when granted a license for further travel. Those having insufficient means to "satisfy competent penalty for their contempt and disobedience" were ordered to submit or abjure the realm. The act provided a form of submission acknowledging "that the bishop or see of Rome hath not, nor ought to have any power or authority over her majesty," and promising to "obey and perform her majesty's laws and statutes, in repairing to the church, and hearing divine service." *Concilia,* IV, 345.

[57] *S.P.Dom.Eliz.* cxviii. 11.

their friends and supporters. "There are," Whitgift wrote Walsingham, "taken here in Worcestershire . . . two old and very ignorant massing priests whose examinations I have sent to you enclosed." But these were pathetic and comparatively harmless figures like "Uncle James." His letter continued:

There are also two brethren . . . Thomas Moore and Rees Moore, poor men but very dangerous. Thomas Moore was Bonner's porter in Queen Mary's time. . . . Many papists resort to their house to hear masses. . . . I have sundry times laid wait for them, but could not by any means have taken them.[58]

There was scarcely any Elizabethan bishop, faithful to the police duties laid upon him by the government, who was not engaged in what must have amounted to a private feud with one or more priests who "could not by any means" be apprehended. The brothers Moore and one Hughes, "the chief sayer of mass" who "came from beyond seas," appear to have been Whitgift's most troublesome problems.[59] All this was a bishop's duty in the interests of national security, and it does not seem that Whitgift found the particular zest in this aspect of episcopal responsibility that was shown by Grindal, Sandys, and others whose hatred of Romanism had been fixed during their exile in Mary Tudor's reign. On the contrary, his attitude mirrored more accurately the government's policy of considerable forbearance when Romanist dissent could be proven to be purely religious. Disapproving strongly of the brutality some would have shown to recusants on the grounds of "Christ's compelle intrare and other suchlike phrases in the New Testament," his objections to vio-

[58] *Ibid.*, clvi. 29.
[59] Strype, *Whitgift*, I, 164.

lence were well enough known to make him the target of considerable criticism. At one time he warned Matthew Hutton of the dangers of having a tolerant attitude mistaken for some deeper sympathy with popery.[60] Martin Marprelate's later epithet "the Pope of Lambeth" was not suggested by any pontifical arrogance Whitgift might have shown, but by his kindness when archbishop to Romanist clergy who were converted to the English Church. For these men he had a special care.

I am moved with Christian pity and compassion [he wrote the bishops] to pray your lordship to move the better and wealthier sort of the clergy within your diocese, to yield some contribution. . . .

Our adversaries plentifully reward and maintain such as fly from us to them; and their priests, while they remained papists, lacked nothing; a great want of charity therefore, and shame it were for us, after their conversion, to suffer them to beg or else to die, or to revolt for lack.[61]

In contrast to the Romanist recusants, Puritans in Worcestershire gave Whitgift little trouble. Few signs had yet appeared in his diocese of the new and alarming activity upon which the Puritans embarked after the *Admonition* controversy. In 1577 Whitgift had received special orders from the Queen to be alert for "a certain public exercise, or, as they call it, prophesying, by certain persons pretending a more purity," and to see that

none other exercise be suffered to be publicly used, than preaching by persons learned, discreet, conformable, and sound in religion, heard and allowed by you without partiality, and reading homilies

[60] Trin. Coll. MSS, 0.3. 53, fols. 7-8.
[61] Cardwell, *Doc. Annals*, II, 45.

in such sort, as is set forth by public authority, by the injunction and order of the book of common prayer.[62]

He responded promptly with the inclusion in his visitation interrogations of a question directed at such exercises, probably the earliest notice of them appearing in any episcopal articles.[63] His prompt action sprang more from awareness of the menace to the good order of the establishment that lurked in these exercises than from any real fear that he would uncover many assemblies in Worcestershire. The nonconformity that prevailed among the Puritans of his diocese was mostly of the older vestiarian sort. Experience had equipped Whitgift to deal firmly and successfully with that kind of discontent, and he had little difficulty securing a large measure of obedience to the ecclesiastical regulations.[64] But he was fully informed of the disorder in other parts of the realm. Grindal's suspension had intensified the activity of the disciplinarian Puritans and brought their disobedience into the open. The moment rapidly approached when they would offer a final and defiant challenge to the established Church.

[62] *Ibid.*, I, 434-5.
[63] Kennedy, *Eliz. Epis. Ad.*, II, 59.
[64] *VCH, Worcestershire*, II, 50-3.

V

THE CHALLENGE OF PURITANISM

IN the 'seventies and 'eighties of Elizabeth's reign the
Puritans offered their decisive challenge to the Queen's
establishment. The revolutionary movement launched by the
appearance of the *Admonition to the Parliament* was led,
not by the Precisions of the vestiarian conflict, but by the
new "Disciplinarians" of the Cartwright faction, those who
demanded the abolition of episcopacy and the establishment
of a "godly seignorie" whereby the Church might be rightly
governed in that "severity of discipline that Christ commanded." Such was the pattern of church order that Cartwright and his followers found prescribed in Holy Scripture.
However much these disciplinarian Puritans differed among
themselves both as to the way of securing their aims and in
the matter of temporary conformity to the Queen's Church,
all agreed that ministry and discipline were not "things indifferent"; without the church order advocated in the *Admonition* "there can be no right religion." Moreover, there
could be no right governance of a Christian commonwealth
except it were related to this essential structure in the Church.

The more closely one investigates the nature of the
Puritan challenge, the more difficult it is to disentangle and
identify all the strands of thought that were woven together

in the ideas behind it. The recent revival of interest in six-teenth-century Puritanism that has produced the works of William Haller, M. M. Knappen, Leonard Trinterud, and others has revealed the complexity of Puritanism and the obscurity that shrouds its origins. Undoubtedly the English Puritans owed their heaviest debt to the theology, political theories, and principles of ecclesiastical polity that were em-braced by the continental reformers in Geneva, Zurich, and the Rhineland cities. Yet in men like Tyndale, Bale, Frith, and Bradford there seems to be an earlier strain of native Protestantism which forms a significant part of the Puritan heritage. Foreign influence, first appearing in England in the reign of Henry VIII and intensified with the coming of Martin Bucer and Peter Martyr under Edward VI, reached its peak during the Marian exile and in the following years when English divines were in close touch with Calvin, Bullinger, Beza, and other religious leaders abroad. The diversity of these influences, however, never elicited a single uniform response, nor did the English Puritans fail to show their capacity for modifying and adapting the ideas of their continental friends and advisors.

Puritanism as a whole defies exact definition. We are concerned, as were Parker, Cooper, and Whitgift, with the activities of various groups of Puritans whose hostility to the Elizabethan Church took different forms and was ex-pressed in varying degrees of intensity. No single united Puritan party took shape in Elizabethan England, a testi-mony perhaps to the diverse character of the forces that helped to fashion Puritan ideas. From the beginning of the Queen's reign a large number of malcontents regarded the religious settlement, in Gualter's words, "an unhappy com-pound of popery and the Gospel." It was therefore to be endured with the hope that the *interim* might be brief, but there was never universal agreement upon what were "things indifferent" or how far they could be borne without renouncing the ministry; what matters cried out for speedy reform; or what was the exact model of a Church "truly reformed."

Out of the vestiarian controversy in which probably the largest number of dissidents were involved—for many could readily identify the "unhappy compound" in the continued use of externals which had been associated with the old order in the Church—came the strong radical minority of Disciplinarians. Their challenge was not only to the ecclesiastical usages and liturgy of the Church, but also to the polity of the establishment and the whole order of the Tudor commonwealth. These are the Puritans with whose campaign for reform and power John Whitgift was embattled. A movement that began with a refusal to wear a surplice ended with a denial of royal supremacy.[1] Yet even the Disciplinarians never presented a united front in Elizabeth's reign, despite all the efforts of John Field and Walter Travers to hammer out an agreed and coherent program for the reconstruction of the English Church. Not until nearly forty years after the Queen's death did Stuart England see this achievement among the presbyterian Puritans.

The scope of the challenge of the Disciplinarians is readily seen in a glance at the literary duel between Whitgift and Cartwright that followed the appearance of the *Admonition to the Parliament*. There nearly every point on which the Puritans and the supporters of the establishment divided is exhaustively treated by the contestants. Cartwright reiterated at length the attacks of the *Admonition* upon the rites, cere-

[1] The interview between the Bishop of Lichfield and the Puritan minister Axton is instructive in this progress from the surplice to the supremacy. *Seconde Parte*, I, 68 ff.

monies, and vestments prescribed in the Prayer Book and other formularies.[2] Deploring the borrowings from "the mass-book" and usages "patched out of the Pope's portuis," he catalogued the numerous complaints which the Puritans repeated for many years.[3] In reply, Whitgift patiently advanced his reasonable arguments. The Prayer Book was not, as the Puritans charged, given an authority equal to that of the Bible.

> I do not think [wrote Whitgift] the communion-book to be such but that it may admit alteration. I do not believe it to be so perfect but that there may be both added to it, and taken from it. But . . . it is a godly book, without any error in substance of doctrine, and nothing in it (that I know) against the word of God. . . .
> Those imperfections, or rather motes, that you say to be in it, not to be such that any godly man ought to stir up any contention in the church for them, much less to make a schism. . . . That very perfection of an outward platform of a church, which you challenge unto yourselves, is one step to Novatianism, and well deserveth the name of Catharism.[4]

As to usages and ceremonies, replied Whitgift, these need not be "a show of papistry," as Cartwright maintained. Kneeling at the Holy Communion, for example,

> is the meetest manner of receiving this sacrament . . . being commonly used in praying and giving of thanks, both which are annexed to this sacrament. . . . The only peril is adoration, which may as well be committed sitting or standing.[5]

[2] Whitgift, *Works*, II, 438; III, 73, 384.
[3] See *Seconde Parte*, I, 70, 93, 197-201, 258-9; *Tracts Ascribed*, pp. 25-7, 31-6.
[4] Whitgift, *Works*, I, 173-4.
[5] *Ibid.*, III, 89-90.

Whitgift was convinced that the greater number of externals over which the controversy raged were "indifferent things, and put in the liberty of the Church," as even Calvin admitted. "It skills not," he answered Cartwright on the subject of the bread used in the Holy Communion, "what kind of bread is used, leavened or unleavened."[6] While Whitgift would have preferred common bread, "for the avoiding of superstition," this and other matters not prescribed by Holy Scripture were "left to the discretion of the church."[7] Over such rites and ceremonies the Church possessed authority, as both the ancient Fathers and the continental Protestant reformers agreed.[8] The Church of England, exercising this liberty, had rejected usages that were superstitious and retained those that were godly. When vestments, Whitgift declares,

were a sign and token of the popish priesthood, then were they evil, even as the thing was which they signified; but now they be the tokens and the signs of the ministers of the word of God which are good, and therefore also they be good. . . .[9]

This church of England [he affirms] abandoned great numbers of papistical rites and ceremonies; but, because it refuseth some, may it therefore retain none? Or, because it rejecteth those which be wicked and unprofitable, may it not therefore keep still such as be godly and pertain to order and decency?[10]

Whitgift was not blind to the faults and imperfections in the established Church, but, he reminded Cartwright,

It must be considered whether the faults be in the things themselves, or in the persons: for we may not with partial and cor-

[6] *Ibid.,* III, 84.
[7] *Ibid.,* I, 243. See also I, 201, 207-12; II, 44.
[8] *Ibid.,* I, 213, 246-7, 251; II, 454.
[9] *Ibid.,* II, 67. See also II, 55.
[10] *Ibid.,* II, 446-7. See also II, 589.

rupt judgment impute the faults of the persons to the things, whether they be offices or ceremonies, for then should we continually be altering the state, and never stand stedfast in any kind of government. Therefore in such cases we must seek to reform abuses in men . . . not pull away the states and offices, or the things themselves, because they be abused by some men.

That such faults were not within the order of the Church of England, he was firmly convinced. He stoutly declared

The state of this church of England at this day . . . is the state of a church reformed, and by authority and consent settled, not only in truth of doctrine . . . but also in order of things external, touching the government of the church and administration of the sacraments . . . All points of religion necessary to salvation . . . and true manner of worshipping God, are as purely and perfectly taught, and by public authority established, in this church of England at this day, as ever they were in any church since the apostles' time, or now be in any reformed church in the world.[11]

The crucial point at issue in this discussion over externals, as ultimately in the whole dispute, was the different view of Holy Scripture. The Puritan could admit no "things indifferent" in a Church truly reformed in accordance with the detailed model he supposed Scripture to provide. While Whitgift and Cartwright agreed that the Bible was the final and self-authenticating authority, the test of all saving truth, the former regarded this scriptural authority as bearing upon matters of doctrine and conduct; the latter, on the other hand, found in the Bible divine ordinances for the Church's worship, discipline, and polity as well. "The chief and prin-

[11] *Ibid.,* I, 4-6.

cipal ground" of the *Admonition,* Whitgift perceived, was that

those things only are to be placed in the church which the Lord himself in his word commandeth . . . nothing is to be tolerated in the church of Christ, touching either doctrine, order, ceremonies, discipline, or government, except it be expressed in the word of God.[12]

Cartwright's view mystified Whitgift.

Many things [wrote the Puritan] are both commanded and forbidden, for which there is no express mention in the word, which are as necessarily to be followed or avoided as those whereof express mention is made . . .

This kind of argument seemed clearly to justify Whitgift's contention that the Puritans made Scripture a "nose of wax," using it as they would, and interpreting the New Testament according to preconceived ideas. They found there what they sought to discover, divine authority for their pattern of ministry and discipline.[13]

The exclusive claim of the Puritans that a presbyterian church order alone was grounded in Scripture created an unbridgeable gulf between them and the defenders of the episcopal establishment. In their controversy over the form of the ministry, Cartwright expressed horror that his opponent made a distinction between "matters of faith necessary to salvation" and "matters of ceremonies, orders, discipline, and government," as though the latter were "things indifferent," not necessary to salvation. Whitgift could only reply

[12] *Ibid.,* I, 176.
[13] See Pearson, *Church and State,* pp. 123-5.

that to make "matters of ceremonies, discipline, and kind of government . . . necessary to salvation is a doctrine strange and unheard of to me."[14] It did not "stand with the truth and with learning." Nevertheless, on this view of Scripture the Puritan advanced his exclusive claim for presbyterianism, and the intolerant and passionate force with which it was proclaimed sprang from the conviction that this form of church order was alone sanctioned by the Word of God. The earliest Anglican defense of episcopacy against such exclusive claims was one that accepted the distinction between those matters of faith set forth by Scripture, and those matters of government "left to the discretion of the church."

That any one kind of government [wrote Whitgift] is so necessary that without it the church cannot be saved, or that it may not be altered into some other kind thought to be more expedient, I utterly deny. . . .

I find no one certain and perfect kind of government prescribed or commanded in the scriptures to the church of Christ; which no doubt should have been done, if it had been a matter necessary unto the salvation of the church . . . Some kind of government may be a part of the church, touching the outward form and perfection of it, yet it is not such a part of the essence and being, but that it may be the church of Christ without this or that kind of government; and therefore the kind of government of the church is not 'necessary unto salvation'. . . .[15]

I condemn no churches that have appointed any order for the electing of their pastors which they think to be agreeable to their state, and most profitable for them; for therefore I say that no certain manner or form of electing ministers is prescribed in the scripture, because every church may do therein as it shall

---

[14] Whitgift, *Works,* I, 180-1. See also I, 224.
[15] *Ibid.,* I, 184-5. See also III, 214, 218.

seem to be most expedient for the same. That may be profitable for the churches of Geneva and France, etc., which would be most hurtful to this church of England.[16]

For nearly fifteen years the characteristic Anglican defense of episcopacy reflected the tolerant and comprehensive spirit of the Elizabethan Church, but under the repeated invective of the Disciplinarians on one hand, and the Romanists on the other, assaulting the establishment with claims for the divine sanction of presbytery or papacy, the Anglican tone changed. In the Third Book of his *Ecclesiastical Polity* Hooker lamented that the continental Churches lacked "that which best agreeth with the sacred Scripture, I mean the government that is by Bishops," though he did not there condemn a polity "which either the irremediable error of former times, or the necessity of the present hath cast upon them."[17] In the Seventh Book, however, there is a closer approximation to the high doctrines of Sutcliffe, Saravia, and Bilson.

A thousand five hundred years and upward the Church of Christ hath now continued under the sacred regiment of bishops. Neither for so long hath Christianity been ever planted in any kingdom throughout the world but with this kind of government alone; which to have been ordained of God, I am for mine own part . . . resolutely persuaded . . .
Some wicked thing hath undoubtedly bewitched us, if we forsake that government, the use whereof universal experience hath for so many years approved, and betake ourselves unto a regiment neither appointed of God himself, as they who favour it pretend, nor till yesterday ever heard of among men . . .

[16] *Ibid.,* I, 369.
[17] Hooker, *Works,* I, 517-8.

Let us not fear to be herein bold and peremptory, that if any-thing in the Church's government, surely the first institution of bishops was from heaven, was even from God, the Holy Ghost was the author of it."[18]

It was the political implications of the Puritan position that alarmed Whitgift most, and aroused the suspicion among many that the program of the Disciplinarians would "overthrow the state both of religion and of the realm." Whitgift's concern was well-founded, for the success of the reforms proposed by the *Admonition* would have destroyed episcopacy and the Queen's supremacy together.[19] The truth is that the controversy involved a clash between two op-posing conceptions of the relations of Church and State. Whitgift and the defenders of the establishment stood fast on the same ground occupied by Stephen Gardiner and the apologists for the national Church and royal supremacy in the days of Henry VIII. At some places Whitgift asserted his convictions in almost the exact words of the *De vera obedientia*.[20]

I perceive [he wrote] no such distinction of the commonwealth and the church that they should be counted, as it were, two several bodies, governed with divers laws and divers magis-trates.[21]

To Whitgift's mind all was comprised within a single Christian commonwealth wherein God had committed the supreme government in both civil and ecclesiastical matters

---

[18] *Ibid.*, III, 173, 175.
[19] Whitgift, *Works,* I, 344, 478; II, 239, 281.
[20] *Ibid.*, II, 85.
[21] *Ibid.*, I, 21-2. See also I, 388; III, 267, 313.

to the Christian prince. The primary duty of the subject was
still Gardiner's "true obedience."[22]

This was not the way Cartwright understood God to have
disposed authority in the commonwealth. The theocratic
principles of Geneva offered a more scriptural example of
Christian order, for the commonwealth "must be made to
agree with the church." Church and State, though intimately
related, were two distinct bodies.[23] The prince or civil magistrate, according to Cartwright, might govern only

according to the rules of God prescribed in his word . . . they
be servants unto the church, and as they rule in the church, so
they must remember to subject themselves unto the church, to
submit their sceptres, to throw down their crowns before the
church, yea, as the prophet speaketh, to lick the dust of the feet
of the church.[24]

Whitgift was quick to see the implications of this appeal
to the "rules of God."

Methink I hear you whisper [he replied] that the prince hath
no authority in ecclesiastical matters: I know it is a received
opinion among some of you. . . .

Cartwright could only say of the Queen, that

Although her authority be the greatest in the earth, yet it is
not infinite, but it is limited by the word of God . . . [The] making of the orders and ceremonies of the church . . . pertain unto
the ministers of the church . . . the civil magistrate hath not to
ordain ceremonies pertaining to the church.[25]

[22] *Ibid.*, II, 263-4; III, 182, 296-301.
[23] *Ibid.*, I, 27.
[24] *Ibid.*, III, 189.
[25] *Ibid.*, III, 295-6.

"Limited by the word of God"—this was where the Disciplinarians stood fast, for there they could interpret in their own fashion the very words in which the *Thirty-Nine Articles* described the royal supremacy as "that prerogative which we see to have been given always to all godly princes in Holy Scripture." Scripture, argued Walter Travers in the *Explicatio,* subjected the godly prince to the discipline, and when Whitgift saw the monarch subordinated "to the seignory . . . ordered and ruled by the pastors," it was evident to him that the prince's God-given authority in both ecclesiastical and civil matters had been overthrown.[26]

This was the Puritan "push at the civil policy," as Parker had put it. Despite Cartwright's protestations of loyalty, among the more fanatical Disciplinarians the "true obedience" was made to depend upon the same testing of the prince's "godliness" that had appeared in John Ponet's *Treatise of Politike Power.* In this tract, written by the Edwardian Bishop of Winchester during his exile in Mary's reign, the old principle of non-resistance to an ungodly prince was turned into a duty of active resistance when the prince's commands were conscientiously felt to be against the Word of God and the welfare of the commonwealth.[27] Echoed in Christopher Goodman's *How Superior Powers ought to be Obeyed* and Anthony Gilby's *Admonition to England and Scotland,* Ponet's ideas won the acclaim of radical reformers as long as their "ungodly prince," the Catholic Mary Tudor, lived. With the accession of Queen Elizabeth their tune changed. Little was said of any qualification of the "true obedience" until it became clear to the Puritans of the disciplinarian faction that in the last resort

[26] *Ibid.,* III, 191, 198.
[27] Hudson, *John Ponet,* p. 155.

it was the Queen who stood between them and the achievement of their goal. Then the text Ponet had chosen for his titlepage came uppermost in their minds: "It is better to trust in the Lorde than to trust in Princes," and the challenge was offered to the royal supremacy and the whole order of the Tudor commonwealth with which it was inseparately linked.[28]

The position to which Cartwright reduced the civil power was familiar to Whitgift. "I have read it," he declared, "in the books of the papists."[29] The supporters of the establishment saw little difference between the attacks of Rome and those of the revolutionary Puritans.[30] Either, if successful, would have repudiated the tolerant principle of comprehension in the Elizabethan settlement, and destroyed the Tudor national Church; both bore marks of a religious spirit foreign to that which was the peculiar genius of Elizabethan Anglicanism.

The *Admonition* controversy that provoked the contest between Whitgift and Cartwright died down, as we have seen, before the publication of Whitgift's final *Defense of the Answer* in 1574. But Bishop Cox was mistaken when he supposed that the Puritans had been vanquished by Whitgift's "learned confutation." Silenced by the repressive activity of the authorities, the ardent Disciplinarians sought other means of disseminating their opinions. At hand was an ideal instrument in the informal assemblies of local clergy, encouraged for their better education in the Scriptures. It was a stroke of genius on the part of Puritan leaders to seize control of the admirable opportunities offered them

---

[28] See *Seconde Parte,* I, 52, 188.
[29] Whitgift, *Works,* III, 301.
[30] *Ibid.,* I, 57, 114-9; III, 160, 171, 267, 296, 308-13.

by these "exercises," and during the years Whitgift was at Worcester the famous "prophesyings" became the chief scene of Puritan activity.

Meetings of ministers for the study and discussion of Holy Scripture were held in some parts of England, particularly in the diocese of Norwich, as early as 1564.[31] In the decade that followed they became increasingly common, spreading rapidly through those areas where Puritanism was strongest. However useful such exercises might have been for improving the education of the clergy and raising the standard of preaching, in the hands of the opponents of the establishment they speedily became a very effective instrument for the spread of Puritan ideas among the people. At the prophesyings ministers expounded the meaning of Scripture passages to their fellow clergy and the lay folk gathered with them, afterwards criticizing each others' expositions in a fashion that suggests the Genevan "censures."[32] Experience shaped common rules of procedure and uniform methods of conducting the exercises, and gradually they were almost wholly directed towards the inconspicuous advance of the Puritan cause under the guise of a godly religious exercise. In the end the prophesyings matured into associations of immense importance in the development of the later classes or presbyteries.

Elizabeth and Parker were not unaware of the potential dangers in the movement, but the archbishop's attempt to suppress the meetings met with little success. His acrimonious correspondence with the Bishop of Norwich reveals that for

[31] Prophesyings were common in the Swiss and Rhineland cities, and the Marian exiles undoubtedly learned their value there. Trinterud, "The Origins of Puritanism," *Church History,* xx, 1, 46.

[32] Strype, *Annals,* II, i, 133 ff.

one reason or another a number of bishops encouraged their clergy in these exercises.[33] Parkhurst was convinced that the assemblies were a strong remedy against clerical ignorance, and Freke, his successor, allowed them to continue. Sandys of London favored the early prophesyings, though he sought to bring them more closely under his authority; Chaderton at Chester hoped they would arm his clergy against the Roman Catholic propagandists who infested his diocese. Even Bishop Cooper of Lincoln permitted them their continuance under a set of regulations which in one particular, at least, bore a surprising resemblance to the similar meetings of the ministers of Geneva.

This done [ran the bishop's orders] the first speaker must be contented to be admonished by the moderator, and the rest of the brethren, of such things as shall seem to the company worthy admonition. The same inquiry is to be made of the life of the speakers in their course. That we may all be reformed both in doctrine and life.[34]

The bishops were not fools, nor were they sympathetic with the phase into which Puritanism entered after the *Admonition* controversy. Any means of improving the character and diminishing the ignorance of his clergy attracted the support of every earnest Elizabethan bishop. The difficulty seems to have been that in some instances they did not realize the use to which the Puritan leaders put the meetings, while in others they overestimated the extent to which their authority could be effectively exerted. The pas-

[33] *Parker Correspondence*, pp. 457-60.
[34] Strype, *Annals*, II, i, 475. For Chaderton's attempt to control the exercises see p. 481.

sionate determination of the Disciplinarians made the prophesyings impossible to control, particularly when their developing program was provided with an authoritative form. In 1574 there appeared a lengthy treatise on the presbyterian polity "of the Churche of Christe ordeyned and appointed of God for the goode administration and government of the same," called *Ecclesiasticae disciplinae et Anglicanae Ecclesiae ab illa aberrationis plena E Verbo Dei et dilucida Explicatio.*[35] Translated by Cartwright under the title *A full and plain declaration of Ecclesiasticall Discipline owt off the word off God and off the declininge off the churche off England from the same,* its tendentious exposition of the Puritan theory of order and discipline in a Church rightly reformed was spread through the assemblies. The *Explicatio* or *Declaration* provided the blueprint for the Puritan reconstruction of the established Church from within; its appearance forged the link between the prophesyings and the classis organization.

At this critical juncture Archbishop Grindal succeeded Parker at Canterbury. Grindal was one of the moderate party of former exiles, and like Jewel, Sandys, and Cox, sympathetic with the Precisians in the earlier vestiarian phase of the Puritan controversy. He never seems to have understood the developments that changed the Puritan program into one challenging the entire structure of the establishment. Kindly and gentle, always willing to think the best of the nonconformists, his chief interest was in the improvement of the education of the clergy and their conse-

---

[35] Bancroft, *Survay,* p. 73. The *Explicatio* should be distinguished from Travers' later and more significant *Disciplina Ecclesiae Sacra* (the famous "Book of Discipline") with which it has sometimes been confused. Paget, *Fifth Book,* pp. 53 ff. See below, p. 180.

quent ability rightly to proclaim the Word of God. When he devised articles in consultation with Whitgift for the Convocation of 1575-6 their major stress was in this direction. According to these regulations none was to be ordained without proper testimonials of soundness in doctrine and honesty of life. Clergy unlicensed to preach were to be examined in their learning; if shown to be ignorant, they were to undertake a course of biblical study under the direction of the archdeacons.[36]

Nothing could convince Grindal that the prophesyings were not a very proper and useful means of raising the standards of clerical learning and behaviour. Furthermore, they were, he said "set down in holy scriptures . . . for the great profit of the church." On this point he was stubbornly immoveable. Confronted by the Queen's repeated demands that he suppress the meetings, he offered his utmost compromise. He would bring his metropolitical authority to bear upon the bishops, forcing them to regulate the prophesyings by a uniform set of injunctions. Accordingly, he drew up a set of articles intended to achieve this end. By these rules, exercises could be used only in such places as the bishop might appoint, at all times under the close supervision of the archdeacon or his deputy, and without the participation of lay persons in the discussions. All mention of matters of state was to be avoided; invective against the ecclesiastical laws or rites of the Church was to be halted. Ministers under sentences of deprivation or inhibition from preaching were in no place to be suffered to speak.[37]

[36] Grindal, *Remains,* pp. 185-92. Whitgift was Prolocutor of this Convocation, the year before his appointment to Worcester, and he and Grindal appear to have worked out together the articles that are sometimes known as the "Canons of 1576." Cardwell, *Synodalia,* I, 132-8.

[37] Strype, *Grindal,* pp. 327-8.

Elizabeth lost all patience with her new archbishop. Her irritation with Parker was mild compared with the exasperation to which Grindal's earnest and naive obstinacy reduced her. Matthew Parker had at least understood her and sought to carry out her orders; this man quoted Scripture at her like a Puritan divine and talked about his conscientious duty. Elizabeth hated the zealous preachers. She knew that assemblies of discontented clerics were dangerous to the peace and good order of the realm. Moreover, the very articles with which Grindal proposed to regulate the prophesyings betrayed the true character of those exercises. Surely deprived and inhibited ministers had no place in innocent meetings arranged to help educate the clergy, and as for the article requiring the moderators immediately to interrupt and silence any speaker who "glanced openly or covertly against the state, or any person public"—matters must be completely out of hand when such orders had to be devised. How far Elizabeth was aware that deprived ministers already dominated the prophesyings in such Puritan strongholds as Norfolk and Northamptonshire, it is difficult to say, but her instincts in respect to the meetings were right.[38] Puritanism had become a conspiracy; the prophesyings were the scenes of an insidious undermining of the Church of England.

Advised by some of the bishops, the Queen issued a sharp command to the archbishop to suppress the exercises.[39] From it there was no appeal and the unhappy Grindal wrestled with his conflict of loyalties. Unable at last to retreat from his conscientious stand, on December 20, 1576 he sent his

[38] *Seconde Parte,* I, 121, 145.
[39] Strype, *Grindal,* p. 404.

famous letter to Elizabeth. Obviously written by a man driven to speak his mind plainly, come what may, one can only admire both the temerity and the earnestness that possessed its author. The Queen can never have received a letter like it.[40]

Protesting his loyalty and gratitude, Grindal began by reminding the Queen, that while her zeal in religious matters is commendable, yet the best princes—King David, good King Ezechias, the godly King Jehoshaphat, and Theodosius the Emperor—have not refused "to be better informed out of God's word." He marveled that she could entertain the opinion that the Church should have few preachers. "Alas! Madam, is the Scripture more plain in any one thing than that the Gospel of Christ should be plentifully preached?"

Public and continual preaching of God's word [he wrote] is the ordinary mean and instrument of the salvation of mankind. St. Paul calleth it the ministry of reconciliation of man unto God. . . . That unable preaching be removed is very requisite. . . . I, for mine own part . . . am very careful in allowing such preachers only as be able and sufficient to be preachers, both for their knowledge in the Scriptures, and also for testimony of their good life and conversation. . . . We admit no man to the office, that either professeth Papistry or Puritanism. . . .

But some there be . . . that are mislikers of the godly reformation in religion now established, wishing indeed that there were no preachers at all . . . some are altogether worldly minded . . . serving Mammon and not God. . . . And another great sum have given over themselves to all carnal, vain, dissolute, and lascivious life. . . . Therefore they wish also that there were no preachers at all.

But God forbid, Madam, that you should open your ears to

[40] *Ibid.,* pp. 558-74.

any of these wicked persuasions, or any way go about to diminish the preaching of Christ's Gospel. . . .

He then informed Elizabeth that he was still of the same mind about the *Homilies* as when they last argued the question; they are "nothing comparable to the office of preaching." He repeated his conviction that the most profitable means of strengthening preaching was through the use of carefully supervised prophesyings. Grounded in both the Old and New Testaments, these exercises not only improved the preaching; they "beat down popery," made the clergy more skillful in the Scriptures and less ignorant, and improved the opinion laymen have of the ministers. "Only backward men in religion and contemners of learning do fret against it"—Elizabeth's imperious temper must have flared at that.

I am forced [Grindal continued] with all humility, and yet plainly, to profess, that I cannot with safe conscience, and without the offense of the majesty of God, give my consent to the suppressing of the said exercises; much less can I send out any injunction for the utter and universal subversion of the same. . . . If it be your Majesty's pleasure, for this or any other cause, to remove me out of this place, I will, with all humility, yield thereunto, and render again to your Majesty that I have received of the same. . . . What should I win, if I gained—I will not say a bishopric—but the whole world, and lose mine own soul?

The bridge is crossed now, and Grindal can speak from his heart. He asks the Queen to leave matters of this kind to the bishops and divines of the realm "according to the example of all godly Christian emperors and princes of all ages." Citing the encounters of St. Ambrose with Theodosius and Valentinian, he begs "Would to God your

Majesty would follow this ordinary course." Finally, with a bluntness that he cannot conceal, he requests that

When you deal in matters of faith and religion, or matters that touch the Church of Christ . . . you would not use to pronounce too resolutely and peremptorily, *quasi ex authoritate,* as ye may do in civil and extern matters. . . . It is the anti-christian voice of the Pope: "So I will have it; so I command; let my will stand for a reason." In God's matters, all princes ought to bow their scepters . . . to serve God with fear and trembling.

Remember, Madam, that you are a mortal creature . . . although ye are a mighty Prince, yet remember that he which dwelleth in heaven is mightier. . . . God hath blessed you with great felicity in your reign, now many years; beware you do not impute the same to your own deserts or policy, but give God the glory. . . . Ye have done many things well, but except ye persevere to the end, ye cannot be blessed.

But I trust in God, your Majesty will always humble yourself under his mighty hand, and go forward in the zealous setting forth of God's true religion, always yielding due obedience and reverence to the word of God, the only rule of faith and religion. . . . I beseech God our heavenly Father plentifully to pour his principal spirit upon you, and always to direct your heart in his holy fear. Amen.

Elizabeth's rage was unbounded. Grindal's stubborn refusal to employ his authority against the assemblies forced her to that which was most distasteful, the direct exercise of the royal supremacy. On May 7, 1577 ignoring the archbishop, she issued orders directly to the bishops, commanding the suppression of the prophesyings.[41] Persons, she wrote, presuming to be teachers and preachers of the Church . . . do

[41] *Ibid.,* pp. 342, 574-6.

daily devise, imagine, propound, and put into execution sundry new rites and forms . . . by procuring unlawful assemblies . . . which manner of invasions they in some places call "prophesying," and in other "exercises." . . .

The bishops are instructed to see that these meetings cease. No minister should be allowed to preach or to teach except he be duly licensed and "conformable." Elizabeth closed her letter in characteristic fashion:

And in these things we charge you to be so careful and vigilant, as by your negligence, if we shall hear of any person attempting to offend in the premises without your correction or information to us, we be not forced to make some example or reformation of you, according to your deserts.[42]

By the Queen's order Archbishop Grindal was sequestered, and for six months was confined to his palace at Lambeth. As he continued to remain obdurate, his suspension was never fully removed, despite the appeals made to Elizabeth by Convocation and the bishops.[43] During the entire six years that John Whitgift was Bishop of Worcester, the Church of England was without effective metropolitical authority. Makeshift arrangements were devised whereby the Bishop of London and Grindal's officials exercised some part of the archbishop's functions, but this did little to lessen the inconvenience or halt the drift towards administrative chaos in the ecclesiastical scene. The resulting disorganization brought the Elizabethan Church into its darkest days; for a time it seemed as though the establishment was to be wrecked on the rock of Edmund Grindal's conscience.

---

[42] Cardwell, *Doc. Annals,* I, 428-31.
[43] *Ibid.,* 441-6; *Synodalia,* II, 543-6.

Puritan sympathy among some of the gentry and their growing antagonism to the bishops was again exhibited in the Parliament of 1581. Five years earlier the Commons had petitioned the Queen for "reformation of Discipline in the Church."[44] The convocational articles of 1576 were devised in part, at least, to answer this petition of the House against the ordination of men "who are not only altogether unfurnished of such gifts as are . . . incident to their calling, but also are infamous in their lives and conversations."[45] More extensive parliamentary articles of similar tenor were delivered to the Queen in 1581. She handed them over to Sandys, now Archbishop of York, who called together five of his brethren to consider them.[46] The extent to which the articles incorporated some of the less inflammatory Puritan proposals for reform is evident from Whitgift's annotations.[47] Elizabeth saw to it that the articles were not returned to the members of the House of Commons who had presented them. As Sandys later recounted the story to the Bishop of Chester, he told the members of the House that the Queen had informed him "her Highness was sufficient of herself to deal with the clergy in matters ecclesiastical; and that the Parliament House should not meddle therein."[48]

Spurred on by the Queen, the bishops labored to check the Puritan agitation, and none more vigorously than the Bishop of London, John Aylmer, who had been made president of the Ecclesiastical Commission. Violent and ill-tempered,

[44] D'Ewes, *Journals,* p. 257.

[45] See Neale, *Elizabeth I and Her Parliaments,* p. 351.

[46] Whitgift was one; the others were John Piers of Salisbury, Richard Davies of St. David's, Nicholas Robinson of Bangor, and Thomas Cooper of Lincoln. It is significant that these men were all bishops who had never shown sympathy with the Puritans, nor had belonged to the party affected by the Marian exile.

[47] Strype, *Whitgift,* III, 47-63.

[48] *Desiderata Curiosa,* p. 102.

Aylmer searched out the Puritan and Romanist recusants with a passion that approached viciousness.[49] His flurry of activity, however, availed little when the Council reversed its sterner decrees without the Queen's knowledge—the same "comfort these Puritans have" that had distressed Parker—and the local authorities gave little cooperation in Puritan strongholds. Archbishop Sandys was convinced that a kind of madness had seized the more violent malcontents. In May 1581 he warned Bishop Chaderton against encouraging any unusual religious exercises that might cloak a conspiracy.

> My lord [he wrote] you are noted to yield too much to general fastings, all the day preaching and praying. Verily a good exercise in time and upon just occasion, when it cometh from good authority. But when there is none occasion, neither the thing commanded by the prince or a synod, the wisest and best learned cannot like of it, neither will her Majesty permit it. There lurketh matter under that pretended piety. The devil is crafty; and the young ministers of these our times grow mad.[50]

Sandys did not exaggerate. If the prophesyings disappeared, the matter that lurked in them sprang up in the secret "conferences" of the early stages of the classis system. Experimental presbyteries came into being, where people had their first full taste of the joys of the Genevan discipline, though perhaps not yet seasoned with all its rigors. Openly flouting the ecclesiastical laws, Puritan ministers took livings only to preach, disregarding the required ministrations of the Prayer Book. New pamphlets appeared, and men counted over again the "hundred points of Poperie

---

[49] Strype, *Aylmer*, p. 36.
[50] *Desiderata Curiosa*, p. 102.

yet remayning, which deforme the Englishe reformation" in Anthony Gilby's *Pleasaunt Dialogue*. It was evident on every side that in the absence of strong central authority the existing ecclesiastical machinery of repression was insufficient to deal with a movement now approaching coherent organization.

It is no surprise, therefore, that the period of Grindal's suspension witnessed the first overt and permanent Protestant separation from the Church of England.[51] While the great majority of Puritans, exerting their influence towards the reformation of the Church from within, never embraced the principles of Separatism, impatient left-wing leaders could not wait for the day when the Queen or her government would be won to the cause. Indeed, their ideas had advanced to the point where there was perhaps little to choose between the existing formularies of the Queen's Church and the proposed discipline of the *Explicatio* or other Puritan programs of reform. Robert Browne gave them their watchword: "Reformation without tarrying!"[52] He and Robert Harrison organized their conventicle at Norwich in 1580, and slowly but surely Separatism sent down its roots into the ground of English religious life. The Separatists could tolerate no feature of the establishment. Harrison's *Treatise of the Church and the Kingdome of Christ* denied the Church of England any spiritual ministry whatsoever; it was not a true Church of Christ.[53] Here

[51] The question whether earlier and isolated congregations of dissenters were actually Separatists in the full sense is discussed by Burrage, *Early English Dissenters*, I, 82 ff.

[52] Browne published his *Treatise of Reformation without Tarying for Anie* in 1582. See *The Writings of Robert Harrison and Robert Browne*, pp. 151-70.

[53] *Ibid.*, pp. 32, 34-5.

was that final dissent to which Bishop Cooper referred as he concluded his description of the opponents of the Elizabethan settlement:

Now break out another sort, earnestly affirming and teaching that we have no Church, no bishops, no ministers, no Sacraments; and therefore that all that love Jesus Christ ought with all speed to separate themselves from our congregations.[54]

Already the ecclesiastical authorities had been active in hunting down other groups of sectaries whose principles were as abhorrent to the Puritans as they were to the bishops. Showing some affiliations with both Anabaptism and the later Quakers, these were members of the "Family of Love" —what Knollys called "the deified men"—and in 1580 Elizabeth issued a stern proclamation against their "damnable heresies."[55] It is small wonder that confronted by what looked to be a steady distintegration of the ecclesiastical settlement, Elizabeth was seized by moments of utter despair. But the tide was on the point of turning, and the very real hold which the established Church had come to have in the lives of the great mass of Englishmen was presently displayed.

On the 6th of July 1583 poor Edmund Grindal, blind and broken in health, at last found peace in death. Edwin Sandys might have been his natural successor were it not that the Queen mistrusted his ability to bring a firm hand to bear upon the rebellious opponents of the Church. Unable to control the London Puritans earlier, Elizabeth doubted that he could do better as Archbishop of Canterbury. Besides,

---

[54] *Admonition to the People,* p. 158.
[55] *Concilia,* IV, 297-8. See also Ellis, *Letters,* 3rd Series, IV, 32-6.

she was determined to have no more archbishops who had been exposed to "Germanical opinions" while in exile during her sister's reign. Only a man of unquestioned loyalty and unflinching resolve would do; only a man who believed that "insolent audacity against states and lawful regiment is rather to be corrected with due punishment than confuted by argument" could deal effectively with the challenge now presented by the activity of the Puritans.[56] John Whitgift was the obvious choice, and the government felt that the sooner he was settled at Lambeth the better. At least six months before Grindal's death negotiations for his resignation and replacement were under way, but the scheme came to naught, in George Paule's opinion, because Whitgift would not accept the office as long as the archbishop lived.[57]

Nominated to Canterbury on August 14th, Whitgift was elected on the 23rd, and a month later confirmation of his election brought him the burden of heaviest responsibility in the Elizabethan Church.[58] The news of his translation filled the Puritans with dismay. "The choice of that man at this time to be archbishop," one lamented, "maketh me think that the Lord is determined to scourge his church."[59] The Puritans never underestimated the capacity of their chief opponent.

With quiet resolution Whitgift went about his preparations for the move to Lambeth. He had no illusions concerning the magnitude of the task that lay before him. His letter of September 17th to his friend Matthew Hutton reveals his determination to accept the charge placed upon

[56] Whitgift, *Works,* II, 188.
[57] Grindal, *Remains,* 397, 402. Paule, p. 35.
[58] The steps in his translation to Canterbury are recorded in Lambeth MS. 807, f. 29. See also *Reg. Whitgift* (Worcester) 32, II, f. 23.
[59] Birch, *Memoirs of Queen Elizabeth,* I, 42.

him with the same resolution in which he had sought to do his duty heretofore.

The burden laid upon me [he wrote] is very heavy and great; yet because it is God's own doing who hath wrought it in her Majesty's heart, my trust is that he will also furnish me with gifts and graces necessary, that I may without fainting perform that whereunto he hath so called me.

Jo Wigorn: Elect Can.[60]

[60] Lambeth MS. 1138 (3). See *Hutton Correspondence,* p. 72.

VI

THE DEFENSE OF THE ESTABLISHMENT

ON the 23rd of October 1583 John Whitgift was solemnly enthroned at Canterbury, the seventy-second occupant of St. Augustine's Chair. Three weeks later, preaching in St. Paul's Cathedral before a brilliant assemblage gathered to honor Elizabeth on the twenty-fifth anniversary of her accession, the new archbishop made it plain that the lax days of Edmund Grindal had passed. His very text alarmed the Puritans: "Warne them to be subject to rule and power, to obey magistrates, to be redie to every good worke." By the time he descended from the pulpit it was unmistakably clear that the best work was conformity to her Majesty's ecclesiastical laws.[1]

Whitgift lost no time in preparing to control the rebellious Puritan clergy. Four days before his enthronement he had finished drafting a series of injunctions designed to close the gaps in the existing formularies through which the Disciplinarians found opportunity to challenge the order and constitution of the Church. Armed with the Queen's approval, he dispatched these *Eleven Articles* to the bishops

[1] Whitgift, *Works*, III, 586-96.

with orders for their strict enforcement.[2] Though the new articles enjoined full application of the laws against Romanist recusants, their main burden fell upon the Puritan malcontents. A direct simplicity left no loopholes for devious interpretation. Incipient prophesyings and private religious assemblies were sternly forbidden; the use of the authorized "Bishops' Bible" was to be enforced against the popular Geneva translation with its subversive notes. No compromise was permitted with the vestiarian requirements of the *Advertisements*. Bishops were instructed to ordain only fit and educated persons, properly beneficed or employed. No man was to be suffered to minister except he be duly admitted priest or deacon "according to the laws of this realm," while preachers who declined to use the services of the Prayer Book and administer the Sacraments were to be inhibited from preaching.[3] The crucial regulation was the sixth article, the hinge on which the Puritan controversy turned for a decade, and eventually the chief instrument of Whitgift's successful defense of the establishment. By it none was permitted to minister in any capacity unless he first subscribed

That her majesty, under God, hath and ought to have the sovereignty and rule over all manner of persons born within her realms, dominions, and countries, of what estate, whether ecclesiastical, or temporal soever they be; and that no foreign power, prelate, state or potentate hath or ought to have any jurisdiction, power, superiority, preeminence, or authority ecclesiastical or spiritual, within her majesty's said realms, dominions, and countries.

That the book of common prayer, and the ordering of bishops,

2 *Concilia,* IV, 303, 307-8.
3 Cardwell, *Doc. Annals,* I, 466-71.

priests, and deacons, containeth nothing in it contrary to the
word of God, and that the same may lawfully be used, and
that he himself will use the form of the said book prescribed
in public prayer, and administrations of the sacraments, and
none other.

3) *That* he allowed the book of the articles of religion, agreed
upon by the archbishops and bishops of both provinces, and
by the whole clergy in the convocation holden at London in
the year of our Lord God MDLXII and set forth by her majesty's
authority, and that he believeth all the articles therein contained
to be agreeable to the word of God.[4]

While the article of subscription added little to what
might be required by the *Canons of 1571,* its careful and
precise wording clarified the ambiguities in the existing
formularies. There was no escape from the "laws of consecration and ordering."[5] No conscientious presbyterian Puritan could subscribe the "consecration and superiority [of
bishops] in Church government, and the ordering of priests,
deacons, and other suchlike points."[6] Moreover, to affirm
that the Prayer Book contained nothing contrary to the word
of God "killed them in their souls." Raising the old com-
plaint that the statutory subscription was exceeded, the
Puritans again demanded freedom to subscribe only the
doctrinal statements of the *Thirty-Nine Articles,* though
some of them were now unwilling to accept even those save
"in that sense that is best."[7] The objections, of course, extended beyond the sixth article. The prescribed vestments
were regarded as "the mark of the beast," and the pro-
hibition of ministrations by men ordained in foreign Prot-

---

[4] *Reg. Whitgift,* I, f. 97a.
[5] *Seconde Parte,* I, 183.
[6] *Ibid.,* I, 184, 204. See Dering's objections in *A parte of a register,* p. 82.
[7] *Seconde Parte,* I, 195.

estant Churches was bitterly resented. The provision that preachers use the Prayer Book services at stated intervals struck at the employment of Puritan ministers as lecturers and special preachers, a popular means of spreading the Genevan doctrines by non-beneficed clergy from whom there was no opportunity to exact a pledge of conformity. Finally, even the question of how far the Queen's ecclesiastical authority was in accord with the word of God was boldly raised.[8]

Well aware that his metropolitical powers alone were insufficient to enforce the *Eleven Articles,* even were the bishops to cooperate fully, Whitgift secured a new authorization of the Ecclesiastical Commission as provided in the *Act of Supremacy.*[9] At the outset of Elizabeth's reign the statutory Commissioners were largely occupied with visitatorial and administrative duties, but gradually adopting the procedures of a church court, after 1580 the body was regularly known as "High Commission." In Whitgift's hands this process of transformation into a permanent ecclesiastical court was speedily completed. The High Commission, emancipated from control by the Privy Council, added to its former responsibilities the censorship of the press, the task of tendering the oaths and forms of subscription, and successfully asserted its right to impose fines and sentences of deprivation and imprisonment. With the machinery of enforcement ready by early December, the archbishop found the man to operate it efficiently. This was Richard Bancroft, an old friend and admirer from the days when he was a senior member of Jesus College while Whitgift was Master of Trinity. Having come to London in 1579

[8] *Ibid.,* I, 177-96.
[9] *S.P.Dom.Eliz.* ccxxviii. 19. See Prothero, p. 472a. The history of the Commission is told in Usher, *Rise and Fall of High Commission.*

in the service of Christopher Hatton, Bancroft soon displayed that zeal for which Andrew Melville called him "the capital enemy of all the Reformed Churches in Europe." As archiepiscopal visitor in the diocese of Ely he led an inexorable search for the East Anglian sectaries. However ambitious, Bancroft was an honest and capable administrator. Whitgift's confidence in him was not misplaced. For twenty years Richard Bancroft was his indefatigable and faithful supporter, ultimately as Bishop of London and Archbishop of Canterbury succeeding to the task of Puritan repression.

On December 12th Bancroft was directed to instruct the bishops to begin visitations, adding the *Eleven Articles* to their own, being particularly diligent in enforcing the new subscription.[10] Thus began the "woeful year of subscription," opening with what the chroniclers of dissent have called the "violent and illegal methods" of a "despotic regime of tyranny," directed by "the Jeffreys of the ecclesiastical bench," a man who "embodied the worst passions of an intolerant state-priest, and stood out in the history of protestant non-conformity as worthy of especial reprobation."[11] Seldom has a discomforted minority heaped such abuse upon its opponent as the Puritans poured upon John Whitgift. Devoting his life to spare the English Church the narrow confines of Puritanism, perhaps more than any other man he made possible the growth of the distinctive ethos of Anglicanism. Yet he did so at the cost of his reputation, a martyr to the unrestrained fury of his enemies. Largely

[10] Whitgift's plan for their enforcement in diocesan visitations is clear in his articles for Bath and Wells in 1583 and for Chichester in 1585. Kennedy, *Eliz. Epis. Ad.*, III, 153-8, 182-5. The bishops, however, often avoiding Article 6, did not always enforce the *Eleven Articles* with the rigor the archbishop desired. *Reg. Whitgift*, I, fos. 335 et seq.

[11] Price, *History of Non-conformity*, I, 470-1. Heron, *Short History of Puritanism*, pp. 128-36.

because Whig historians accepted the Puritan propaganda uncritically, Archbishop Whitgift has come down in history as "an inquisitor as merciless as Torquemada."[12] In Gardiner's judgment he was "narrow-minded to an almost incredible degree";[13] in Macaulay's phrases he was a "mean and tyrannical priest, who gained power by servility and adulation, and employed it in persecuting both those who agreed with Calvin about Church Government, and those who differed from Calvin touching the doctrine of Reprobation."[14]

While one may not agree that Harington told the whole story when he described the archbishop as winning divers Puritans "by sweet persuasions to conformity . . . ever leaning to the milder censure as best became his calling," and thus, in Arthur Wilson's words, leaving "a name like sweet perfume behind him," the fact is that the remarks of these seventeenth-century writers are nearer the truth than the Puritans would have had men believe.[15] Even the mass of documents gathered into *The Seconde Parte of a Register,* favorable to the Puritan cause and *ex parte* in nature, gives a clear picture of a tolerant forbearance in Whitgift that few Puritans showed. The material in *The Seconde Parte,* for example, records in detail a visit to the archbishop of a deputation of suspended clergy from Chichester. He listened patiently on a bitter winter's day as they sat around a "good fire of coles," the Puritans making an issue of every difference in the Prayer Book from the three changes ordered

[12] Beesly, *Queen Elizabeth,* p. 228.

[13] *History of England 1603-1642,* I, 33.

[14] *Critical and Historical Essays,* II, 135.

[15] Harington, *Nugae Antiquae,* II, 23. Wilson, "The Life and Reign of James I" in Kennet, *Complete History of England,* II, 665. See also *Reliquiae Wottonianae,* p. 172, and Camden's remarks in *Britannia,* p. 338 and *Elizabeth,* p. 288.

in the statute of 1559. They were troubled by the omission
of the "Black Rubric"; they would allow no liberty of conscience to hold any doctrine of the Real Presence. They refused to accept Whitgift's assurances that the *Advertisements*
had long ago modified the ornaments rubric; they talked
tendentiously of the requirement of vestments abandoned
for years. "You are unlearned," said Whitgift, not unkindly,
"and but boys in comparison of us, who have studied
divinity before you for the most part were born." He sent
them to walk in the garden, to go home and think it over.
In the end he allowed them to subscribe on their own terms,
generous enough to accept their declaration that "their subscription was not required to any other sense than such as
was not against the word of God"—a qualification that was
capable of almost limitless interpretation in the Puritan
mind. Afterwards Whitgift found that they had spread reports of a triumph over him in which he was made to accept
their subscription under protest.[16] Nonetheless, he kept his
word with them, though repeated efforts to deal courteously
with non-conformists taught him that those who flatly refused to subscribe would ordinarily yield only to sharper
measures.

Consequently, in May 1584, the use of the *ex officio* oath
was revived by High Commission, and a set of two dozen
articles was devised for the examination of suspects under
it.[17] The *ex officio* oath was one which the ecclesiastical
authorities by virtue of their office might administer to an
accused person, forcing him if guilty to incriminate himself.
Originally borrowed from Roman law, it had long been in
use in the church courts. Bonner and Gardiner were examined under it in King Edward's reign, as Whitgift was quick

[16] *Seconde Parte,* I, 210-20.
[17] Strype, *Whitgift,* III, 81-7.

to point out when its use was challenged. Unhappily, it gave the court an advantage over the honest and conscientious Puritan, while the man willing to perjure himself could escape. Yet there was no other instrument in the canon law wherewith to curb effectively those who refused every reasonable overture made to them. The use of this oath, of course, redoubled the clamorous outcry against the new archbishop. Demanding the restoration of deprived ministers, the Puritans launched savage attacks upon the *Eleven Articles* and their enforcement by High Commission. Despite the most rigorous censorship, tracts poured from the press, and the members of the Council were showered with pamphlets and petitions, some reiterating every old grievance with the establishment, others pleading for the abolition of episcopacy and the speedy erection of a presbyterian church government.[18] An ominous opposition to the bishops appeared at Court, compounded partly out of sympathy for the Puritans, partly out of a fear that the archbishop's severity would alienate the loyalty of many of the Queen's subjects at a time when Romanist activity and the menace of Spain imperiled the national security, and partly out of a new anti-clericalism spreading among the common lawyers. Jealous of the Church's independent jurisdiction and alarmed at the growth of the prerogative courts, an alliance began between the Puritans and the lawyers that was to come to full maturity in the reigns of the Stuart monarchs.

The opposition came quickly to a head. Robert Beale, clerk of the Council, subjected the archbishop to a withering torrent of abuse, taxing him with illegal proceedings. Leicester and Walsingham openly showed their animosity. Francis Knollys, according to Fuller, "bred a banished man in Germany during the reign of Queen Mary, and . . .

[18] Lambeth MS, 577, fos. 245-7.

never after fond of episcopacy,"[19] and who regarded the dissident clergy as bulwarks against Romanism, was eager "to open the mouths of all zealous preachers, that be sound in doctrine, howsoever otherwise they refuse to subscribe to any tradition of man, not compellable by law."[20] Though supported by Hatton alone among the councillors, Whitgift was unmoved by the clamor. Strengthened by the single-minded constancy he had learned from John Bradford in the first years at Cambridge, he was prepared to suffer for his principles. In June 1584 he assured Burghley that he would not be swerved from his duty to protect the Church. "I am content," he wrote, "to be sacrificed in so good a cause: which I will never betray, nor give over, God, her majesty, the laws, my own conscience and duty being with me."[21] Everyone at Court was aware that the Queen stood behind her archbishop, but could he be brought down, she might let him fall. Once before, in 1559, she had given some ground to the opposition; she might be forced to yield again. It was the moment when Whitgift's steadfast courage preserved the integrity of the Elizabethan settlement. Weakness would have precipitated a crisis in which the unique character of the Elizabethan Church might have disappeared.

Burghley's reply to the archbishop's unyielding stand indicated the extent of his own distaste for clerical government.

I am sorry [he wrote] to trouble you so often as I do, but I am more troubled myself, not only with many private petitions of sundry ministers . . . but also I am now daily charged by councillors and public persons to neglect my duty in not staying

---

[19] *Church History,* V, 31.
[20] Strype, *Whitgift,* III, 104. See also *S.P.Dom.Eliz.* clxxiv. 52.
[21] HMC, *Bath MSS,* II, 26-7.

of these your Grace's proceedings, so vehement and so general against ministers and preachers . . .

By chance I am come to the sight of an instrument of twenty-four articles of great length and curiosity, found in a Romish style, to examine all manner of ministers in this time, without distinction of persons. Which articles are entitled *Apud Lamhith, May 1584, to be executed ex officio mero, etc.* . . . which I have read, and find so curiously penned, so full of branches, and circumstances, as I think the Inquisitors of Spain use not so many questions to comprehend and to trap their preys. I know your canonists can defend these . . . but surely under your Grace's correction this judicial and canonical sifting of poor ministers is not to edify or reform.

Now, my good Lord, bear with my scribbling. . . . I favour no sensual and wilful recusants. But I conclude that, according to my simple judgment, this kind of proceeding is too much savouring of the Romish inquisition, and is rather a device to seek for offenders than to reform any. . . . It may be, as I said, the canonists may maintain this proceeding by rules of their laws, but though *omnia licent,* yet *omnia non expediunt.* . . .[22]

Whitgift, who had prudently retired to Croydon, replied at length, assuring Burghley that ministers were deprived, not for refusing subscription but only for stubborn nonconformity. He wrote:

I would not touch any for not subscribing only, but for breach of order in celebrating divine service . . . not according to the form by law prescribed. . . .

Touching the twenty-four articles which your Lordship seemeth so much to mislike. . . . I cannot but greatly marvel at your Lordship's vehement speeches against them, I hope without cause, seeing it is the ordinary course in other courts likewise, as in Star Chamber. . . . I think these articles to be more tolerable,

[22] Strype, *Whitgift,* III, 104-7.

and better agreeing with the rule of justice and charity, and less captious, than those in other courts. . . .

I know your Lordship desireth the peace of the Church; but how is it possible to be procured, after so long liberty and lack of discipline, if a few persons, so meanly qualified as most of them are, should be countenanced against the whole state of the Clergy of greatest account. . . .[23]

Burghley's reply did not press the point of the character of Whitgift's articles of inquiry; he confined himself to expressing the opinion that "your Grace's proceeding . . . is scant charitable." Fuller ascribed the tone of irritation in Burghley's letter to "the fit of the gout,"[24] but it was much more likely due to the fact that Elizabeth, remembering that by his advice she had been inflicted with Edmund Grindal, was not disposed to listen to any complaints about her new archbishop.

By the middle of July Burghley had weakened considerably in his opposition.

God knoweth [Whitgift wrote him] how desirous I have been from time to time to satisfy your Lordship in all things, and to have my doings approved by you. For which cause, since my coming to this place, I did nothing of importance without your advice. I have risen early and set up late, to write unto you such objections and answers as are used on either side. I have not done the like to any man. . . . My Lord, an old friend is better than a new; and I trust your Lordship will not so lightly cast off your old friends, for any of these new fangled and factious sectaries. . . .

Your Lordship further seemeth to burden me with *willfulness.*

[23] *Ibid.,* III, 107-12.
[24] *Church History,* V, 48.

. . . There is a difference between *willfulness* and *constancy*. I have taken upon me defense of the religion and rites of this Church; the execution of the laws concerning the same; the appeasing of the sects and schisms therein; the reducing the ministers thereof to uniformity and due obedience. Herein I intend to be constant.

Reminding Burghley that it was under the Queen's charge and protection that he enforced the laws, a duty, he hinted, in which the members of the Council should assist him, he continued:

And now, my singular good Lord, I heartily pray you, not to be carried away from the cause, or from myself, upon unjust surmises or clamours; lest thereby you be some occasion of that confusion, which hereafter you will be sorry for. For my own part, I am determined to my duty and conscience without fear. Neither will I therein desire further defense of any of my friends, than justice and law will yield unto me . . . In these public actions I see no cause why I should seek friends, seeing they, to whom the care of the commonwealth is committed, ought therein to join with me . . .[25]

Burghley ceased to object, but other members of the Council continued their "Machiavel governance." They forced the unfortunate Aylmer to indemnify at least one suspended minister for his imprisonment, and ordered the Bishop of Chester to extend the organization of ecclesiastical exercises—scarcely distinguishable from the prophesyings— in his diocese. As might be expected after the agitation in the Commons in 1576 and in 1581, the conflict was carried to the Parliament that assembled in November 1584. Whit-

[25] Strype, *Whitgift*, III, 112-5.

gift successfully averted any action on the clamor raised over the ignorance of the clergy and the necessity for more careful scrutiny of those ordained, by the adoption of the *Canons of 1585* in Convocation.[26] Promulgated with royal approval and designed to eliminate a number of abuses in ecclesiastical administration, these canons were supplemented by the archbishop's own injunctions for the increase of preaching and the continued training of non-graduate ministers.[27]

These, however, were secondary skirmishes. The main points of Puritan attack were soon revealed. While the "Bill and Book" for the revision of the Prayer Book, introduced by Dr. Peter Turner, son of the once troublesome Dean of Wells, was not pressed, a number of Puritan demands were edited into articles for reform. These petitioned for a ministry more learned in the Holy Scriptures, the abolition of the use of the *ex officio* oath, the restriction of subscription to the statutory form only, a regulation that six ministers of good report assist the bishop in the laying-on-of-hands at ordinations, and the freedom for ministers to make small changes and omissions in the Prayer Book services.[28] Other petitions openly attacked the constitution of the Church, some demanding the erection of the entire classis system within the framework of episcopal polity.

When the petitions reached the House of Lords, Archbishop Sandys delivered the bishops' answers to the several points, conveying to the members of the Commons a gentle reminder that some of his brethren were preachers "when many of the House of Commons had been in their cradles,"

[26] Cardwell, *Synodalia,* I, 139-46.
[27] *Ibid.,* II, 562-4. See below, p. 201.
[28] D'Ewes, *Journals,* pp. 357-9.

a remark not calculated to soothe the passions of the Puritan sympathizers.[29] But the petitions disappeared into committees, and Elizabeth brought the turmoil to an end in characteristic fashion. Proroguing Parliament on March 29, 1585, she admitted the justice of some of the complaints. Aware that a number of bishops had given Whitgift little assistance, she rebuked them severely. To the supporters of the Disciplinarians she gave a sharp warning.

If I were not persuaded [she said] that mine were the true way of God's will, God forbid that I should live to prescribe it to you . . . I see many overbold with God Almighty, many too many subtle scannings of his blessed will . . . The presumption is so great, as I may not suffer it . . . nor tolerate newfangleness . . .

I must pronounce them dangerous to a kingly rule, to have every man according to his own censure to make a doom of the validity . . . of his Prince's government, with a common veil and cover of God's Word, whose followers must not be judged but by private men's exposition.[30]

The opposition retired in defeat. Whitgift had withstood both the intrigues of the members of the Council and the challenge delivered through the Parliament. Quarrels with the Privy lords ceased, at least partly because of the new influence of Christopher Hatton, the Archbishop's firm supporter, soon to become Lord Chancellor.[31] With his machinery for good order secure, Whitgift could, perhaps with some relief, concede much in its operation. He informed Walsingham that subscription would be required only at

29 *Ibid.*, p. 360.
30 *Ibid.*, pp. 328-9.
31 Strype, *Whitgift*, I, 426. Brooks, *Hatton*, p. 334.

ordination or upon admission to livings. As for the more stubborn Puritans, he would not force them to declare the Prayer Book to be agreeable in every point with Scripture if they, on their part, gave a solemn promise to use it faithfully.[32] This liberality eased the tension, and when in the following year Whitgift became a member of the Privy Council the machinery of ecclesiastical government operated more smoothly.

In these circumstances the Puritans had but one recourse, to court obscurity and hasten the development of their classis system against the day when the presbyterian organization would be ready to supplant the episcopal constitution of the Church. The classis was the outcome of a dozen years' education in the prophesyings and presbyterian experiment in the conferences. It was a presbytery of twelve local ministers, joined with whom were a number of "godly and grave laymen"—churchwardens and justices of the peace where they could be had—who were to exercise the office of Elder in the new model establishment.[33] Beyond the local classis plans were laid, though never fully developed, for provincial synods and a national assembly. In the years immediately following 1585 the main Puritan effort was directed towards spreading the system and securing uniform practice among the classes. As far as possible the "Holy Discipline" was used and enforced. Sympathetic clergy assumed office only after being accepted by their parishioners, and episcopal ordination was reduced to a civil rite by the use of a supplemental presbyterial service. Ministers met frequently to work out their own principles of uniformity in the use of

[32] Strype, *Whitgift*, I, 432.
[33] See Usher, *Presbyterian Movement*; also *Seconde Parte*, 164-8.

portions of the Geneva rites or modifications of the Prayer Book services.[34]

The guiding hand in this organizational activity was that of John Field, one of the authors of the *Admonition,* who labored indefatigably to induce the Puritans to agree on a single coherent program for the reconstruction of the national Church.[35] In these efforts he had considerable assistance from exiled Scottish ministers, and from sympathetic noblemen who were induced to present leading Puritans to the lectureships and livings within their gift. Within a few years, the Puritan minority contrived an organization by which they hoped to capture the entire establishment.

Meanwhile the archbishop was embroiled in a controversy that brought to the fore the thorny question of the recognition of nonepiscopal orders. In August 1584 the influential post of Master of the Temple fell vacant. Lord Burghley, apparently at the urging of some of the lawyers, pressed for the appointment of the Puritan leader, Walter Travers. Travers had returned to England in 1580 as tutor to young Robert Cecil, Burghley's son, and soon afterward was made afternoon lecturer or reader at the Temple Church. When his name was proposed as Master, Whitgift, remembering the troublesome days when Travers was a Fellow of Trinity under him and certain that he had written the *Explicatio,* hastened to warn the Queen. He is, said the archbishop,

one of the chief and principal authors of dissension in this Church; a contemner of the Book of Prayers and other orders by authority established; an earnest seeker of innovation; and

[34] Bancroft, *Dangerous Positions,* p. 68; *Survay,* p. 67.
[35] *Ibid.,* p. 369.

either in no degree of the ministry at all, or else ordered beyond the seas, not according to the form in this Church of England used.[36]

In vain Travers protested that the ministry of men ordained in any reformed Church should be recognized throughout Protestant Europe, exactly, he pointed out, as in the Roman Church "whosoever hath taken their unholy orders, is acknowledged a sufficient Priest in any Church of their communion." The Marian clergy, he argued, have been allowed to continue their ministry with no further requirement than the subscription enjoined in 1571. Similar recognition should be extended to the ministry of "the Churches professing the Gospel." Travers was willing to subscribe the *Thirty-Nine Articles* in the limited statutory form, and should thus be enabled "for dealing in the ministry, as if I had been at the first made Minister by the form established in this Church."[37] This argument came strangely from him for nothing was more detestable to the Puritans than the recognition of the orders of those ordained by the Roman rites. Much of their dissatisfaction was directed to this point of the continuity of the English Church with its own past.

Whitgift was not persuaded. He would consent to Travers' appointment only if he testified his conformity by the subscription required of all upon entering into ecclesiastical livings, and gave proof to the archbishop that he was a "minister ordered according to the laws of this Church of England," which Whitgift "verily believed he was not."[38] When Travers asserted that no question had ever been raised

[36] Strype, *Whitgift*, I, 341.
[37] *Ibid.*, III, 115-8.
[38] *Ibid.*, I, 344.

about the foreign orders of William Whittingham, for some years Dean of Durham, the archbishop denied the truth of this contention. Had Whittingham lived, Whitgift maintained, he would have been deprived, "without special grace and dispensation."[39]

Whitgift's objections were sufficient for Elizabeth. The appointment at the Temple was finally given to an obscure but promising young scholar, Richard Hooker, inaugurating that period in the Temple Church when, as Fuller remarked, "the pulpit spake pure Canterbury in the morning, and Geneva in the afternoon, until Travers was silenced."[40] The silencing came speedily. Before a year had passed Whitgift succeeded in depriving Travers, rejecting his final plea for recognition of the ministry conferred upon him abroad.[41] The archbishop's disciplinary action, however, was not a condemnation of the validity of orders bestowed and exercised within the continental Protestant Churches. The problem for him was not the determination of what particular kind of ministry was essential to the being of the whole Church. As is clear in the earlier controversy with Cartwright, Whitgift believed the three-fold ministry of the Church of England to be allowable, traditional, and maintained in the interests of good order in the Church and in

[39] *Ibid.*, III, 185. Whittingham died before Archbishop Sandys and Bishop Barnes of Durham concluded the process of deprivation for disobedience to the Durham statutes, and for being a minister only after the "form of Geneva." The case is complicated by the attempt to show that Whittingham's ministry was simply that of "reader" or "doctor," the implication being that had he been in Genevan minister's orders, he would have been suffered to hold his place. See Strype, *Annals*, II, ii, 167-75, 620; *The Life and Death of William Whittingham;* and *Seconde Parte,* I, 188. Dean Hutton and Whitgift certainly regarded him as fully ordained according to the Genevan form, but probably the whole story will never be known.

[40] *Worthies* (Devonshire), p. 264.

[41] *Seconde Parte,* I, 267. See Hooker, *Works,* III, 682 ff.

the realm.[42] Travers had sought his ministry elsewhere—
"gaddeth into other countries to be ordained"—a manifest
act of schism. By such action he had not only brought the
ministry of the national Church into contempt, but clearly
revealed his adherence to the Puritan claim of divine sanction
for the presbyterian polity alone. The assertion that "any
one kind of government is so necessary that without it the
Church cannot be saved" was intolerable to the archbishop;
as he found "no one certain and perfect kind of government
prescribed or commanded in the Scriptures," he condemned
no Churches "that have appointed any order for the electing
of their pastors, which they think . . . most profitable for
them."[43] The Puritan conspiracy, he was convinced, would
deny this liberty to the Church of England and overthrow a
church order for whose "sacred regiment" there was overwhelming scriptural and patristic evidence, reinforced by the
testimony of fifteen hundred years of the Church's life.[44]

The archbishop's suspicions of the Puritan activities of
Walter Travers were amply justified. His writings made him
"one of the chief and principal authors of dissension." John
Field's most useful instrument in spreading the presbyterian
principles and tightening the classis organization was a new
schematic outline of the Puritan discipline contained in a
small tract of which Travers was probably the chief author,

[42] See above, pp. 139-41.

[43] Ibid., I, 184-5, 369. See also Cooper, Admonition to the People, pp.
74-5.

[44] Among the papers reprinted in Strype's Whitgift (III, 222-3) is one
that contains a famous passage: "If it had pleased her Majesty, with the wisdom of the realm, to have used no Bishops at all, we could not have complained justly of any defect in our Church . . ." Despite the fact that the
error of ascribing this document to Whitgift has been repeatedly pointed
out for a number of years, it is still occasionally presented as indicating his
views. The paper was composed by Hammond and sent by him to Burghley.
HMC, Salis. MSS, III, 754.

the *Disciplina Ecclesiae Sacra*,[45] circulated after 1584, and translated by Cartwright in a form commonly called "The Book of Discipline."[46] The *Disciplina* was designed to supplant the longer descriptive discussion of government in a truly reformed Church that had appeared a decade earlier in Travers' *Explicatio*, as well as other tentative forms of discipline more recently drafted.[47] Providing a brief and concise exposition of presbyterial organization, it also contained a form of subscription and pledge of uniformity of use. Thus it was ideally adapted to bind the Disciplinarians together on a single coherent platform of church order and practice. With it was generally used either a *Book of Common Prayer* from which the objectionable portions were expurgated or a modification of the Genevan service book. It is hard to exaggerate the importance of the *Disciplina* in shaping the minds of that minority of Puritans who remained implacably opposed to the episcopal establishment throughout the reign of Elizabeth. The full impact of its influence is seen only when the controversy with Puritanism is renewed in Stuart England.

Inevitably the Puritan demands were brought to Parliament in 1587, this time with more extensive preparations. Petitions were sent in from all quarters, and draft bills to introduce the Puritan discipline and reform the ministry were prepared.[48] To impress their sympathizers with the desperate plight of the Church, the Puritans compiled some

---

[45] *Disciplina Ecclesiae Sacra ex Dei Verbo descripta.* Paget, *Fifth Book*, pp. 228-51. See Bancroft, *Survay*, 153, 231, 305.

[46] Neal, *History of the Puritans*, III, 490-501. Cartwright's translation was printed in 1644 under the title *A Directory of Church Government Anciently contended for . . . in the daies of Queen Elizabeth.*

[47] *A parte of a register*, pp. 421-505.

[48] *Seconde Parte*, I, 304-11; II, 1-4, 196-8.

remarkable surveys, purporting to cover over two thousand parishes and exposing the alleged moral offenses, ignorance, and pastoral incompetence of the clergy.[49] Despite the obvious bias, the documents are of considerable value, though less for their catalog of clerical weaknesses than for the picture given of the incumbents of Elizabethan parishes in the mid-'eighties. We find, for example, that a surprising number of Marian priests are still active. The records reveal that Elizabeth's clergymen are drawn from every class in society. The former university don rubs shoulders with the ex-baker, tailor, and button-maker. Here and there are intensely human touches that illuminate the life of the country clergy better than almost any other records we possess. The incumbent of one parish who "professeth physicke" doubtless cares as much for the bodily health of his people as for their spiritual welfare. He is matched in another village by the parson-apothecary who, like Shakespeare's Friar Lawrence, must have up-filled his osier cage "with baleful weeds and precious-juiced flowers." In one place is the farming vicar, whose knowledge of husbandry surely increased his usefulness among the country folk; in another is the clergyman noted "the best wrastler in Cornwall"—perhaps only one in a long line of Anglican ministers whose spiritual exercises have been judiciously combined with athletic prowess. The chief Puritan concern was not, however, with these men. The ministry, according to the surveys, was crowded with lewd and "dumbe" ministers, drunkards, and those "scarce able to read." "Massman" and "suspected of poperie" were frequent notations, while more than a few were labelled "whoremaisters," "gamsters," and "worldlinges." Every whispered suspicion and scandalous report seems to have

[49] *Ibid.,* II, 88-184.

been entered. The exaggeration is obvious—no Church could have survived the array of blackguards paraded in the surveys.

There is an unmistakable note of desperation in the Puritan preparations for this Parliament, the urgent advocacy of a cause that is on the brink of failure. The truth is that the appeal of Puritanism was at last declining. Continued contentious agitation had wearied some supporters; the new and more rigid classis discipline was uncongenial to others. Moreover, the parliamentary Erastians, while willing to make use of Puritan discontent to extend their control over ecclesiastical affairs, were by no means eager to exchange episcopacy for another and more stubborn kind of clericalism. Finally, the supporters of the royal supremacy, devoted to the principle of obedience to constituted authority in Church and State alike, had been increasingly alarmed by the tone of the Puritan challenge. The question Whitgift had raised with Cartwright was now framed openly, and it spelled doom to Puritan hopes in Elizabeth's England: "Wherein differ these men, in this case, from the Papists? The Pope denieth the supremacy of princes: so do, in effect, these."[50]

It speedily became evident that the Puritans had reason to be desperate. The best chance of success had passed three years before, when Archbishop Whitgift had withstood the pressure put upon him. Amid the growing conviction that the real object of their attack was the Crown's ecclesiastical authority, the extreme measures proposed to Parliament in 1587 stood little chance of passage. Nevertheless, in February Anthony Cope, "first using some speeches touching the necessity of a learned ministry and the amendment of things

[50] Strype, *Whitgift*, III, 193. See also Cooper, *Admonition to the People*, pp. 77-8, 82.

amiss in the Ecclesiastical Estate," introduced "a Bill and a Book," which provided for the abolition of episcopacy and the establishment of the presbyterian classis and synodical discipline.[51] The three most objectionable of the *Thirty-Nine Articles*—those concerning the traditions of the Church, the use of the *Homilies,* and the consecration of bishops and ministers—were to be removed; the Genevan service book, or some alteration of the liturgy in that direction, was to be made the uniform use in the realm. Parliament showed little sympathy, however, with these proposals, and despite the determined efforts of Mr. Cope and his few supporters, the bill was not read. The Speaker reminded the Commons that "her Majesty before this time had commanded the House not to meddle with this matter." Elizabeth promptly confiscated the "Bill and a Book," detaining Cope and his friends in the Tower, and the last serious Puritan parliamentary campaign came to naught.

Blocked from achievement of their goal, the Puritan organization began to disintegrate. A group of young and uncontrollable extremists led by John Penry, Giles Wiggington, John Udall, and others gave vent to their disappointment and impatient wrath in the scurrilous Martin Marprelate tracts. The immediate object of their attack was John Bridges' *A Defense of the Government Established in the Church of England,* a learned and temperate, though somewhat ponderous defense of episcopacy by the Dean of Salisbury. By October 1588 a coarse, rollicking reply was circulated, entitled *O read over D. John Bridges for it is a worthy work.* In it the bishops were abused as "profane, proud, paltry, popish, pestilent, pernicious, presumptuous

---

[51] D'Ewes, *Journals,* p. 410. See also Strype, *Whitgift,* III, 186-94; *Seconde Parte,* II, 212-8.

Prelates."[52] Then in rapid succession came the torrent of Martinist pamphlets. The *Epitome* continued the attack upon Bridges, *Schoolpoints* directed a blast of scorn at Richard Bancroft, and Bishop Cooper's serious attempt to refute the slanders in his *Admonition to the People of England* only provoked a malicious tract called *Ha' y' Any Work for Cooper?* The archbishop was the target for the greater part of the insulting abuse. "John of Kankerbury, the Pope of Lambeth" was a mild epithet compared with the mounting crescendo of hatred that likened him to Hildebrand, Lucifer, and finally branded him "the forerunner of Antichrist."[53]

Thoroughly aroused by the activities of the unknown Marprelate authors, the authorities made every effort to track down the hidden Puritan press, while Elizabeth issued a stern proclamation against seditious and schismatical books and libels.[54] When it was clear that Cooper's temperate *Admonition to the People* had no effect in countering the slanders, the bishops resorted to the desperate expedient of persuading Tom Nashe and John Lyly to answer the malicious libels in kind. The result was a spate of tracts embarrassing the bishops by the zealous indecency in which their defense was undertaken.[55] The whole affair, however, was

[52] The Martinist *Epistle*. The tracts are reprinted in *The Marprelate Tracts*, ed. William Pierce, and in *Puritan Discipline Tracts*. For a discussion of the controversy see Arber, *The Marprelate Controversy* and Bonnard, *La Controverse de Martin Marprelate*. Whitgift thought that Penry and Udall were the chief authors. Paule, p. 32. Perhaps the question of authorship will never be satisfactorily settled. See *Notebook of John Penry*, pp. vii-xxv.

[53] Strype, *Whitgift*, III, 218-20. The archbishop was said to be as ambitious as Wolsey, proud as Gardiner, and tyrannical as Bonner. *Notebook of John Penry*, p. 22n.

[54] *Concilia*, IV, 340.

[55] The pamphlets ascribed to Nashe are reprinted in Grosart, *Complete Works of T. Nashe*, I, 73-253, and McKerrow, *Works of T. Nashe*, I, 50-136; IV, 42-65. See also Bond, *Works of J. Lyly*, III, 388-426. A number of other anti-Martinist tracts are in the Lambeth collection 30.6.23.

of brief duration. When Bancroft's agents seized the press at Manchester the Marprelate outburst was quelled. In the end the chief significance of the tracts was the fact that they marked the beginning of the rapid collapse of organized Puritanism.

By 1593 nearly all the Puritan leaders had been silenced. Field died in 1588, and John Udall, arrested for challenging the Queen's authority by his attack upon the bishops, died in prison in 1592 while under sentence of banishment. Henry Barrow, John Greenwood, and John Penry, all of whom deserted conservative Puritanism to embrace the principles of Separatism, perished on the scaffold in 1593. Their bitter opposition to the ecclesiastical establishment led them to repudiate the Queen's supremacy and to deny the Church of England the name of a true Church.[56] If to a later generation they were martyrs for the principles of Independency, in Elizabeth's England they were "maintainers of sedition." Cartwright was arrested in 1590, but prolonged interrogation could not establish his connection with the *Disciplina* or the classis movement.[57] He was released in 1592, retiring into an obscurity from which he emerged a decade later to assist in preparing the Puritan demands for presentation to James I at the Hampton Court Conference. Robert Browne, having found in Scotland "the preachers having no names of bishops did imprison me more wrongfully than any bishop would have done," returned to make his submission, albeit with misgivings, and ended his days in a country parish.[58] So it went with nearly all the others. Archbishop Whitgift showed remarkable patience and no sign of personal resentment at the abuse he had received at Puritan hands. In his

---

[56] *Harleian Misc.*, II, 20.
[57] *Cartwrightiana*, pp. 21 ff. See Strype, *Whitgift*, III, 242-60.
[58] Burrage, *Early English Dissenters*, I, 111.

hour of triumph he has been made to appear a vindictive judge, partly because in the renewed controversy of the next century men were willing to accept without question the statements of his opponents. The Puritan in early Stuart England recalled that Barrow had condemned the archbishop as "a monster, a miserable compound, I know not what to make him; he is neither ecclesiastical or civil, even that second beast spoken of in the Revelation."[59] He remembered Penry's remark, "I know that prelate to be a great enemy of God, his saints and truth";[60] he read over the pages of Giles Wiggington's own record of Whitgift's persecution of him.[61] There was no one then to recall, even had Puritan ears been open to reason, that Barrow's intolerance and tendentiousness would have tried the patience of a saint; that Penry, however sincere and ardent, was a fanatic with whom few men could agree; and that even the sympathetic Sandys had found Wiggington a malcontent who "laboureth, not to build, but to pull down; and by what means he can, to overthrow the state ecclesiastical."[62] Nowhere does the evidence justify the reputation the archbishop's enemies fixed upon him. When men are judged by the standards of their age Whitgift's forbearance was unusual. When we recall the frenzied passions of cruelty and intolerance that marked religious strife and controversy in most areas of sixteenth-century Europe, there is a singular liberality in the Queen's policy of comprehension that Whitgift strove so valiantly to maintain in the Elizabethan Church.

The decade of conflict that closed in 1593 brought an end to the Puritan challenge to Elizabeth's ecclesiastical settle-

---

[59] *Harleian Misc.,* II, 27.
[60] *Notebook of John Penry,* p. 64.
[61] *Seconde Parte,* II, 241-58.
[62] *Desiderata Curiosa,* p. 115.

ment. Its force was spent; its threat ebbed away. The surprising rapidity with which Puritanism declined is not, of course, wholly explained by the firm measures of Archbishop Whitgift or by the administrative vigilance of Bancroft and his officers. A number of reasons combine to explain the success that crowned the efforts of the authorities. The silencing of the leading Puritans, for example, stripped the party of its leadership, while the death of Leicester and the decline from influence of Walsingham and Knollys left few warm supporters of the Puritan cause at Court. Moreover, the lack of unity among various groups of Puritans often prevented the coordination of their efforts to achieve reforms. Cartwright and the more earnest men, shocked by the tactics of the authors of the Marprelate tracts, repudiated them vehemently. At the same time a wide breach opened between the main body of Puritans, always seeking to reform their Church from within, and the small group of ardent Separatists with whose condemnation of the Church of England they were in thorough disagreement. Even beyond these open quarrels there was sufficient division of opinion in the Puritan ranks to prevent the formation of an organization strong and coherent enough to survive the frustrations of continuous defeat. Despite Field's labors, no single form of discipline had been accepted by all the Puritans, nor was there common agreement on the methods by which the Reformed system should be put into effect.

On February 9, 1589 Richard Bancroft at Paul's Cross made public exposure of the extent to which the Puritans had set up "their Discipline secretly in most shires of the Realm, their Classes, their Decrees, and Book of Discipline."[63] His sermon came as considerable shock to a num-

[63] Baker MSS, Mm.1.47, fos. 333-5. See Bancroft, *A Sermon Preached at Paules Crosse.*

ber of influential laymen who had been inclined to favor the Puritan proposals for reform, less because they fully grasped the ecclesiastical principles involved than because they were advanced by men whose earnestness and sincerity were both attractive and compelling. Bancroft's exposure of the extent of the challenge to constituted authority with its implicit denial of the royal supremacy turned the tide of lay opinion strongly against the Puritans. Elizabeth reflected more than her own adamant opposition to Puritanism when she wrote to James I on July 6, 1590:

Let me warn you that there is risen, both in your realm and mine, a sect of perilous consequence, such as would have no kings but a presbytery, and take our place while they enjoy our privilege . . . Yea, look we well unto them. When they have made in our people's hearts a doubt of our religion and that we err if they say so, what perilous issue this may take I rather think than mind to write.[64]

When Bancroft in 1593 added to his denunciations the two detailed reports of his struggle against the extension of the classis system, *A Survey of the Pretended Holy Discipline* and *Dangerous Positions and Proceedings,* the great majority of Elizabeth's subjects who thought about Puritanism at all agreed that it was fraught with "perilous consequence." They did so more readily in the early 'nineties because the execution of Mary Stuart in 1587 and the resounding defeat of the Spanish Armada in the following year had dispelled the fears of Romanist plots and the menace of Spain that haunted Englishmen for over two decades. The Protestant confidence of the nation no longer

[64] *Letters of Elizabeth and James I,* pp. 63-4. Did Elizabeth teach James his favorite maxim "No bishops, no king"?

needed Puritanism as a possible foil to papist activity. It was really to rid itself of a counterweight to Rome that had proved dangerous to cherish. Any lingering doubts of the seditious activity of Puritans were cleared from the minds of Londoners by the unhappy conspiracy of Hackett, Coppinger, and Arthington to overthrow the government of the Church by violence and release the imprisoned ministers, if not to attack the Queen herself.[65] Though it might be best to look upon the half-mad religious fanatic who was proclaimed Messiah in Cheapside on July 16, 1591 as Richard Hooker did—"with much commiseration and pity" for a "poor seduced creature"[66]—the fact that Hackett and his companions were in close touch with Puritan leaders did much to bring the whole movement under suspicion of sedition.

The reaction against the implications of anarchy in the Puritan challenge found decisive expression in the stringent penal legislation of the *Act to Retain the Queen's subjects in Obedience* of 1593, directed against the practices of "seditious sectaries and disloyal persons."[67] Closing the long decade of conflict, the statute imposed severe penalties upon those who denied the Queen's ecclesiastical supremacy, obstinately refused to attend the services of the Church, or who joined in "unlawful assemblies, conventicles, or meetings, under color or pretense of any exercise of religion, contrary to her Majesty's said laws and statutes." The form of submission provided in the act significantly included not only a pledge of conformity, but also a conscientious affirmation that "no other person hath or ought to have any power

---

[65] Cosin, *Conspiracie for Pretended Reformation*, pp. 58-61.
[66] *Works*, II, 5.
[67] 35 Eliz. c. 1. *Statutes*, IV, ii, 841-3.

or authority over her Majesty."[68] Here was raised on the Puritan side the same defense of penal legislation that was erected against Romanist activity. The law against dissenters was a parallel statute to the *Act against Popish Recusants* passed in the same Parliament. From the administrative point of view the chief importance of the statute was that it lifted the burden of dealing with refractory Puritans from the bishops and ecclesiastical authorities and made it the concern of the ordinary courts. At long last the Elizabethan Church was eased from intense controversy to devote its energies and resources to those matters more properly part of its spiritual life. The remnant of Puritanism, driven underground, waited the passing of Elizabeth, its leaders hoping for better things from the Scottish monarch who year by year emerged more clearly as the inevitable successor to the throne of the Tudors.

Whitgift could rest from a struggle with Puritanism that had been almost continuous for twenty years. The defense of the Church on the administrative level had been successful; it was another's task to take it up on an intellectual and spiritual level far removed from the passions of controversy. In 1591 the archbishop received an earnest and plaintive appeal from Richard Hooker, pleading that he be set free from "the noise and oppositions of the Temple Church." Said Hooker, "God and nature did not intend me for contentions."[69] He had begun his work on the *Laws of Ecclesiastical Polity* and sought a place where he might "pray for God's blessing upon my endeavours, and keep myself in peace and privacy." Whitgift gave him Boscombe rectory in

[68] *Concilia,* IV, 345. Compare the form of submission with that to be used with Romanist recusants. See above, p. 129n.
[69] Walton, *Life of Mr. Rich. Hooker,* p. 112.

the diocese of Salisbury; four years later the Queen appointed him to Bishopsbourne in Kent. The first four books of the *Ecclesiastical Polity* appeared in 1593, entered in Stationers' Hall on the 29th of January, and were nicely timed to provide convincing and learned justification for the statute passed against seditious sectaries in the parliamentary sessions of that year.[70]

When one surveys the thirty-five years of Elizabeth's reign from the vantage point of 1593, the survival of the Elizabethan settlement appears to be due to the combination of a number of forces. Most obvious was surely the determination of the Queen herself that "none should be suffered to decline either on the left or on the right hand." Hooker did not overstate the conviction of many churchmen when he roundly declared "By the goodness of Almighty God and his servant Elizabeth, we are."[71] Political situations contributed to the continued maintenance of the Queen's policy of comprehensiveness, and no doubt the divisive elements within Puritanism blunted the attacks its adherents levelled against the establishment, but the chief instrument of Elizabeth's fixed purpose was her third archbishop. His courage and tenacious devotion to duty lay behind the successful defense of the establishment.

There are, however, other factors that play roles of some consequence in the reaction against the intensity of the Puritan challenge, though they are perhaps less easy to evaluate. One is the influence of that alliance between the *politique* spirit and the secularism of the Renaissance that operated to subordinate the claims of religious loyalties to those of the national welfare. To no small degree the passage of time brought into greater prominence such *politique* elements as

[70] See Sisson, *Judicious Marriage of Mr. Hooker,* pp. 60-6.
[71] *Works,* II, 11.

were present from the outset in the Queen's ecclesiastical policy. They combined with the secular values of the late Renaissance world to begin that process whereby in time religion became peripheral to man's other corporate activities. While the frequent assertion that in the last years of Elizabeth's reign nationality had come to replace a common religious loyalty as the deepest bond among Englishmen is not wholly true—as the stormy events of the first half of the seventeenth century show—yet the movement in the direction of modern secular society is already discernible. We do not need the journal of the French ambassador, Sieur de Maisse, to tell us that Englishmen in 1593 cared less about religion than they did fifty years earlier, but neither can we accept his remarks without some qualification. He and his master, Henry IV, belong to a generation of Frenchmen who, having already sacrificed the ancient ideals of religious unity, are ready to place their own construction upon the English religious scene. What is plain enough is that Elizabeth refused to force her people to pay the terrible prices of persecution, religious strife, and the disruption of the national life which was exacted in those states where a single conscientious religious allegiance was maintained. This alone meant that in Elizabethan England there was a point beyond which even the pressures of the penal legislation would not be applied. It is not without significance that whereas the religious convictions of Thomas More on one side and John Milton on the other are quite plain for men to see, those of William Shakespeare are veiled in obscurity. Equally revealing as a measure of the *politique* spirit in the policy of the Queen is the fact that both Puritanism and Roman Catholicism survived the forty-five years of Elizabeth's reign to become permanent elements in the religious tradition of Englishmen.

However important these influences were in cooling the religious passions of sixteenth-century England, in the end the Elizabethan settlement endured by reason of its own spiritual integrity. By 1593 the Church of England possessed an ethos peculiar to itself, characterized less by mere negations on the side of Rome or Geneva than by a coherent and distinctive embodiment of the Christian tradition that claimed continuity with all that was best in the Middle Ages and in the ancient Catholic Church. Bred within the comprehensive limits of the Elizabethan formularies, nurtured upon the spirituality of the *Book of Common Prayer,* the generation that came to manhood in the 'nineties brought Anglicanism to its maturity. A scornful condemnation of the late Elizabethan Church as a position born of compromise, timorously defended, and maintained only because the political exigencies admitted no deeper commitment, cannot stand in the face of the piety, learning, and loyalty that flowered in the first generation of men whose religious experience was wholly within the life of Elizabethan Anglicanism. Bilson, Field, Mason, Hall, Morton, Montague, Overall, Andrewes, Laud—here is a numbering of the stars in the firmament of the early Stuart Church. Yet all came to manhood in the days of Whitgift's defense of the establishment against the Puritan challenge. The light that they shed over the first years of the seventeenth century was a brilliance reflected from the Elizabethan sunset.

What emerged in that generation was a Christian tradition still recognizably in continuity with the Catholic order England had known for centuries, now enriched and widened by the religious and intellectual challenges that stretched men's minds in the Tudor Age. Possibly the uniquely distinctive feature of the Reformation experience of the English Church was the achievement of a synthesis between the

Christian elements in the Renaissance awakening and the truth that was preserved and transmitted through the medieval order. In that invigorating synthesis Anglicanism finds its justification. In its appeal to Scripture the evangelical spirit of John Colet triumphed over the narrow biblicism of Thomas Cartwright. In its appeal to tradition a faithfulness to history, informed and controlled by the claims of reason, opened to Richard Hooker not only the whole range of classical and patristic learning, but the creative insights of the medieval schoolmen as well. The line of spiritual continuity is clear—from Colet to Cranmer to Jewel to Hooker, and then to the Caroline divines.

But the character of the new tradition was determined by the continuing shape of the old Church out of whose life it came. There is another succession—from Warham to Gardiner to Parker to Whitgift—the line of institutional continuity, the identity of the Church of England with its own past. In the long run it was the continuing life of the ecclesiastical institution that mattered most. As has often been pointed out, all institutions mould men to their nature, assert their true being in the lives of those whom they nurture. Out of the unbroken and continuing life of *Ecclesia Anglicana* what we call Anglicanism came, received the determining imprint of all that had gone before, and entered upon its uniquely Catholic witness to the claim on all men of the wholeness of Christian truth. It is well to remember that what came to maturity in the massive learning and simplicity of spirit of Richard Hooker is the constant potential of the ecclesiastical institution to which John Whitgift devoted his life.

VII

THE LAST DECADE

AS the intensity of controversy diminished, John Whitgift relinquished the task of vigilant watch over the
Puritans to Richard Bancroft, whose zeal in exposing the
classis movement and suppressing the sectaries had brought
him an experience in the ways of the Puritans which surpassed even that of the archbishop.[1] Participation in affairs
of state, chiefly through membership in the Privy Council,
claimed a greater share of Whitgift's interest after 1593,
though his earlier refusal to accept the post of Lord Chancellor upon Bromley's death in 1587 was a wise recognition
of his limited capacity for that responsibility. Ecclesiastical
administration was no longer plagued by interference from
members of the Council. Walsingham died in 1590, two
years after Leicester's death, and the officers of state during
the last years of Elizabeth's reign were nearly all loyal adherents of the established Church.[2] Relieved, therefore, from

[1] In 1597, at Whitgift's repeated urging, Elizabeth made Richard Bancroft
Bishop of London. See *Tracts Ascribed*, pp. xvii-xx.
[2] Robert Cecil was well-disposed; Christopher Hatton, a firm supporter
until his death; John Puckering, Hatton's successor as Chancellor, was "a
friend to the Church, the archbishop and his proceedings"; and Thomas
Egerton, in turn, "a most constant favourer of the clergy and Church government established." Paule, pp. 76-7. See DeMaisse, *Journal*, p. 21.

both the assaults of the Puritans and the opposition encountered at the hands of their former friends at Court, the archbishop was able to turn his administrative energies to matters of paramount importance to the inner life of the Church.

The years of the last decade are those in which Whitgift's correspondence reveals his unceasing concern for the appointment of men of ability and integrity to high office both in the Church and in the universities.[3] He did not hesitate to condemn the preferment of unworthy men to vacant sees or deaneries—those, as he once put it, "more learned in husbandry than in divinity"; he ignored the appeals of importunate friends for places in Cambridge, preferring "the good of the University before private affection."[4] His injunctions and orders display his determination to reduce the evils of clerical non-residence, to control the practice of holding benefices in plurality, and to increase the support that clergy with generous incomes were expected to provide for university scholars. The central effort in all this activity was Whitgift's program for the improvement of the character of the clergy, their fitness and education. In the end his achievements in this respect might be reckoned his most significant contribution to the Church he served and loved. While the success that attended some of his reform measures was transitory, the results of his effort to improve clerical education were extensive and permanent. The successful maintenance of the peculiar ethos of the Church of England in the late Elizabethan and early Stuart age required of its defenders and interpreters the endowment of sound learning, scriptural, patristic, and historical. Whitgift's

[3] Samples of this correspondence may be seen in HMC, *Salis. MSS*, III, 153; V, 18, 31, 215; VI, 116-7; VII, 147; VIII, 332.
[4] *Ibid.,* X, 1. See also X, 6; XV, 150.

measures did not transform all Elizabethan parsons into scholars, but between 1575 and 1600 he planted their feet firmly on that path which eventually made a highly-educated ministry one of the distinguishing marks of the Church of England.

Everywhere in the sixteenth century a reawakened interest in learning and intellectual activity spread among the peoples of western Europe. In Protestant lands the Reformation gave a tremendous impetus to popular education; the Catholic revival brought the same impulse to areas still loyal to the old faith. Englishmen were in the forefront of this movement. Closely associated with their intense national self-consciousness and pride, education on all levels and in many new fields was an absorbing passion with the Elizabethans. English grammar schools increased, new collegiate foundations appeared, old establishments were reformed, and educational endowment became a favorite form of both philanthropic and patriotic activity. Whitgift's England was not only the land of Shakespeare, Marlowe, Sidney, Spenser, and the familiar figures of the literary renaissance; it was also the England of Tallis and the musicians; Camden, Hakluyt, and the geographers; Mulcaster, Kemp, and the schoolmasters. William Harvey's medical studies, John Gerarde's *Herball,* John Maplet's *Naturall Historie,* Christopher Saxton's cartography, Dr. John Dee's scientific enquiry—all bore witness to the breadth and vigor of Elizabethan knowledge and learning. This was the climate of Whitgift's educational activity, and the archbishop's name deserves a place among those that are inseparable from this glory of Elizabethan England. He set an example for similar foundations in his new schools at Eastbridge Hospital, Canterbury, and at the Hospital of the Holy Trinity in Croydon. He encouraged the increase of university scholarships, himself participating in their establishment, and turned Lambeth Palace into a house of studies for young men whom he assisted later at the Universities of Oxford and Cambridge. As we might expect, however, his greatest efforts were directed towards religious education, and here the education of the clergy was the primary task.

There is abundant testimony to the lamentable condition of the English clergy at the beginning of Elizabeth's reign. A serious shortage in the number of priests was in part the legacy of the turbulent decade preceding the Queen's accession, and in part due to the social changes that accompanied the Reformation. The violent shattering of the old patterns of church life altered the course of vocation for many men. The gradual social and economic depression of the lower clergy proved a strong deterrent to many, while the expanding opportunities for achievement, wealth, and power in new and adventurous careers attracted the eyes of Tudor youth away from the Church. Moreover, Parker and his bishops were confronted not only with a shortage of priests, but with widespread ignorance among the parish clergy. Few parsons were able to preach. Many knew little or no Latin and less Scripture—indeed, some could barely read the English services of the new Prayer Book. It is evident that at least some of the non-conformity in the early years of the ecclesiastical settlement was due less to Puritan or Romanist sympathies than to sheer ignorance.

The first steps taken to improve this condition and secure a wider knowledge of the Scriptures were not notably successful. By the *Injunctions* of 1559 all clergy under the degree of master of arts were required to possess the New Testament both in Latin and in English, and periodically to be examined on their study of it by the bishop or his officers. Though most bishops issued orders to implement these regulations,[5] the continued ordination of ignorant men prevented much real improvement. The licensing of "Readers," an expedient to which the bishops resorted in order that services might be held in vacant parishes, further complicated the problem.[6] A large number of these "Readers" were eventually ordained, bringing into the ranks of the clergy men with little sound education behind their superficial familiarity with the Prayer Book services. The *Canons of 1571,* therefore, made a fresh approach to the difficulty. Only those having a sufficient learning both of Latin and the Scriptures —university training if possible—were to be admitted to ordination, while those already in the ministry were to continue, as Grindal's orders for the Province of York expressed it, "everyday with good advisement [to] confer one chapter of the Latin [New Testament] and English together."[7]

Significant advance over these early attempts to deal with clerical ignorance coincides with Whitgift's emergence from the University of Cambridge to a position of influence on the broader scene of church life. In the year before his nomination to Worcester, Whitgift was Prolocutor of the Lower House of Convocation. There the matter was debated, and Whitgift drew up a set of injunctions in conference with Grindal, newly-translated to Canterbury. Promulgated under Grindal's mandate in 1576, these convocational articles laid

---

[5] Parkhurst, for example, at Norwich ordered two chapters of the New Testament to be learned each week. Guest laid out a scheme by which the Rochester clergy were to study the epistles of St. Paul in order. *Visitation Articles,* III, 99, 159. Parker's *Advertisements* required the archdeacons to set New Testament passages "to be conned without book." *Ibid.,* III, 178.

[6] "Readers," who pledged themselves to study the Scriptures daily and promised sobriety and quietness of life, were licensed to read the daily offices, and hold burial services and churchings. They were strictly enjoined not to minister the Sacraments or to preach. They might in some cases retain their ordinary secular employment if it were not "mechanical." *Ibid.,* III, 67-8.

[7] *Ibid.,* III, 260.

down sterner measures for the better education of the clergy.[8] Daily study of the New Testament was enjoined upon all non-preachers, an exercise in which they were to be periodically examined by the archdeacons. The previous regulations governing the sufficiency of learning for ordination were made more precise, a candidate in future being required not only to profess the doctrine of the *Thirty-Nine Articles,* but also "able to answer and render . . . an account of his faith in Latin, agreeable and consonant to the said articles." Livings above the value of £30 were to be open only to licensed preachers or men holding advanced degrees, while the bishops were to deny any benefice to those who could not reach the minimum educational standards, except where "stipends and livings be very small, they must admit the best that can be found in such case of necessity."

Incorporated into Grindal's metropolitan visitation articles of 1576, the new injunctions were used as the basis of diocesan orders. Barnes at Durham held two meetings of his clergy annually in each deanery for the examination of their progress in Biblical study, with apparently surprising results.[9] At Lincoln, Whitgift as dean undoubtedly had a hand in the orders of his friend Bishop Cooper. In that diocese it was not only commanded that "ministers bend themselves diligently to the study of the Holy Scriptures," but also those lacking university degrees or preaching licenses were to acquire Heinrich Bullinger's *Decades* in Latin or English. Each week, in addition to a chapter of the Bible, one of Bullinger's sermons was to be perused in such a way as to enable the minister to give a reasonable account of it

---

[8] Cardwell, *Synodalia,* I, 133.

[9] Kennedy, *Eliz. Epis. Ad.,* I, cii; II, 75. Three quarters of Barnes' clergy participated and half that number did their work with commendable earnestness.

to the archdeacons at visitation time.[10] An English translation of the "Fiftie Godlie and Learned Sermons" of the
Decades appeared in 1577, coinciding with this effort to increase the theological literacy of the parish clergy, and the
entry in the Northill churchwardens' accounts for that year
is one frequently met—five shillings for "a boke called
Bullinger's *Decads* to the use of our curat."

Whitgift's translation to Canterbury placed him in a position to shape and enforce a more effective program for clerical education than had yet been devised. Seven years in
Worcester brought him considerable experience in the administration of such regulations from the side of the bishop,
and the articles he issued from Lambeth in 1586 show both
the influence of the earlier injunctions worked out with
Grindal and Cooper, as well as the practical lessons in enforcement learned in a bishopric. For the last fifteen years
of Elizabeth's reign Whitgift's orders of 1586 remained the
standard injunctions respecting the education of the clergy.[11]
His constant pressure upon the bishops, and his frequent
inquiries concerning the state of learning among the clergy
in the various dioceses secured widespread episcopal cooperation in both provinces.[12] Within three or four years the
archbishop not only succeeded in securing enforcement of
the new articles everywhere, but also taught the bishops the
value of taking counsel together to make their own injunctions more effective by united action.[13]

The archbishop's articles were framed, as we might expect, with the precision of the schoolmaster and the rigor

[10] *Ibid.*, II, 45-6. See also III, 150.

[11] They are reflected in the provisions of the *Canons of 1597*. See Cardwell,
Synodalia, I, 147-63.

[12] See *Concilia,* IV, 318. Strype, *Whitgift,* III, 292-3.

[13] Kennedy, *Eliz. Epis. Ad.,* III, 266. See also III, 224, 237, 240, 255-6,
and *Concilia,* IV, 341-2.

of the disciplinarian.[14] All clergy (not preachers or masters of arts) were given two months to secure the materials of study: a Bible, Bullinger's *Decades,* and a notebook.[15] Each day one chapter of the Bible was to be read, and each week one sermon of the *Decades,* careful notes being made in the copybook. Aware that the archdeacons had insufficient time and opportunity to examine the clergy, Whitgift set up a kind of "tutorial" system. Licensed preachers were given oversight of the studies of unlearned clergy in their vicinity, each "tutor" having a half-dozen men assigned him from parishes within a radius of six or seven miles. Quarterly reports from the preachers on the extent and character of each parson's study were to be turned in to the diocesan authorities. There was an admirable practicability about the plan, and behind it was the full force of ecclesiastical authority. Repeated refusal to comply with the requirements for study was to be punished with inhibition or other censure.

The articles did not ignore the religious education of the people. Licensed preachers were enjoined to exercise their office more frequently on pain of forfeiting their licenses, and bishops were ordered to assume the responsibility of arranging the quarterly sermons required in parishes where the incumbent were unlicensed. The bishop was to secure the visiting cleric; the parish was to pay the "charge for the dinner and hossemeate of the said preacher." Incentive was given non-preachers of proved ability by permitting them to expound points of the catechism to their people, a

---

[14] Cardwell, *Synodalia,* II, 562-4.

[15] Whitgift neglected no detail. The *Decades,* published for a second time in English in 1584, was again printed in 1587 to provide copies for study in accordance with the new articles. Whitgift caused two editions of the Bishops' Bible to be printed in the same year, and bishops were commanded to make certain that all parishes possessed the authorized Bible. Cardwell, *Doc. Annals,* II, 31-2.

way of practice that might lead to their eventual licensing as preachers.

The ultimate success that attended Whitgift's attempts to raise the level of clerical learning was not easily won. Though as early as 1588 he might confidently assert that learning among the clergy "now flourisheth in England more than it ever did," it was a dozen years and more before the effects of his regulations were apparent on a wide scale. The program continued beset with difficulties to the end of Elizabeth's reign. A shortage of clergy persisted, bringing to the bishops the constant temptation to relax the standards for ordination, and the Church was increasingly forced to share the best men with the newer professions and careers of the Elizabethan world. A certain amount of resistance to the improvement of the clergy was offered by many gentry who were not averse to seeing the parson in a place of inferiority and dependence.[16] Clericalism was an ever-present fear to the class in power in Elizabethan England, and men who enjoyed the impropriation of what Whitgift calculated to be no less than £100,000 of annual income belonging to the Church, did not look with favor on any attempts to bring the whole body of the clergy up to their level.

The chief factor against which Whitgift struggled was an economic one. So many livings were impoverished that at the beginning of his campaign for better clerical education the archbishop complained that more than half the benefices in England were worth no more than £8 to £10 annually. No less than a thousand of these yielded the miserable pittance of £2. The other half of the Church's livings—something over four thousand—possessed incomes ranging between £10 and £25 annually, with only about four hundred

[16] *Concilia*, IV, 283.

of them worth more than £30. This meant that there were under a thousand benefices with really adequate stipends. The loss of the old fees, the impropriations of ecclesiastical incomes, the inroads that taxes, first-fruits, and benevolences made upon incumbents, and the rise in prices which continued gradually through the latter years of Elizabeth's reign so reduced the financial condition of the clergy that the Church had little chance of commanding the services of large numbers of able and learned men. The gradual increase of married clergy, rising from about one-fifth of the total number in 1560 to something near two-thirds in 1585, only intensified the difficulties. The vicarage family that was to play so large a part in English church life in the next three centuries emerged upon the scene in Whitgift's day, but it did so at the cost of considerable sacrifice and hardship on the part of devoted men and women. The custom of allowing benefices to be held in plurality eased the situation, though the abuses to which it was subject worried Whitgift constantly. Yet he was aware that it could not be stopped without, as he said, "the utter overthrow of a learned ministry." Regulation of pluralities, not abolition, was the only possible course, for as Whitgift demanded wrathfully, "What man of reason will think that eight pounds yearly is able to maintain a learned Divine? When as every scull in a kitchen, and groom of a stable, is better provided for?"[17]

In the face of such odds the archbishop's achievement is the more extraordinary. Perhaps only that same capacity for unrelenting toil and dogged devotion to duty that characterized all his activity crowned with success these efforts to turn the Anglican clergy into a body of educated men. Statistics are incomplete and often unreliable; anything more

[17] Strype, *Whitgift,* I, 534.

than the simplest generalization is likely to give a false picture. Yet it is clear that when Whitgift came to Canterbury about two-thirds of the clergy were non-graduates, the majority of whom had no university training at all. Less than one-sixth of the total number were sufficiently learned to be licensed as preachers. After fifteen years of Whitgift's leadership, about half the clergy held preaching licenses, the greater part of these being at least graduates and many having proceeded to higher degrees; the rest, though non-graduates, had considerable university training. Of the other half, the majority were considered sufficiently educated, a large number having had some study at one of the universities, and only a small minority could compare in ignorance with the unlearned clergy of two decades earlier.[18] Much was still said in 1604 about the ignorance of the clergy, but to a large degree that was the result of the higher standards which Whitgift's efforts induced men to accept. The ignorant parson of the end of Elizabeth's reign attracted far more unfavorable attention than his many predecessors had aroused twenty years before.

Though the diminution of Puritan agitation allowed the archbishop to devote closer attention to the state of the Church and the clergy, he did not escape the intermittent distractions of religious controversy during his last decade at Lambeth. Disputes arose that were more confusing to Whitgift's mind than the struggle with the Disciplinarians. One of these quarrels was provoked by Richard Bancroft's

[18] Some knowledge of the state of clerical education may be gained from the records and articles already cited, from *Lincoln Episcopal Records*, the *State of the Church*, the Puritan surveys in *Seconde Parte*, II, Strype's *Annals*, III and IV, and from Usher, *Reconstruction*, II. The numerous sermons John Manningham heard and recorded in 1602-3 give a picture of Elizabethan preaching in these last years that bears out conclusions concerning the improvement in the education of the clergy. See *Diary, passim.*

provocative sermon at Paul's Cross on February 9, 1589. Bancroft pointed up his exposure of the political threat of Puritanism with some remarks about the "miserable Church of Scotland" and the taint of sedition that clung to the Scottish presbyterian allies of the English Disciplinarians.[19] The anger of a number of his unsympathetic listeners was not lessened by the vigorous defense of episcopacy upon which Bancroft launched before the sermon was over.

Sir Francis Knollys, ever vigilant for a stick with which to beat the bishops, at once raised the voice of Puritan opposition. Bancroft, he charged, had maintained the superiority of bishops *jure divino,* "avouching it to be of God's own ordinance, though not by express words, yet by necessary consequence."[20] While the Puritan divines took themselves to Scripture to frame their answers, Knollys informed Burghley that this doctrine was an offense against "her Majesty's prerogative royal." The pride of the bishops, he demanded,

must be pulled down, and made subject to her Majesty's supreme government . . . they must confess that they have no superiority of government at all, but by commission from her Majesty: for otherwise their claimed superiority is treasonable to her and tyrannous over the inferior clergy.[21]

Bancroft's sermon did not advance an exclusive claim for the divine institution of the episcopal church order, except as it might appear "by necessary consequence," as Knollys put it. In Bancroft's *Survay* the remarks of the sermon were amplified. Episcopacy was defended as apostolic and tradi-

[19] Donaldson, "Whitgift and Bancroft and the Scottish Church," *Transc. Royal Hist. Soc.,* xxiv (1942), pp. 95-115. See also Burrage, *Early English Dissenters,* II, 130-2.

[20] Strype, *Whitgift,* I, 559.

[21] *Ibid.,* II, 52.

tional, finding its warrant in Christ's institution of the apostleship, and having a

general and continual allowance, both of God himself, and of all godly and rightly zealous men, ever since there was any outward form of church government appointed.[22]

Knollys was mistaken when he accused Bancroft of finding his doctrine in the book of "Dr. Whitgift against Cartwright," but he was nearer the truth when he asserted that the archbishop agreed with the views expressed in his friend's sermon. Defending Saravia, Sutcliffe, and the other supporters of episcopacy in the early 'nineties, Whitgift replied to Theodore Beza's criticism of them:

We make no doubt but that the episcopal degree (which we bear) is an institution apostolical and divine; and so always hath been held by a continued course of times from the Apostles to this very age of ours . . .

You may remember, learned Sir . . . the beginnings of that episcopacy, which you make to be only of human institution, is referred by the Fathers, with one mouth, to the Apostles, as the authors thereof; and that the Bishops [were appointed] as successors of the Apostles; especially in certain points of their functions. And what Aaron was to his sons and to the Levites, this the Bishops were to the Priests and Deacons; and so esteemed of the Fathers to be by divine institution.[23]

Whitgift did not challenge the right of the Church at Zurich to determine its own order of ministry, but he expressed rather sharply the wish "that every particular Church would mind its own business, and not prescribe the laws of

[22] *Survay*, p. 144; See also pp. 124, 142-3; *Sermon*, pp. 10, 68-9, 99.
[23] Strype, *Whitgift*, II, 170.

rites and the manner of government to others."[24] The archbishop's views had advanced beyond those which he formu-
lated in the heat of the *Admonition* controversy two decades
before. Church government was no longer defended as
among the "things indifferent," but on all sides a positive
note characterized the apologetic for episcopacy presented
by the supporters of the establishment in the last decade of
the reign. The episcopal church order was grounded in its
apostolic foundation under divine guidance.

Elizabeth silenced Knollys, but the controversy was not
stilled. Hadrian Saravia and Matthew Sutcliffe carried the
defense of episcopacy a step further in the direction of an
exclusive claim for this form of church order,[25] and Thomas
Bilson in the *Perpetual Government of Christ's Church* in
1593 went far beyond the cautious language of Hooker's
first books of the *Ecclesiastical Polity*. The controversy, however, over what Knollys called a view of the divine institution of episcopacy "by necessary consequence," and the dispute among the divines of the Church of England in respect
to non-episcopal orders belongs to the seventeenth century
and later ages. Here in Whitgift's last years we see only the
first exploration of the implications of their position by the
first generation that has come to maturity entirely within the
life of the Elizabethan Church.

The first flurry of a controversy that reached its height in
the next century was mild compared to the acrimonious debate over the doctrines of predestination and election that
arose in Cambridge in the mid-'nineties and resulted in the
brief appearance of the famous Lambeth Articles. It is not
easy to do justice to the issues and implications of this dis-

[24] *Ibid.*, II, 172.
[25] Saravia in *De Diversis Gradibus Ministrorum, etc.* (1590; English
translation, 1592), and Sutcliffe in *Treatise of Ecclesiastical Discipline*
(1592).

pute in summary fashion. Yet because Whitgift's participation has been misinterpreted and his intentions misrepresented, we must catch at least a glimpse of this controversy in its proper perspective.

In the spring of 1595 Archbishop Whitgift was aroused by an unseemly wrangle in the University of Cambridge. For some time the divinity professors, William Whitaker and Peter Baro, had contested the extent to which the high Calvinistic doctrines were properly received in the Church of England.[26] In April 1595 William Barret, one of the ardent supporters of Baro's challenge to the rigors of extreme Calvinism, savagely attacked the views of the majority of Cambridge divines in a sermon *ad clerum* at Great St. Mary's. Barret denied, among other things, the indefectibility of grace and the absolute decree of predestination without respect to sin. Moreover, he declared in "very unhandsome terms" that Calvin and Beza were blasphemers and false guides.[27] Barret's friends were jubilant, but the university authorities stood aghast. Here was clear evidence that Baro had not "sown the seed of his new and outlandish opinions in a barren soil." The Heads, in Heylyn's phrase, "took fire immediately." Led by the Regius professor, William Whitaker, Roger Goade of King's, Richard Some of Peterhouse, and Laurence Chaderton of Emmanuel, they forced the preacher to recant opinions "raked out of the dunghill of Poperie and Pelagianisme."[28] The recantation devised for Barret by the Heads aroused Baro's followers; its statements went far beyond the Anglican formularies on the points in dispute. On the other hand, the offensive manner of Barret's submission angered the authorities of the University. Both

[26] Heylyn, *Quinquarticular History*, III, xx, 5.
[27] Strype, *Whitgift*, II, 229-30; III, 320.
[28] Cooper, *Ath. Cantab.*, II, 237.

sides complained to the archbishop, and Whitgift, alarmed by a disturbance which threatened the good order he had wrought so mightily to preserve in Cambridge, intervened to still the controversy. Without careful investigation of the dispute, he rebuked the Heads for their "consistorian-like kind of proceeding" against Barret, censuring them, after consultation with Saravia on the points of the recantation, for having made the preacher "to affirm that which was contrary to the doctrine holden and expressed by many sound and learned divines in the Church of England."[29] When the Heads remonstrated with him, the archbishop's tone became more threatening.

It is a most vain conceit [he informed them] to think that you have authority in matters of controversy to judge what is agreeable to the doctrine of the Church of England; what not, the law expressly laying that upon her Majesty, and upon such as she shall by commission appoint to that purpose, and how far my authority under her Highness reacheth therein, I hope you will not give me occasion to try.[30]

Though Whitgift, when more accurately informed of Barret's opinions in the course of the correspondence, acknowledged his own dissent from them and admitted the justice of punishing Barret's "manner of dealing, and giving occasion of these questions," he would not permit the Heads to attempt to determine what was orthodoxy on these matters nor to continue a controversy that threatened to disrupt the life of the University. If Barret deserved punishment, so likewise did others "that shall continue these controversies either on one side or the other." The matter, however, had gone too far to be stilled by the voice of ecclesiastical authority

[29] Cooper, *Annals*, II, 530-1. See also Strype, *Whitgift*, II, 238-43.
[30] *Ibid.*, II, 252.

alone. Burghley was brought in on the side of the Heads, Dr. Some preached his "intemperate and indiscreet" sermon suggesting a fit comparison between the archbishop and the Jewish persecutors of the disciples, and Whitaker's passionate concern with "that question bandied amongst the divines, whether true and justifying faith may be lost" could not be silenced.[31] The upshot of it all was the conference held at Lambeth Palace in November during which Whitgift, Whitaker, Richard Fletcher, Richard Vaughan, and Humphrey Tyndal framed for circulation among the Heads some propositions dealing with the disputed points.[32]

The uncompromising tone of the nine Lambeth Articles clearly allowed the Puritan divines to maintain their opin-

---

[31] Camden, *Elizabeth*, p. 507. Camden ascribed Whitaker's death in this same year 1595 to the fact that he "much weakened his body with study" in the dispute.

[32] The text of the articles ran:

I. Deus ab aeterno praedestinavit quosdam ad vitam, quosdam ad mortem reprobavit.

II. Causa movens aut efficiens praedestinationis ad vitam non est praevisio fidei, aut perserverantiae, aut bonorum operum, aut ullius rei, quae insit in personis praedestinatis, sed sola voluntas beneplaciti Dei.

III. Praedestinatorum praefinitus et certus numerus est, qui nec augeri nec minui potest.

IV. Qui non sunt praedestinati ad salutem necessario propter peccata sua damnabuntur.

V. Vera, viva, et justificans fides, et Spiritus Dei sanctificans non extinguitur, non excidit, non evanescit in electis, aut finaliter aut totaliter.

VI. Homo vere fidelis, id est, fide justificante praeditus, certus est plerophoria fidei, de remissione peccatorum suorum, et salute sempiterna sua per Christum.

VII. Gratia salutaris non tribuitur, non communicator, non conceditur universis hominibus, qua servari possint, si voluerint.

VIII. Nemo potest venire ad Christum, nisi datum ei fuerit, et nisi Pater eum traxerit. Et omnes homines non trahuntur a Patre, ut veniant ad Filium.

IX. Non est positum in arbitrio aut potestate uniuscujusque hominis servari.

Strype, *Whitgift*, II, 280. See Trin. Coll. MSS. B. 14. 9, fos. 81-2. There were some variations in texts of the articles. See Heylyn, *Quin. Hist.*, III, xxi, 2, and Fuller, *Church History*, V, 220-1.

ions, despite Whitgift's modification, in the interests of the
anti-Calvinist party, of Whitaker's original and more stringent proposals.[33] How far these articles were an advance in
the direction of the full rigors of Calvinism over the more
moderate statements of the *Thirty-Nine Articles* may readily
be seen from a few of their assertions. It is not placed within
the will or power of every man to be saved (stated the
articles) nor is saving grace given to all men. God has from
eternity predestined some to life; others He has reprobated
to death, and those who are not predestined to salvation will
necessarily be damned for their sins. The moving cause of
predestination to life is only the good will of God's pleasure.
A true, living, and justifying faith is not extinguished in the
Elect, either totally or finally, and a man who is endowed
with a justifying faith is certain, by the full assurance of
faith, of the remission of his sins and eternal salvation
through Christ.

Lacking authorization or official publication, the Lambeth
Articles disappeared from view almost as quickly as they
were framed, though they were secretly cherished by the
Calvinistic divines through the remaining years of the
Queen's reign. When Whitaker and Tyndal brought them
to Cambridge, a storm of opposition arose. Baro, Lancelot
Andrewes, Samuel Harsnet, John Overall, and others made
such vigorous objection that the agitation spread to the court.
Elizabeth ordered their immediate withdrawal and Whitgift
suppressed them.[34] The truth of Fuller's quaint story that
the Queen jestingly threatened him with the penalties of
Praemunire is impossible to ascertain.[35] Certainly it would
have tickled Elizabeth's sense of humor to do so.

[33] Hardwick, *Articles of Religion,* pp. 319-23.
[34] Trin. Coll. MSS. B. 14. 9, fos. 118-20.
[35] *Church History,* V, 221n.

How far Whitgift was moved by pressure from the University authorities to lend himself to what were later called "Whitaker's doctrines" is difficult to determine.[36] That he believed them to represent a position tenable under the formularies of the established Church, and perhaps close to his own views, is clear enough, but unhappily his association with the articles has caused considerable misunderstanding of his motives in consenting to their appearance. It is commonly stated that the archbishop "countenanced an endeavour to reform the Creeds of the Church and impart to them a more pronounced Calvinistic colouring."[37] There is, however, no evidence for this contention. The Lambeth Articles were neither promulgated by archiepiscopal authority, nor published in any form—nor, indeed, as Whitgift carefully pointed out, were they "sent down to the University to be disputed upon." They were communicated to the Heads with a covering letter which, as we shall see presently, explained the archbishop's intentions. The attempt to give authoritative status to these propositions, making them interpretative of the statements in the *Thirty-Nine Articles,* was not made by Whitgift, but by Dr. Reynolds and the Puritan leaders at the Hampton Court Conference.[38] Forestalled then by Bancroft and Overall, who explained to James I the original purpose of the articles, apparently with Whitgift's approval, the Calvinistic divines were forced to wait until the Westminister Assembly before the *Thirty-Nine Articles* were revised to their satisfaction.[39] Equally, there is no justification for Macaulay's absurd statement that Archbishop

[36] Strype, *Whitgift,* II, 282-3.
[37] *Camb. Mod. Hist.,* III, 346.
[38] Heylyn, *Quin. Hist.,* III, xxii, 2. See Cardwell, *Conferences,* p. 178.
[39] Green, *Thirty-Nine Articles,* App. iv; Neal, *History of the Puritans,* III, App. i.

Whitgift employed his power persecuting those "who differed from Calvin touching the doctrine of Reprobation."[40] On the contrary, the members of the anti-Calvinistic party in Cambridge were invariably the recipients of his patronage and ecclesiastical favor. Harsnet, Overall, Saravia, and Andrewes were all Whitgift's chaplains and constantly advanced in preferment by archiepiscopal influence. He protected Peter Baro from ill-treatment at the hands of the Cambridge authorities, and upon the death of Whitaker the archbishop offered no objection to the appointment of John Overall, who "openly and freely professed his consent" with Baro, to the Regius professorship of divinity.

The truth is that the reasons for the archbishop's action are by no means as obscure as they have been made to appear, nor need we depend upon ingenious conjecture to reconstruct them. His first motive in sending the Lambeth Articles to the Heads in Cambridge was to secure peace and concord as rapidly as possible among the disputants there. Well aware how far the passions of controversy could disrupt the ordered life of the University, Whitgift seized upon the readiest means to quiet the stubborn group of extreme Calvinists. His letter of November 24, 1595 to the Heads of the colleges made his intentions clear.

Mr Drs Tyndall and Whitaker [he wrote] can signify unto you what is done in the matter for which they came hither, which I doubt not but that they will faithfully relate unto you. My earnest and hearty desire is to have the peace of the Church generally observed in all places, and especially in that University whereof I am a member. And for the better observation and nourishing of the said peace we have with some care and diligence drawn out and set down certain propositions which we

---

[40] *Critical and Historical Essays*, II, 135.

are persuaded to be true and the copy whereof I send unto you here inclosed, praying you to take care that nothing be publicly taught to the contrary; and that also in teaching of them, that discretion and moderation be used, that such as shall be in some points differing in judgement be not of purpose stung or justly grieved; and especially that no bitterness, contention or personal reproofs or reproaches be used by any towards any. Which propositions nevertheless must so be taken and used as our private judgement, thinking them to be true and correspondent to the doctrine professed in this Church of England, and established by the laws of the land; and not as laws and decrees. Touching Mr Barret, I persuade myself that you shall find him willing to perform that which is prescribed unto him, the rather if he be used courteously and without bitterness. And so being ready and willing to assist you in any thing fit for the good government of that University, I commit you to the tuition of Almighty God.

. . . your assured loving friend Jo: Cantuar:[41]

If any further evidence beyond this letter is needed to establish Whitgift's primary motive in consenting to the Lambeth propositions, it is provided by the reiteration of these points to Queen Elizabeth,[42] and by a letter a few weeks later to Thomas Neville of Trinity in which the archbishop asserted the baseless character of accusations that he entertained some ulterior purpose.[43]

Yet there is something further to be said about the whole controversy that illustrates the climate of doctrinal opinion in the Elizabethan Church, and illuminates some passages of Whitgift's letter of November 24th. The real background of the dispute that provoked the Lambeth Articles was the

[41] HMC, *Salis. MSS,* V, 465.
[42] Heylyn, *Quin. Hist.,* III, xxi, 3.
[43] Whitgift, *Works,* III, 616.

non-confessional character of the Church of England. The Queen's religious settlement committed her establishment to no doctrinal definitions beyond those of the few essential formularies. The *Act of Supremacy* declared nothing to be accounted heresy except what had been so adjudged "by the authority of the Canonical Scriptures, or by the first four General Councils," or what might be so determined "by the High Court of Parliament . . . with the assent of the Clergy in their Convocation." The *Canons of 1571* enjoined the clergy to teach only doctrines contained in the Scriptures, and those in the sense held by "the Catholic fathers and ancient bishops." The *Thirty-Nine Articles* at once affirmed the influence of Reformed theology in respect to some doctrines bitterly contested in the sixteenth century, and guarded traditional beliefs concerning others, staking out, so to speak, the limits within which the Church of England steered its moderate course. The doctrinal position of the *Book of Common Prayer* and the explicit assurances of the Queen's *Declaration* made one thing emphatically plain. Within both an allegiance to the authority of Scripture and the faith of the Creeds, and a broad acceptance of certain Reformation theological positions in that aspect which linked them more closely to the doctrines of the ancient Church than to the definitions of confessional Protestantism, a wide liberty of thought was allowed. This toleration was the keystone of Elizabeth's policy of comprehension. Her original settlement of religion had been constructed to rest on the broadest possible base of agreement on the essentials of Christian doctrine rather than on the precise and rigid theological definitions familiar in sixteenth-century confessional systems.

The Elizabethan Church, therefore, was open to theological influence from all sides, and no pressure was stronger than that which came from continental centers of Reformed opinion. The wide use of Bullinger's *Decades* brought one doctrinal influence into England; Calvin's *Institutes,* warmly recommended by Cartwright as the chief place for the study of doctrine, brought another.[44] The extraordinary number of editions and translations of Calvin's writings that appeared in Elizabethan England testifies to the reverence in which he was held by a majority of the Queen's divines. It is not surprising that the Genevan doctrines concerning predestination and election captured the minds of Calvin's admirers, perhaps the more readily because of the general acceptance of Augustinian principles from which the Reformation churches attacked a Pelagianism commonly ascribed to Romanist theology. Yet there was no received orthodoxy on these matters, even among the ardent Puritans, until the appearance in the 'eighties and 'nineties of a minority party of rigorists represented by the Heads who censured Barret at Cambridge. For the most part Puritans were content with the cautious and moderate statements of the *Thirty-Nine Articles* and the *Homilies* on what were often called these "deep points," until the group of extreme Calvinists came to believe that the statements of the formularies were dangerously insufficient. Such a man, for example, was William Perkins, Fellow of Christ's College and a famous popularizer of Calvin's doctrines, whose lectures, according to Heylyn, brought the decree of reprobation "so home in the ears of his auditors that it made their hearts fall down, and, yea, their hair to stand almost upright."[45]

On the other side, many of the Elizabethan churchmen refused to relax their hold on the doctrines of "the Catholic fathers and ancient bishops," even when confronted with the

[44] *Cartwrightiana,* pp. 114-5.
[45] *Quin. Hist.,* III, xx, 3.

plain words of John Calvin. Whitgift himself, whose sympathy was often with Reformed opinion, nevertheless informed Cartwright in their earlier controversy:

I reverence M. Calvin as a singular man, and worthy instrument in Christ's church; but I am not so wholly addicted unto him, that I will condemn other men's judgments that in divers points agree not fully with him, especially in the interpretation of some places of the scripture, when as, in my opinion, they come nearer to the true meaning and sense of it in those points than he doth.[46]

In the course of the controversy over Barret's sermon the archbishop was equally firm. He would not approve preachers "to traduce Calvin and other learned men in pulpits," but neither did he like "the same towards Augustine, Jerome, and other learned Fathers" who had "often and many times been abused in the University without control."[47]

Perkins, Whitaker, and their friends had their critics from this side. Robert Abbot of Oxford declared Perkins' description of divine predestination to be "contrary not only to the doctrine of the primitive times, but also unto that of the Church of England."[48] As early as 1584 Samuel Harsnet publicly challenged the increasing severity with which the Genevan doctrines were held. In a sermon at Paul's Cross he attacked the absolute decree of reprobation as contrary to Scripture, describing the "Calvinian Gospel" in some points a

Goliath, so huge and monstrous, that many quake and tremble at it, but none, that is to say, but few or none . . . durst take up David's sling to throw it down.[49]

[46] Whitgift, *Works,* I, 436.
[47] Strype, *Whitgift,* II, 240.
[48] Heylyn, *Quin. Hist.,* III, xx, 3.
[49] *Ibid.,* III, xvii, 8.

This is the conflict apparent in the background of the dispute in 1595. The Heads, disturbed by the increasing extent to which younger men opposed more traditional doctrines of grace and salvation to their high Calvinism, began to make claims of the same exclusive nature as those the Disciplinarians had advanced for the presbyterian church order. Following the line taken by the extreme Genevans two decades earlier, some of the Calvinistic party openly asserted their form of the doctrines of predestination and election to be the only orthodox formulation of saving truth.[50] Barret's revolt encouraged a display of the surprising strength acquired by the anti-Calvinists between Harsnet's sermon in 1584 and the publication of the first four books of Hooker's *Ecclesiastical Polity* nine years later. The Cambridge authorities were thereupon stimulated to attempt a definition of orthodoxy in their own terms, an effort that arose at least partly from the fear that their own rigorous position might be declared intolerable. Whitgift's problem was posed not only by a disturbance which destroyed the peace of the University, but also by a challenge on both sides that offered a potential threat to the principle of comprehension enshrined in the moderate formularies of the Queen's settlement. While he forbade the Heads to judge what was alone agreeable to the doctrine of the established Church, at the same time he would not deprive them of the assurance that, maintained as of "private judgement" and "not as laws and decrees," their views were "correspondent to the doctrine professed in this Church of England." He warned them, however, against denying others the right to hold opinions that differed in some points, so long as they too were regarded as of private judgment. Perhaps Whitgift knew that

[50] Heylyn, *Ecclesia Restaurata*, pp. 63-4.

only a set of carefully phrased propositions could quiet the anxieties of the Calvinistic divines, whereas Overall, Andrewes, Harsnet, Saravia, and other of his younger friends might be sufficiently assured by the archbishop's evident favor that acceptance of the most rigid formulation of the doctrines in dispute was not required by the official formularies.

Whitgift's mistake was to suppose that a set of theological definitions could be successfully used as an administrative weapon. Here Whitgift's usual perspicacity seems to have deserted him. His approach to the problem was on one level; their controversy was on another. While to the great majority of Englishmen these "deep matters" were irrelevant abstractions, to the theologically minded divines they were fast becoming the central issue between those who embraced the full "Calvinian Gospel" and those whose position anticipated that of the Arminian party of the next century. As a guide to what might be held of private judgment and taught with "moderation and discretion," and with a tolerant charity towards those who differed, the Lambeth Articles satisfied no one. Elizabeth undoubtedly understood Whitgift's explanation of their purpose, but she would tolerate nothing that might be construed in that "evil sense" which the archbishop disavowed to Neville. The formularies of her settlement would stand to the end without interpretive glosses on one side or the other.

The controversy bewildered Whitgift. He did not understand the theological cleavage between the churchmen with whom he surrounded himself and the Cambridge Heads for whom he had approved the propositions. On the points at issue the patterns of his thinking had been formed years earlier, when Englishmen had not yet fully explored the implications of predestination and election under Genevan tutelage, and, on the other hand, before the heritage of Catholic and patristic theology had begun its gradual reassertion in the Elizabethan Church. The new controversies eluded Whitgift's understanding. Men's minds, he complained to Matthew Hutton, were exercised on points that "were never doubted by any Professor of the Gospel during all the time of your abode and mine in the university."[51] He took refuge from this confusing scene in the familiar peace of Croydon.

There, ten miles from London in the Kentish countryside, was an ancient manor, enjoyed by the archbishops since the days of Pecham as their chief residence after Lambeth. In the village that nestled among the low wooded hills, John Whitgift built the tangible monument by which he is best remembered in England today, the School and Hospital of the Holy Trinity. Work on the quadrangle of buildings comprising the almshouse, school, and chapel took nearly four years to finish, and Whitgift scrutinized its progress carefully at every stage.[52] Upon its completion in 1599 the almshouse accommodated thirty-five to forty indigent men and women, each allowed a generous pension. The school, attached to the hospital in the fashion of Whitgift's own former school, St. Anthony's, offered free education to the poor children of Croydon. Drawn with meticulous care, the provisions of the archbishop's statutes centered the life of the whole community in the chapel services. Eventually endowed with an annual income of nearly £200 in addition to the initial building costs of almost £3000—a staggering sum in those days—the Croydon foundation was used by Whitgift's enemies to give verisimilitude to their malicious charge

[51] Trin. Coll. MSS. 0. 3. 53, f. 9.
[52] Garrow, *Croydon*, pp. 118 ff.

that he was amassing a fortune out of the archbishopric.
Whitgift deeply resented the accusation.

The archbishopric [he declared] is no better to me than it was
to my late predecessors; who died not very wealthy, for anything
I can learn: and I hope I bestow it as well as they did. But
whosoever saith that this archbishopric is yearly worth £6000 or
worth anyway, in ordinaries or extraordinaries, £3000, must
answer to God at the least for vain speeches, that I term them
no worse. And yet out of that which any way I receive, there
goeth in annuities, pensions, subsidies, and other duties to her
Majesty, £800 at the least. And then what remaineth is soon
known.

And other ways I receive not one penny. The land which
I had before mine advancement, and which I have purchased
since, my brethren have, those excepted which I have bestowed
upon mine hospital.[53]

The income of the archbishopric was actually £2200, of
which about £1500 remained after all annual pensions, subsidies, and annuities were paid. Even with this large sum,
however, careful stewardship was required if Whitgift, after
meeting the necessary charges of his office and see, were to
be able to devote funds to good works on the scale which he
conceived to be his obligation. Christian duty, he once remarked, led a man rather "to do good and charitable deeds
by himself whilst he liveth, than to hope that others will
do the same for him after his death."[54]

During the last five years of his life Archbishop Whitgift
spent much of his time at the Croydon Hospital, in "that
chamber over the hall, and the two chambers over the inner
gatehouse" which his statutes provided "shall be reserved

[53] Strype, *Whitgift,* II, 422.
[54] Garrow, *Croydon,* p. 90.

to myself and to my own use during my life." There, re-moved from the scene of controversy and the cares of his office, surrounded by his books, he looked out on the little quadrangle as twenty-five years before he had watched over the courts of Trinity College. This was the atmosphere where John Whitgift found a peace and contentment he had not known since the day he bade farewell to the University of Cambridge. Whitgift cared little for the stately magnificence of Lambeth or the ceremonious splendour that attended the Archbishop of Canterbury in his palace. Such things were "the outward show" of official dignity, "the countenance of [a bishop's] degree, whereunto he is called of God, by his prince." However carefully to be maintained and cherished, the symbols of high office and power should be—and here Whitgift penned an appropriate motto for his own life—"no impediment to a godly man for doing his duty."[55] The simplicity of Croydon was much more to his taste. He en-joyed hearing the school children at their lessons, walking the paths of the quadrangle with his pensioners, and kneel-ing among them all at chapel prayers each morning and evening.

There was loneliness mingled with the happiness of these last few years. Most of the archbishop's old companions had gone, including his only intimates, Dr. Perne and Bishop Cooper. Matthew Hutton still lived, a friend from their first association nearly forty years earlier in Cambridge, but he was in York, since 1595 archbishop of the northern province. A new generation had stepped into the places of leadership and responsibility in the Church—Bancroft, Bishop of Lon-don; Andrewes, Dean of Westminster; Overall, Dean of St. Paul's; Bilson, Bishop of Winchester. Following them were the younger men, Francis White at St. Peter's, Cornhill,

[55] Whitgift, *Works,* I, 153; II, 383.

Richard Montague and Thomas Morton at Cambridge, and at Oxford the youthful William Laud, newly-ordained and a Fellow of St. John's College. Many of the new figures owed their advancement to Whitgift, but that did not entirely curb their impatience with the restraining hand of the aging archbishop. Manningham in 1602 might have heard a preacher at Paul's Cross fulsomely describe the Archbishop of Canterbury as "the sun amongst the ministers," but Whitgift knew there were many who thought that sun a long time going down.[56] His only comment, however, was a dry prophesy to Hutton. "Peradventure when we are gone," he wrote, "they will wish us alive again."[57] During the troubles that descended upon them in the years that followed it is entirely possible that some of them did.

In the third week of March 1603 the summons came that brought to a close the most notable chapter of Whitgift's life, his long association with Elizabeth Tudor. The Queen lay dying at Richmond, and as the archbishop journeyed from Lambeth his mind must have been full of the memories of their friendship. Years before, in characteristic fashion, Elizabeth had roundly declared her affection for her "little black husband." She liked him because he was unmarried, kept a good house, and had about him a company of tall young men.[58] This was Elizabeth at her gayest, a mood that perhaps Whitgift least understood. But Elizabeth the monarch had shrewdly gauged the extent of the archbishop's loyalty to his sovereign and to the principles upon which she had erected her ecclesiastical establishment. She had watched his courage tested; she knew the depth of his single-minded and inflexible sense of duty. Elizabeth trusted Whit-

[56] Manningham, *Diary,* p. 35.
[57] Trin. Coll. MSS. 0. 3. 53, f. 9.
[58] *S. P. Dom. Eliz.* clxxxv. 79.

gift as few others among her public servants, and it may well be, as Walton suggested, that her confidence rested upon her recognition that his virtues were armed by the strength of his piety.[59] Where her trust was placed, the Queen yielded her respect. She valued Whitgift's counsel, acted upon his advice, and bore without resentment his occasional blunt reminder of her duty as a Christian prince. The relationship between the Queen and her archbishop is curiously hard to penetrate, perhaps because, unlike many Elizabethans, neither Whitgift nor Elizabeth readily laid bare their inward religious life. Whether, as many people thought, the archbishop was the Queen's confessor or not, he was her constant spiritual counsellor as well as the chief ecclesiastical administrator of her settlement.

Whitgift, Bancroft, Bishop Watson of Chichester, the Queen's Almoner, and three or four of the great officers of state were present at Richmond on March 23rd to join Elizabeth's chaplain, Dr. Parry, in his prayers for their dying mistress. Manningham saw few dry eyes in the chapel that afternoon.[60] At about six o'clock in the evening, when Elizabeth made it known that she wanted her old friend, Whitgift went into her. Her power of speech was gone, but she clasped his hand tightly as he knelt to pray. For over an hour she held him in the darkening chamber until the archbishop's aged knees were weary. As the Queen sank into her last sleep, Whitgift's voice filled the room and echoed through the adjoining corridors.

O most heavenly Father and God of all mercy, [he prayed] we most humbly beseech thee to behold thy servant our Queen with the eyes of pity and compassion. Give unto her the com-

[59] *Hooker,* p. 79.
[60] *Diary,* p. 145.

forts of thy Holy Spirit, work in her a constant and lively faith, grant her true repentence, and restore unto her, if it be thy will, her former health and strength of body and soul. Let not the enemy nor his wicked instruments have any power over her to do her harm. O Lord, punish her not for our offenses, neither punish us in her. Deal not with us, O Lord, as we have deserved, but for thy mercy's sake, and for thy Christ his sake forgive us all our sins and prolong her days, that we may still enjoy her to the glory of thy Holy Name, and the joy of all such as truly fear thee; through Jesus Christ our Lord.[61]

Late in the night the archbishop rose sadly from his knees and blessed the unconscious Queen. For others the dawn might bring the promise of a new era; for him it could bring only the passing of an order with which his whole life had been bound. Between two and three o'clock in the morning of March 24, 1603, Elizabeth Tudor died, and Sir Robert Carey began his famous ride to Holyrood House where James Stuart impatiently awaited the news that the age of Elizabethan England was over. So departed Elizabeth I, and if we appraise her influence upon the Church of England in cautious and moderate terms today, the truth is nonetheless conveyed in the more colorful accents of her contemporaries. "What can be devised," asked the author of *England's Mourning Garment,*

more near the mean than she hath in all things followed? For in religion, as in other things, there hath been an extreme erring from the truth, which, like all virtues, being indeed the head of all, keepeth place in the midst. So hath she established the true Catholick and Apostolical Religion in this land . . .

But here I shall be carped at, in that I call the religion pro-

[61] *Reg. Whitgift,* III, f. 148 b. See Nichols, *Progresses of Queen Elizabeth,* III, 610.

fessed in her time, true Catholick and Apostolical, considering the see of Rome . . . think that seat all one to hold the apostolical faith, excluding her Majesty and all other Christian princes with their subjects, that have not fallen before that chair, as people worthy to be cut off from Christ's congregation; given them names of Protestants, Lutherans, and I know not what. And on another side, a selected company, that would needs be counted saints and holy ones . . . condemned her sacred government for Antichristian . . .

I was born and brought up in the religion professed by that most Christian princess Elizabeth . . . [who] taught all her people the undoubted truth; that faith in Christ alone, the way, the door, and the life; not turning either to the right hand, or to the left; and in this, being the best mean, her temperance chiefly appeared. This rule she taught her kingdom . . . by excellent pastors, to whom humbly she gave public ear.[62]

Her most excellent pastor could perform only one more service for his mistress. On the 28th of April the funeral procession of the last of the Tudor monarchs wound its way through the streets to Westminister Abbey. Near the end of the long procession, ahead of the Great Banner of England borne before the chariot that carried Elizabeth's body, walked the Archbishop of Canterbury alone. John Whitgift and the people of England together laid their great Queen to rest.

[62] *Harleian Misc.*, II, 496-7.

EPILOGUE

John Whitgift survived Queen Elizabeth by only a few days short of a year. The last months of his life were those in which the nation adjusted itself to the Stuart monarchy, and the chief administrative burden in ecclesiastical affairs during this period fell almost entirely upon Richard Bancroft, Bishop of London, soon to be named Whitgift's successor. The story of the simultaneous death of Puritan hopes at the Hampton Court Conference and the beginnings of the reconstruction of the Elizabethan Church belongs to Bancroft's life and the record of a new alignment of forces in Church and State. Whitgift was but the nominal leader of the supporters of the establishment when the conference opened at Hampton Court in January 1604. His strength exhausted by the responsibilities of the previous summer and autumn during which he had initiated James I into the intricacies of the relation between the Crown and the Church, the archbishop willingly allowed Bancroft and Overall to assume the task of leadership in the debates of the conference.

By February 1604 Whitgift was seriously ill. Preparations for sessions of Parliament and Convocation took a heavy toll of his remaining vitality, as day after day in the bitter winter weather he travelled in his barge from Lambeth to Fulham or Whitehall. Near the end of the month, on the first Sunday in Lent, he was rowed from his palace to Whitehall for a discussion of the ecclesiastical agenda for Parliament with the King, Bancroft, and some of the great officers of state. The day was bitingly cold. Suffering from a severe chill, Whitgift found the meeting almost unbearably wearisome. Finally, as they rose to go in to dinner, the archbishop suddenly collapsed. Bancroft sprang to his assistance, and with the help of the Lord Chancellor and the Treasurer, the archbishop was borne into the latter's chamber. There he lay in a coma, bereft of speech, his right side paralyzed. Towards evening, when they were able to move him, a barge carried Whitgift back to his palace at Lambeth.

All day Monday he lay as still as death in his bed. On Tuesday King James, in his own sentimental way much moved, came to see him. Whitgift rallied and tossed in his bed, unable to speak coherently. On the next day, February 29th, he took a sharp turn for the worse; by evening the end was very near. Attended by his household chaplains, Barlow, Charior, and Buckeridge, and his friend and Comptroller, Sir George Paule, the archbishop fought his last and losing battle. But as death approached his mind cleared momentarily and his strength returned. As his voice rang out loudly, Archbishop Whitgift spoke an epitaph on his own life and work. "Pro ecclesia dei! Pro ecclesia dei!" cried the old man, and at eight o'clock in the evening he "quietly departed in the Lord." On the 27th of March his body was interred at Croydon. His monument is not so much the stone that there still perpetuates his memory, as it is the firm loyalty which he gave to the religious principles of the Elizabethan Church, maintained with such integrity of mind and devotion of spirit, that in one form or another they have ever remained a central element in the Anglican Tradition.

BIBLIOGRAPHY

Books Cited in the Text and Other Works

Manuscript citations are sufficiently identified in the notes. The following list includes books, articles, and printed records referred to by short title in the notes, together with a number of other works useful in a study of the material presented in these lectures.

Acts of the Privy Council, ed. J. R. Dasent. 32 vols. London, 1890-1907.

Addleshaw, G. W. O., and Etchells, F. The Architectural Setting of Anglican Worship. London, 1948.

Allen, J. W. A History of Political Thought in the Sixteenth Century. Second edition. London, 1941.

Alumni Cantabrigiensis, ed. John Venn and J. A. Venn. Cambridge, 1922-.

An Admonition to the Parliament. 1572. *S.T.C.* 10847.

Arber, E. An Introductory Sketch of the Marprelate Controversy: 1588-1590. *English Scholars' Library*, viii. London, 1879.

Ascham, Roger. Works, ed. J. A. Giles. 4 vols. London, 1865.

Athenae Cantabrigiensis, ed. C. H. and T. Cooper. 2 vols. Cambridge, 1858-61.

Attwater, A. Pembroke College, Cambridge, ed. S. C. Roberts. Cambridge, 1936.

Bacon, Francis. Works, ed. B. Montague. 17 vols. London, 1825-34.

Ball, W. W. R. Trinity College, Cambridge. London, 1906.

Bancroft, Richard. A Sermon Preached at Paules Cross . . . the 9th of Februarie . . . 1588. London, 1588.

———. A Survay of the Pretended Holy Discipline. London, 1593.

———. Dangerous Positions and Proceedings . . . under pretence of Reformation, and for the Presbiteriall Discipline. London, 1593.

———. [*See* Tracts Ascribed, etc.]

Barnard, E. A. B. The Prattington Collections of Worcestershire History. Evesham, 1931.

[Barnes, Richard] The Injunctions and other Ecclesiastical Proceedings of Richard Barnes, ed. J. Raine. *Surtees Society,* 1850.

Baskerville, Geoffrey. English Monks and the Suppression of the Monasteries. London, 1937.

Baumer, F. LeV. The Early Tudor Theory of Kingship. New Haven, 1940.

Beesly, E. S. Queen Elizabeth. London, 1892.

Benham, William. The Prayer-Book of Queen Elizabeth. Edinburgh, 1911.

Bentham, James. The History and Antiquities . . . of Ely. Cambridge, 1771.

Beresford, J. R. "The Churchwardens' Accounts of Holy Trinity, Chester," *Journal of the Chester and North Wales Architectural Archeological and Historic Society,* xxxviii, 1951.

Bicknell, E. J. A Theological Introduction to the Thirty-Nine Articles. London, 1944.

Bilson, Thomas. The True Difference, etc. Oxford, 1585.

———. The Perpetual Government of Christe's Church. London, 1593.

Birch, Thomas. Memoirs of Queen Elizabeth. 2 vols. London, 1754.

Birt, H. N. The Elizabethan Religious Settlement. London, 1907.

Bishop Redman's Visitation 1597. *Norfolk Record Society,* xviii, 1946.

Black, J. B. The Reign of Elizabeth 1558-1603. *The Oxford History of England: Vol. VIII.* Oxford, 1936.

Blunt, J. H. The Reformation of the Church of England. 2 vols. New York, 1870.

Bond, R. W., ed. The Complete Works of J. Lyly. 3 vols. Oxford, 1902.

Bonnard, G. La Controverse de Martin Marprelate 1588-1590. Geneva, 1916.

Brewer, J. S. The Reign of Henry VIII. 2 vols. London, 1884.

Bridges, John. A Defence of the Government established in the Church of England, etc. London, 1587.

Brook, Benjamin. Memoir of the Life and Writings of Thomas Cartwright. London, 1845.

Brooks, E. St. J. Sir Christopher Hatton. London, 1946.

[Broughton, Hugh] An Anonymous Pamphlet concerning his Disagreement with Whitgift. London, 1599.

Brown, J. H. Elizabethan Schooldays. Oxford, 1933.

Bullinger, Heinrich. Decades, ed. Thomas Harding. 4 vols. *Parker Society,* 1848-52.

[Burghley State Papers] A Collection of State Papers . . . left by William Cecil, Lord Burghley, ed. Samuel Haynes. London, 1740.

Burne, R. V. H. "Chester Cathedral in the Reigns of Mary and Elizabeth," *Journal of the Chester and North Wales Architectural Archeological and Historic Society,* xxxviii, 1951.

Burnet, Gilbert. The History of the Reformation of the Church of England, ed. Nicholas Pocock, 7 vols. Oxford, 1865.

Burrage, Champlin. The Early English Dissenters. 2 vols. Cambridge, 1912.

Butterworth, C. C. The English Primers (1529-1545). Philadelphia, 1953.

Cabala, sine Scrinia Sacra, Mysteries of State and Government, etc. London, 1663. Another edition, 1691.

Calendar of State Papers, Domestic Series, of the Reigns of Edward VI, Mary, and Elizabeth, ed. R. Lemon. London, 1856.

Calendar of State Papers, Domestic Series, of the Reign of Elizabeth, ed. M. A. E. Green. London, 1872.

Calendar of State Papers, Domestic Series, of the Reign of James I, 1603-10, ed. M. A. E. Green. London, 1857.

Cambridge Modern History, The, Vol. II: The Reformation. Cambridge, 1934.

Camden, William. Britannia, etc. London, 1610.

———. Elizabeth. Third edition, 1675.

Canon Law of the Church of England, The. *Report of the Archbishop's Commission.* London, 1947.

Cardwell, Edward. A History of Conferences . . . 1558-1690. Oxford, 1841.

———. The Two Books of Common Prayer . . . Edward VI [Liturgies]. Oxford, 1841.

———. Synodalia. 2 vols. Oxford, 1842.

———. Documentary Annals of the Reformed Church of England. 2 vols. Oxford, 1844.

———. Reformatio Legum Ecclesiasticarum. Oxford, 1850.

Cartwright, Thomas. A Replye to an answere made of M. Doctor Whitgifte Agaynste the Admonition to the Parliament. [Wandsworth?], 1573.

———. The Second replie of T[homas] C[artwright] against Maister Doctor Whitgiftes second answer. [Zurich?], 1575.

———. The rest of the second replie of T[homas] Cartvvrihght. [Antwerp?], 1577.

[Cartwright, Thomas] A full and plaine declaration of Ecclesiasticall Discipline owt off the word off God and off the declininge off the churche off England from the same, 1574. A translation of Walter Travers' *Ecclesiastica disciplinae et Anglicanae Ecclesiae ab illa aberrationis plena E Verbo Dei et dilucida Explicatio,* 1574.

Cartwrightiana, ed. Albert Peel and L. H. Carlson. *Elizabethan Nonconformist Texts,* I. London, 1951.

Certaine Sermons appoynted, etc. London, 1563 [The Book of Homilies].

Child, G. W. Church and State under the Tudors. London, 1890.

The Chronicle of Queen Jane, etc., ed. J. G. Nichols. *Camden Society,* 1850.

Clay, W. K., ed. Liturgies and Occasional Forms of Prayer . . . Queen Elizabeth. *Parker Society,* 1847.

———. ed. Private Prayers . . . during the Reign of Queen Elizabeth. *Parker Society,* 1851.

Clayton, H. J. Archbishop Whitgift and His Times. London, 1911.

Collection of Original Letters, ed. M. Bateson. *Camden Society,* 1893.

Collier, Jeremy. An Ecclesiastical History of Great Britain, ed. Thomas Lathbury. 9 vols. London, 1852.

Collins, W. E., ed. Queen Elizabeth's Defense of Her Proceedings in Church and State. *Church Historical Society,* lviii. London, 1899.

————. The Canons of 1571. *Church Historical Society,* xl. London, 1899.

Constant, G. La Réforme en Angleterre (Vol. I translated into English by R. E. Scantlebury as *The Reformation in England: The English Schism,* London, 1934; Vol. II by E. I. Watkin as *Introduction of the Reformation into England: Edward VI.* New York, 1942).

Cooper, C. H. Annals of Cambridge. 5 vols. Cambridge, 1842-1908.

Cooper, Thomas. An Admonition to the People of England, etc. London, 1589.

Cosin, Richard. Conspiracy for Pretended Reformation, etc. London, 1699.

Creighton, Mandell. Queen Elizabeth. London, 1908.

Cremeans, C. D. The Reception of Calvinistic Thought in England. *Illinois Studies in the Social Sciences,* xxxi, 1. Urbana, Illinois, 1949.

Davies, Horton. The Worship of the English Puritans. Westminster, 1948.

DeMaisse [André Hurault], Journal, ed. G. B. Harrison and R. A. Jones. London, 1931.

Desiderata Curiosa, etc., ed. Francis Peck. London, 1779.

D'Ewes, Simonds. The Journals of all the Parliaments during the Reign of Queen Elizabeth. London, 1682.

Dixon, R. W. History of the Church of England. 6 vols. Oxford, 1902.

Donaldson, Gordon. "The Attitude of Whitgift and Bancroft to the Scottish Church," *Transactions of the Royal Historical Society,* 4th Series, xxiv, 1942.

Dugdale, H. G. The Life and Character of Edmund Geste. London, 1840.

Durham Parish Books (Churchwardens' Accounts). *Surtees Society,* lxxxiv, 1888.

Ellis, Henry, ed. Original Letters Illustrative of English History. 11 vols. London, 1846.

Elizabethan Churchwardens' Accounts, ed. J. E. Farmiloe and R. Nixseaman. *Bedfordshire Historical Record Society,* xxxiii, 1953.

Ely Episcopal Records, ed. A. Gibbons. London, 1891.

Figgis, J. N. The Divine Right of Kings. Second edition. Cambridge, 1914.

Fox, John. Acts and Monuments, ed. S. R. Cattley and G. Townsend. 8 vols. London, 1837-41.

Foxe, Richard. Opus eximium de vera differentia regiae potestatis et ecclesiasticae, etc., 1534.

Frere, W. H. The English Church in the Reigns of Elizabeth and James I (1558-1625). London, 1911.

Frere, W. H., and Kennedy, W. M., ed. Visitation Articles and Injunctions, 1559-1575. 3 vols. *Alcuin Club*. London, 1910.

Fuller, Thomas. The Church History of Britain, ed. J. S. Brewer. 6 vols. Oxford, 1845.

———. The History of the University of Cambridge, ed. J. Nichols. London, 1840.

———. The History of the Worthies of England. London, 1662.

Gairdner, James. The English Church in the Sixteenth Century from the Accession of Henry VIII to the Death of Mary. London, 1902.

Gardiner, S. R. History of England: 1603-1642. 10 vols. London, 1883-4.

Gardiner, Stephen. Contemptum humanae legis, etc. London, 1541. (Reprinted in Janelle's *Obedience in Church and State*.)

———. De vera obedientia oratio. London, 1535. (Reprinted in Janelle's *Obedience in Church and State*.)

———. Another edition. Roane, 1553.

———. Letters, ed. J. A. Muller. Cambridge, 1933.

Garrett, C. H. The Marian Exiles. Cambridge, 1938.

Garrow, D. W. The History and Antiquities of Croydon. Croydon, 1818.

Gasquet, F. A., and Bishop, E. Edward VI and the Book of Common Prayer. Third edition. London, 1891.

Gee, Henry. The Elizabethan Clergy and the Settlement of Religion, 1558-1564. Oxford, 1898.

———. The Elizabethan Prayer-Book and Ornaments. London, 1902.

Gee, Henry and Hardy, W. J. Documents Illustrative of English Church History. London, 1921.

Gewirth, Alan. Marsilius of Padua. New York, 1951.

Gilby, Anthony. An Admonition to England and Scotland. Geneva, 1558.

A Glass of the Truthe. London, 1531. (Reprinted in Pocock, *Records*, II, cccxx.)

Godwin, Francis. A Catalog of the Bishops of England. London, 1615.

Goodman, Christopher. How Superior Powers Oght to be Obeyd. Geneva, 1558.

Grace Book Δ (1542-1589), ed. J. Venn. Cambridge, 1910.

Gray, Arthur. Cambridge University. Cambridge, 1926.

Green, E. Tyrrell. The Thirty-Nine Articles. London, 1896.

Gregory, I. L., ed. Hartland Church Accounts, 1597-1706. London, 1950.

Grey Friars of London Chronicle, ed. J. G. Nichols. *Camden Society,* 1852.

Grindal, Edmund. Remains, ed. W. Nicholson. *Parker Society,* 1843.

Grosart, A. B., ed. The Complete Works of T. Nashe. 6 vols. London, 1883-4.

Gwatkin, H. M. Church and State in England to the Death of Queen Anne. London, 1917.

Hall's Chronicle, ed. Henry Ellis. London, 1809.

Haller, William. The Rise of Puritanism. New York, 1938.

Hardwick, Charles A. A History of the Articles of Religion. Philadelphia, 1852.

Harington, John. Nugae Antiquae, ed. Thomas Park. 2 vols. London, 1804.

Harleian Miscellany, ed. J. Malham. 12 vols. London, 1808-11.

Heron, James. A Short History of Puritanism. Edinburgh, 1908.

Heylyn, Peter. Ecclesia Restaurata; or The History of the Reformation in the Church of England. London, 1661.

————. Aerius Redivivus; or The History of the Presbyterians. Oxford, 1670.

————. Historia Quinqu-Articularis; or A Declaration . . . of the Church of England, etc. London, 1681.

Heywood, B. A. The Royal Supremacy in Matters Ecclesiastical. London, 1870.

Heywood, J., and Wright, T. Cambridge University Transactions during the Puritan Controversies. 2 vols. London, 1854.

Holinshed's Chronicles. Second edition. 2 vols. London, 1586.

Hooker, Richard. Works, ed. John Keble. 3 vols. Oxford, 1836.

Hopf, Constantin. Martin Bucer and the English Reformation. Oxford, 1941.

Hudson, W. S. John Ponet, Advocate of Limited Monarchy. Chicago, 1942.

Hughes, Philip. The Reformation in England. Vol. I: *The King's Proceedings.* London, 1950.

————. Rome and the Counter-Reformation in England. London, 1944.

[Hutton Correspondence] The Correspondence of Dr. Matthew Hutton, ed. J. Raine. *Surtees Society,* 1843.

Janelle, Pierre. L'Angleterre Catholique à la Vielle du Schisme. Paris, 1935.

————. Obedience in Church and State [Three Political Tracts by Stephen Gardiner]. Cambridge, 1930.

Jewel, John. Works, ed. J. Ayre. 4 vols. *Parker Society,* 1845-50.

Joyce, J. W. A Constitutional History of the Convocations of the Clergy. London, 1855.

Keir, D. L. The Constitutional History of Modern Britain: 1485-1937. London, 1950.

Kennedy, W. M. The "Interpretations" of the Bishops. *Alcuin Club,* 1908.

Kennedy, W. P. M. Elizabethan Episcopal Administration. 3 vols. *Alcuin Club,* 1924.

Kennet, W. A Complete History of England, etc. 3 vols. London, 1706.

Ketley, J. S., ed. The Two Liturgies, etc. *Parker Society,* 1844.

[The King's Book] *See* A Necessary Doctrine and Erudition, etc.

Knappen, M. M. Tudor Puritanism. Chicago, 1939.

Knight, Samuel. The Life of Erasmus. Cambridge, 1726.

Lacey, T. A., ed. The King's Book. London, 1932.

Leach, A. F. English Schools at the Reformation 1546-48. Westminster, 1896.

————. The Schools of Medieval England. London, 1915.

Leatherbarrow, J. S. The Lancashire Elizabethan Recusants. *Chetham Society,* cx (New Series). Manchester, 1947.

LeNeve, John. Fasti Ecclesiae Anglicanae. London, 1716.

Letters and Papers, Foreign and Domestic, of the Reign of Henry VIII, ed. J. S. Brewer et al. London, 1862-1910. Addenda, 1929-32.

Letters of Queen Elizabeth and King James VI of Scotland, ed. John Bruce. *Camden Society,* 1849.

Liber Cleri 1576. Exchequer Gate, Lincoln.

Lincoln Episcopal Records, ed. C. W. Foster. *Lincoln Record Society,* ii. Lincoln, 1912.

Lloyd, Charles, ed. Formularies of Faith during the reign of Henry VIII. Oxford, 1825.

Macaulay, T. B. Critical and Historical Essays, ed. F. C. Montague. 3 vols. London, 1903.

McDonnell, M. F. J. The History of St. Paul's School. London, 1909.

Mackie, J. D. The Earlier Tudors 1485-1558. *The Oxford History of England: Vol. VII.* Oxford, 1952.

McGinn, D. J. The Admonition Controversy. New Brunswick, 1949.

Machyn, Henry. Diary, ed. J. G. Nichols. *Camden Society,* 1848.

Manningham, John. Diary, ed. J. Bruce. *Camden Society,* 1868.

Marprelate Tracts, The, ed. William Pierce. London, 1911.

Memoirs of Christopher Hatton, ed. N. H. Nicholas. London, 1847.

Meyer, A. O. England und die katholische Kirche unter Elisabeth und den Stuarts. (Translated into English by J. R. McKee under the title *England and the Catholic Church under Queen Elizabeth.* London, 1916.)

Morris, Christopher. Political Thought in England: Tyndale to Hooker. Oxford, 1953.

Mulcaster, Richard. Positions, etc., ed. R. H. Quick. London, 1888.

———. The First Part of the Elementarie, etc., ed. E. T. Champagnac. London, 1925.

Muller, J. A. Stephen Gardiner and the Tudor Reaction. New York, 1926.

Mullinger, J. B. St. John's College, Cambridge. Cambridge, 1901.

———. The University of Cambridge. 2 vols. Cambridge, 1884.

Neal, Daniel. The History of the Puritans. 3 vols. London, 1837.

Neale, J. E. Elizabeth I and Her Parliaments 1559-1581. London, 1953.

———. Queen Elizabeth. London, 1934.

———. "Parliament and the Articles of Religion," *English Historical Review*, lxvii, 1952.

———. "Sir Nicholas Throckmorton's Advice to Queen Elizabeth," *English Historical Review*, lxv, 1950.

———. "The Elizabethan Acts of Supremacy and Uniformity," *English Historical Review*, lxv, 1950.

Necessary Doctrine and Erudition for any Christian Man, A. London, 1543. [The King's Book.]

Nichols, John. The Progresses and Public Processions of Queen Elizabeth. 3 vols. London, 1823.

Notebook of John Penry, The, ed. A. Peel. *Camden Society*, 1944.

Oliphant, James. The Educational Writings of Richard Mulcaster. Glasgow, 1903.

Original Letters relative to the English Reformation, ed. Hastings Robinson. 2 vols. *Parker Society*, 1846.

Paget, Francis. An Introduction to the Fifth Book of Hooker's . . . Ecclesiastical Polity. Oxford, 1899.

[Parker Correspondence] The Correspondence of Matthew Parker, ed. J. Bruce and T. T. Perowne. *Parker Society*, 1853.

Parker, T. M. The English Reformation to 1558. Oxford, 1950.

Parte of a register, A, etc. [Middleburg, 1593.]

Paule, George. The Life of John Whitgift. London, 1612. Second edition, 1699.

Peachman, Henry. The Compleat Gentlemen. London, 1661.

Peacock, George. Observations on the Statutes of the University of Cambridge. London, 1841.

Pearson, A. F. S. Church and State. Cambridge, 1928.

———. Thomas Cartwright and Elizabethan Puritanism: 1535-1603. Cambridge, 1925.

Perry, G. G. A History of the English Church. 3 vols. London, 1887-1894.

Pickthorn, Kenneth. Early Tudor Government Henry VIII. Cambridge, 1934.

Pierce, William. An Historical Introduction to the Marprelate Tracts. London, 1909.

———. John Penry. London, 1923.

Pocock, Nicholas, ed. Records of the Reformation. 2 vols. Oxford, 1870.

Pollard, A. F. Political History of England: 1547-1603. London, 1910.

Pollen, J. H. The English Catholics in the Reign of Elizabeth. London, 1920.

Ponet, John. Short Treatise of Politike Power. Strasbourg, 1556.

Powicke, F. M. The Reformation in England. Oxford, 1941.

Previté-Orton, C. W. The Defensor Pacis of Marsilius of Padua. Cambridge, 1928.

Price, Thomas. The History of Protestant Non-conformity. 2 vols. London, 1836.

Primer, in Englishe and Latyn, set foorth by the Kjnges majestie & his Clergie . . . etc., The, 1545.

Prothero, G. W. Select Statutes and Other Constitutional Documents. Fourth edition. Oxford, 1949.

Pullan Leighton. The History of the Book of Common Prayer. London, 1900.

Puritan Discipline Tracts, ed. John Petheram. 6 vols. London, 1843-7.

Puritan Manifestoes, ed. W. H. Frere and C. E. Douglas, *Church Historical Society,* lxxii. London, 1907.

Records of the Northern Convocation. *Surtees Society,* 1907.

Register Matthew Parker. *Canterbury and York Society,* xxxv, 1928.

Reliquiae Wottonianae. *See* Wotton, Henry.

Rice, G. P. The Public Speaking of Queen Elizabeth. New York, 1951.

Robert Parkyn's Narrative, ed. A. G. Dickens. *English Historical Review,* lxii, 1947.

Rowse, A. L. The England of Elizabeth. London, 1950.

Rupp, E. G. Studies in the Making of the English Protestant Tradition. Cambridge, 1947.

Rymer, Thomas. Foedera, etc. 1741-2.

Sampson, Richard. Oratio quae docet hortatur admonet omnes potissimum Anglos regiae dignitatis cum primis ut obediant, etc. 1533. (Reprinted in Strype's Ecclesiastical Memorials, I, ii, XLVII.)

Sander, Nicholas. De origine ac progressu schismatis Anglicani. Cologne, 1585. (Translated into English by D. Lewis under the title *The Rise and Growth of the Anglican Schism.* London, 1877.)

Schramm, P. E. A History of the English Coronation. Oxford, 1937.

Seconde Parte of a Register, The, ed. Albert Peel. 2 vols. Cambridge, 1915.

Sisson, C. J. The Judicious Marriage of Mr. Hooker. Cambridge, 1940.

Smith, H. Maynard. Henry VIII and the Reformation. London, 1948.

———. Pre-Reformation England. London, 1938.

Smith, L. C. Tudor Prelates and Politics 1536-1558. Princeton, 1953.

Smyth, Charles. Cranmer and the Reformation under Edward VI. Cambridge, 1926.

Somers Tracts, The, ed. Walter Scott. 13 vols. London, 1809-15.

Sparrow, Anthony, ed. A Collection of Articles, Injunctions, Canons, etc. London, 1684.

Spedding, James. An Account of the Life and Times of Francis Bacon. 2 vols. Boston, 1878.

State of the Church in the Reigns of Elizabeth and James I, The, ed. C. W. Foster. *Lincoln Record Society,* xxiii. Lincoln, 1926.

Statutes of the Realm. 11 vols. London, 1810-28.

Statutes of the University and Colleges of Cambridge, ed. J. Heywood. London, 1840.

Stowe, A. R. M. English Grammar Schools in the Reign of Elizabeth. New York, 1908.

Strype, John. Annals of the Reformation. 4 vols. Oxford, 1824.

———. Ecclesiastical Memorials. 3 vols. Oxford, 1824.

———. Historical Collections of the Life and Acts of John Aylmer, Oxford, 1821.

———. The History of the Life and Acts of Edmund Grindal. Oxford, 1821.

———. The Life and Acts of Matthew Parker. 3 vols. Oxford, 1821.

———. The Life and Acts of John Whitgift, D. D. 3 vols. Oxford, 1822.

Stubbs, William. Registrum Sacrum Anglicanum. Oxford, 1858.

Sturge, Charles. Cuthbert Tunstal. London, 1938.

Sykes, Norman. The Church of England and Non-Episcopal Churches in the Sixteenth & Seventeenth Centuries. London, 1948.

Tanner, J. R., ed. Tudor Constitutional Documents 1485-1603. Second edition. Cambridge, 1948.

Thompson, B. M. H. The Consecration of Archbishop Parker. London [n.d.].

Thompson, J. V. P. Supreme Governor. London [1940].

Tracts Ascribed to Richard Bancroft, ed. A. Peel. Cambridge, 1953.

[Travers, Walter] Ecclesiasticae disciplinae et Anglicanae Ecclesiae ab illa aberrationis plena E Verbo Dei et dilucida Explicatio, 1574. (*See* Cartwright, Thomas.)

———. Disciplina Ecclesiae Sacra ex Dei Verbo descripta, 1584.

Trinterud, Leonard J. "The Origins of Puritanism," *Church History,* xx.1, 1951.

Tudor and Stuart Proclamations, ed. R. Steele. 2 vols. Oxford, 1910.

Tudor Parish Documents of the Diocese of York, ed. J. S. Purvis. Cambridge, 1948.

Tunstal, Cuthbert. A Sermon of Cuthbert Bysshop of Duresme, etc. London, 1539.

Tyndale, William. The Obedience of Christen man, etc. London [1548].

Usher, R. G. "The People and the Puritan Movement," *Church Quarterly Review,* cxv, 1904.

————. The Presbyterian Movement . . . illustrated by the minute book of the Dedham Classis. *Camden Society,* 1905.

————. The Reconstruction of the English Church. 2 vols. New York, 1910.

————. The Rise and Fall of High Commission. Oxford, 1913.

Valor Ecclesiasticus, ed. J. Caley and J. Hunter. 6 vols. London, 1810-34.

Venn, John. Admissions to Trinity College. London, 1913.

————. Early Collegiate Life. Cambridge, 1913.

Venn, J. A., and John. Cambridge University: Matriculations and Degrees 1544-1659. Cambridge, 1913.

Victoria County Histories: *Lincolnshire.* 2 vols. London, 1906.
  Worcestershire. 4 vols. London, 1906.

Visitation Articles [*See* Frere, W. H.].

Walker, T. A. A Bibliographical Register of Peterhouse Men. Cambridge, 1927.

————. Peterhouse. London, 1906.

Walton, Isaac. The Life of Mr. Rich. Hooker. London, 1665.

Ware, S. L. The Elizabethan Parish in its Ecclesiastical and Financial Aspects. *Johns Hopkins Studies in History and Political Science,* xxvi, 7-8. Baltimore, 1908.

Watson, Foster. The English Grammar Schools to 1660. Cambridge, 1908.

————. Tudor Schoolboy Life. London, 1908.

White, F. O. Lives of the Elizabethan Bishops. London, 1898.

White, H. C. The Tudor Books of Private Devotion. Wisconsin, 1951.

Whitgift, John. An answere to a certen Libel intituled, An admonition to the Parliament. London, 1572.

————. The defense of the Answere to the Admonition against the Replie of T. C. London, 1574.

————. Works, ed. J. Ayre. 3 vols. *Parker Society,* 1851-3.

Whitney, E. A. "Erastianism and Divine Right," *Huntington Library Quarterly,* II, iv, 1939.

[Whittingham, William] The Life and Death of Mr. William Whittingham, etc., ed. M. A. E. Green. *Camden Society,* 1871.

Wilkins, D. Concilia Magnae Britanniae, etc. 4 vols. London, 1737.

Wilson, Arthur. "The Life and Death of James I" (*See* Kennet's *Complete History,* II).

Wilson, J. D. "The Marprelate Controversy," *Cambridge History of English Literature,* III. Cambridge, 1909.

Wood. A. C. Memorials of the Holles Family. *Camden Society,* 1937.

Wordsworth, Christopher. Ecclesiastical Biography. 6 vols. London, 1853.

Wotton, Henry. Reliquiae Wottonianae. Third edition. London, 1672.

Wriothesley, Charles. A Chronicle of England, ed. W. D. Hamilton. 2 vols. *Camden Society,* 1875.

Writings of Robert Harrison and Robert Browne, The, ed. A. Peel and L. H. Carlson. *Elizabethan Nonconformist Texts,* II, London, 1953.

Zurich Letters, The, ed. Hastings Robinson. 2 vols., *Parker Society,* 1842-5.

Selected Names and Topics

Abbot, Robert, 218

Acts of Parliament, *Henry VIII:* Act Against Papal Authority, 11n; Act for the Submission of the Clergy, 6n; Act in Conditional Restraint of Annates, 22; Act in Restraint of Appeals, 11-13, 22; Dispensations Act, 11n, 22; First Succession Act, 13n; Six Articles Act, 34; Supremacy Act, 8; *Edward VI:* Uniformity Acts, 35-7; *Mary I:* Statutes of Repeal (1st & 2nd), 38-9, 50; *Elizabeth I:* Act Against Jesuits, Seminary Priests, etc., 127-8; Act Against Papal Bulls, 125; Act Against Popish Recusants, 129n, 190; Act Against Seditious Sectaries, 189; Act for the Thirty-Nine Articles, 86-7; Act to Retain the Queen's Subjects in Due Obedience, 126-7; Supremacy Act, 1-2, 53-4, 60, 110, 164, 216; Treasons Act, 124; Uniformity Act, 53, 57, 59, 60n, 86, 110

Admonition controversy, The, 87-100, 131, 135-45, 147

Admonition to England and Scotland, An (Anthony Gilby), 144

Admonition to the Parliament, An (Field and Wilcox), 87-91, 94-5, 98, 133, 135, 139, 142, 176

Admonition to the People of England, An (Thomas Cooper), 68, 90, 106, 158, 182n, 184

Advertisements, The (Matthew Parker), 75-6, 87, 111, 113, 162, 167

Allen, William, 127

Alva, Duke of, 122

Anabaptism, 158

Andrewes, Lancelot, 193, 212, 214, 220, 223

Anglicanism; *see* Elizabethan Anglicanism

Answere to a certen Libel, etc., An; *see* Whitgift

Anti-Calvinist party, The; *see* Lambeth Articles

Apologia Ecclesiae Anglicanae (John Jewel), 67, 106, 114

Ascham, Roger, 29-30

Articles; *see* Ten Articles; Eleven Articles; Forty-Two Articles; Thirty-Nine Articles; Lambeth Articles

Articles for the education of the clergy (Whitgift), 201-3

Augustinian Canons, 4

Aylmer, John, 52, 155-6, 172

Bancroft, Richard, 105, 164-5, 185, 187-8, 195, 205-7, 213, 223, 225, 229-30

Barnes, Richard, 116, 200

Baro, Peter, 209, 212, 214

Barret, William, 209-10, 217-19

Barrow, Henry, 185-6

Beale, Robert, 168

Becket, Thomas, 10

Beza, Theodore, 134, 207, 209

Bilson, Thomas, 105, 141, 193, 208, 223

Bishops; see Elizabethan episcopate

Bishops' Bible, The, 162, 202n

Bishops' Book, The, 34

"Black Rubric," The, 58

Bonner, Edmund, 28, 167, 184n

Book of Common Prayer, *Edward VI,* 35-7, 57-8; *Elizabeth I, see* Elizabethan Prayer Book

Book of Discipline, The; see Disciplina Ecclesiae Sacra

Book of Homilies, The, 36, 114-5, 152, 183

Book of Martyrs (John Foxe), 43

Bradford, John, 39, 41-2, 134, 169

Bridges, John, 183-4

Browne, Robert, 157, 185

Bucer, Martin, 20, 41-2, 44, 134

Bullinger, Heinrich, 76, 91-2, 134, 200-2, 217

Bullingham, John, 104

Bullingham, Nicholas, 101, 104

Burghley, Lord (William Cecil), 49, 64, 101, 103, 176, 211; his "Admonition to simple men, etc.," 55-6; and the vestiarian controversy, 66, 70, 73-5; and Cambridge affairs, 81-2, 84; correspondence with Whitgift, 99, 169-72

Calvin, John, 134, 137, 166, 209, 214, 217-8

"Calvinian Gospel," The; see Lambeth Articles

Calvinism, 209, 212-4, 219-20; see Lambeth Articles

Cambridge, University of; in the reign of Edward VI, 40-2; under Mary I, 43; Elizabeth's visit to, 64-5; and Puritanism, 65-6, 74-5, 81-4; Whitgift's statutes for, 80-1, 83; Whitgift's concern for, 196

Campion, Edmund, 126

Canon Law, 6-7, 11n, 12n

Canons of 1571, The, 60, 87, 111, 118, 163, 199, 216

Canons of 1576, The, 149n

Canons of 1585, The, 173

Canons of 1597, The, 201n

Cartwright, Thomas, 43-4, 97; activities in Cambridge, 65, 81-4; propositions for reformation, 82-3; and the *Admonition,* 90, 94; *A Replye,* 95, 98; *The Second Replie,* 99n; controversy with Whitgift, 133-45; later Puritan activity, 148, 180, 185

Cecil, Robert, 176, 195n

Cecil, William; see Burghley

Chaderton, Laurence, 81, 209

Chaderton, William, 81, 121, 147

Cheke, John, 20

Cheney, Richard, 105

Christ Church, Oxford, 73

Christ's College, 217

Church and State, 7, 9-16, 18-9, 23, 31-2, 142-5; see royal supremacy

Church services, 116-8

Churchwardens, 110

Churchwardens' accounts, 115, 201

Clare Hall, 43

Classis movement, The, 175, 179, 182, 185, 188

Colet, John, 26, 108, 194

"Concealers," The, 109

Conditional Restraint of Annates, Act in; see Acts of Parliament

Convocation of the Clergy, The, *Henrician,* 5-7; *Elizabethan,* 52, 60, 69-70, 73, 86-7, 111, 149, 154, 173, 199, 229

Cooke, Anthony, 1, 52, 62

Cooper, Thomas, 68, 85, 90, 102, 105-6, 134, 147, 155n, 158, 182n, 184, 200-1, 223

Cope, Anthony, 182-3

Cox, Richard, 42, 52, 58, 61, 91-2, 94, 98, 104, 145, 148

Cranmer, Thomas, 4, 24, 31, 35-7, 45, 47, 194

Cromwell, Thomas, 5, 10, 17, 32

Croydon Hospital and School, The, 197, 221-3

Curteis, Richard, 102n, 104

Dangerous Positions and Proceedings, etc. (Richard Bancroft), 188

Davies, Richard, 155n

De Maisse, Sieur, 104, 108n, 192

Derby, Earl of, 121

De vera differentia, etc. (Richard Foxe), 16-7

De vera obedientia, etc. (Stephen Gardiner), 16, 19, 142

Decades (Heinrich Bullinger), 200-2, 217

Declaration of Certain Principle Articles of Religion, A, 110-1

Declaration of the Queen's Proceedings, 56-7, 60-1, 216

Defense of the Answere, etc., The; see Whitgift

Defense of the Government Established, etc., A (John Bridges), 183

Defensor Pacis (Marsiglio of Padua), 17

Dering, Edward, 96-7

Device for the Alteration of Religion, The, 51n, 67

Disciplina Ecclesiae Sacra, etc., 180

Disciplinarians, The, 133, 135, 141-2, 144-5, 148, 161, 180, 205, 219; *see* Precisians; Puritans

Dispensations Act; *see* Acts of Parliament

Divine right of kings, 17-8

Douai, 127

Durham Cathedral, 123

Eastbridge Hospital, Canterbury, 197

Ecclesiasticae Disciplinae et Anglicanae Ecclesiae . . . Explicatio (Walter Travers); *see Explicatio*

Ecclesiastical Commission, The, 56, 75, 87, 110, 164; *see* High Commission

Education of the clergy, 196-205

Edward VI, 15, 28, 31-42, 53, 69, 108

Egerton, Thomas, 195n

Eleven Articles, The (Whitgift), 161-5, 168

Elizabeth I, 29-30, 46-7, 51-2, 174, 188, 208, 212, 224-7; ecclesiastical policy, 15, 48-9, 52n, 56-8, 60-2, 70-1, 121, 125, 130, 141, 150, 154-5, 191-2; settlement of religion, 1-2, 46-61, 67-8, 191-4, 216-7

Elizabeth's *Defense of Her Proceedings; see Declaration of the Queen's Proceedings, etc.*

Elizabeth's *Injunctions; see* Injunctions of 1559

Elizabethan Anglicanism, 24, 106-8, 118-9, 191-4, 216-7

Elizabethan clergy, The, 101-9, 120, 181-2, 198-205

Elizabethan Church and the Romanists, The, 120-131

Elizabethan church life, 112-120, 181-2, 203-5

Elizabethan ecclesiastical legislation; *see* Acts of Parliament

Elizabethan episcopate, The, 101-9, 129-30

Elizabethan parish, The; *see* Elizabethan church life

Elizabethan Prayer Book, The, 57-9, 69, 86, 90, 114-5, 123, 136, 156, 162-5, 173, 176, 180, 193, 199, 216

Elizabethan settlement of religion, The, 1-2, 46-61, 67-8, 216-7; *see* English Reformation; Elizabethan Anglicanism

Ely Cathedral, 61, 78

Ely, Humphrey, 128

Emmanuel College, 209

England's Mourning Garment, 226-7

English Reformation, The; separation from Rome, 9-13; the Crown and the Church, 4-8, 11-23, 54-7, 142-5; Edwardian reformation, 31-2, 35-8; Elizabethan settlement, 46-61, 67-8, 216-7; character of, 32-3, 48-9, 106-8, 118-9, 191-4, 216-7

Episcopacy controversy, The, 176-9, 206-9

Erasmus, 27

Erasmus' *Paraphrases,* 36, 114

Erastianism, 23, 85, 182

Ex-officio oath, The, 167-70

Explicatio (Walter Travers), 144, 148, 157, 180

Field, John, 89, 97, 135, 176, 179, 185, 187

First Succession Act; *see* Acts of Parliament

Fletcher, Richard, 104, 211

Forty-Two Articles, The, 21, 37

Foxe, Richard, 16

Freke, Edmund, 101, 104, 147

Frith, John, 3, 134

Fuller, Thomas, 168, 171, 178, 212

Gardiner, Stephen, 6, 35-6, 43, 45, 106-7, 167, 184n, 194; defense of the royal supremacy, 16-21, 142

Gardiner, S. R., 166

Gilby, Anthony, 144, 157

Glasse of the Truthe, A, 4

Goade, Roger, 209

Goodman, Christopher, 144

Greenwood, John, 185

Gregory XIII, Pope, 126

Grey, Lady Jane, 42

Grindal, Edmund, 42, 52, 58, 72, 82, 87, 93, 104, 132, 161, 171; concern for the education of the clergy, 199-201; Archbishop of Canterbury, 101, 148; defense of the prophesyings, 148-53; suspension from office, 132, 154, 157-8

Gualter, Rudolph, 62, 66, 91-3, 134

Guest, Edmund, 105

Hackett conspiracy, The, 189

Haddon, Walter, 59

Haller, William, 134

Hampton Court Conference, The, 213, 229

Harington, John, 166

Harrison, Robert, 157

Harsnet, Samuel, 212, 214, 218, 220

Hatton, Christopher, 165, 169, 174, 195n

Henry II, 10

Henry VIII, 1, 4, 25, 28, 31-5, 39, 42, 50, 52, 55, 121, 142; and the English Reformation, 1-25; and the submission of the clergy, 5-8; and the separation from Rome, 9-13; and the nationalization of the Church, 14-15; and the royal supremacy, 4-13, 15-24

Heylyn, Peter, 209, 217

High Commission, 164, 167-8; *see* Ecclesiastical Commission

Holy Trinity, The School and Hospital of; *see* Croydon Hospital and School

Homilies; *see Book of Homilies*

Hooker, Richard, 49, 106, 141-2, 189-91, 194, 208; controversy with Travers, 178; *see Laws of Ecclesiastical Polity*

Hooper, John, 36n, 37

Horne, Robert, 77, 102n, 105

How Superior Powers ought to be Obeyed (Christopher Goodman), 144

Humphrey, Lawrence, 73, 77, 93

Hunne, Richard, 4

Hutton, Matthew, 74, 131, 221, 223; correspondence with Whitgift, 159-60

Injunctions of Henry VIII, 26

Injunctions of 1559, 54-6, 59, 68-9, 111, 113, 117, 198

Institutes (John Calvin), 217

"Interpretations of the Bishops," The, 69, 75, 110

James I, 18, 185, 188, 213, 229-30

Jesuits, 127-8

Jesuits, Act Against; *see* Acts of Parliament

Jesus College, 164

Jewel, John, 52, 58, 72, 103, 105, 148, 194; correspondence with Peter Martyr, 62-3; *see Apologia Ecclesiae Anglicanae*

Jones, Hugh, 105

King's Book, The, 19, 22, 28, 35

King's College, 42, 64, 209

Knappen, M. M., 134

Knollys, Francis, 52, 127, 158; and the Puritans, 97, 168-9, 187; and the episcopacy controversy, 206-8

Knox, John, 37

Laceby parish, 84

Lambeth Articles, The, 208-15, 220

Laneham, Robert, 27

Latimer, Hugh, 31, 45

Laud, William, 107, 119, 193, 224

Laws of Ecclesiastical Polity (Richard Hooker), 106, 141-2, 190-1, 208, 219

Leicester, Earl of, 73, 97, 168, 187, 195

Lever, Thomas, 43-4

Liber Precum Publicarum, 59

Lincoln Cathedral, 84

Litel Treatise ageynste the mutterynge of some papistes, etc., A, 25

Lollardy, 3

Lyly, John, 184

Lyly, William, 27

Macaulay, T. B., 166, 213

Magdalen College, 73

Maitland, F. W., 47

Manningham's *Diary,* 205n, 224-5

Marprelate Tracts, The, 44, 131, 183-5

Marsiglio of Padua, 17

Mary I, 1, 34-5, 38-9, 42-5, 47, 108, 144

Mary Stuart, 85, 122, 126, 188

May, John, 82

May, William, 42

Mayne, Cuthbert, 126

Milton, John, 192

Montague, Richard, 224
More, Thomas, 5, 26, 192
Morton, Cardinal, 106
Morton, Thomas, 224
Mulcaster, Richard, 26-7, 197

Nashe, Tom, 184
Neale, J. E., 49, 50n, 51
Neville, Thomas, 78, 215, 220
Northern Rebellion, The, 56, 85, 123
Northumberland, Duke of, 32, 37-8, 42, 109

Oratio, etc. (Richard Sampson), 16
Order of the Communion, The, 28
Ornaments rubric, The, 58-9, 69
Overall, John, 193, 212-3, 220, 223, 229

Papal Authority, Act Against; *see* Acts of Parliament
Papal Bull of deposition of Elizabeth I, 123-4, 126
Papal Bulls, Act Against; *see* Acts of Parliament
Parish churches, 112-4
Parish life; *see* Elizabethan church life
Parker, Matthew, 42, 48, 56, 62, 94, 101, 103, 105-6, 148, 194, 198; and Elizabeth I, 71-2, 75, 150; and the Puritans, 66-7, 72-4, 94-6, 144, 146; *see Advertisements*
Parkhurst, John, 58, 73, 104, 147
Parsons, Robert, 126
Paule, George, 29, 39, 159, 230
Pembroke Hall, 39, 78n
Penry, John, 183, 185-6
Perkins, William, 217-8
Perne, Andrew, 41, 44, 64, 82, 94, 223

Perpetual Government of Christ's Church, The (Thomas Bilson), 208
Peter Martyr, 1, 62-3, 134
Peterhouse, 44-5, 61
Philip II, 46
Pickthorn, Kenneth, 12
Pierce, William, 40
Piers, John, 155n
Pilkington, James, 72, 93, 105
Pius V, Pope, 122-4
Pleasaunt Dialogue, A (Anthony Gilby), 157
Pole, Reginald, 17, 22, 39, 45, 47
Ponet, John, 144
Popish Recusants, Act Against; *see* Acts of Parliament
Praemunire, Statute of, 6, 12n, 87, 124n, 212
Precisians, The, 66, 70, 73, 76, 90, 93, 133, 148; *see* vestiarian controversy; Puritans; Disciplinarians
Primer, *Henry VIII,* 26, 28; *Edward VI,* 59; *Elizabeth I,* 59
Proclamation Against the Despisers and Breakers of Orders, etc., A (Elizabeth I), 97
Prophesyings, The, 131-2, 146-50, 153-4
Puckering, John, 195n
Puritanism, 133-5; in Cambridge, 66, 74-5, 81-4; later, 90-4, 96-8, 135-8; *see* Puritans; Precisians; Disciplinarians
Puritans, The; activity in Parliament, *1559,* 1, 52-3; *1571-2,* 85-7; *1581,* 155; *1584-5,* 172-4; *1587,* 180-3; the classis movement, 156, 175-6; and the Elizabethan settlement, 77, 81-3, 87-94, 97-8; the vestiarian controversy, 63, 66-70, 72-7; in Convocation, 69-70; the

Admonition controversy, 87-94; challenge to the Queen's establishment, 133, 135-58, 161; and the Prayer Book, 136-7, 156, 164; and the authority of Scripture, 138-40, 144; and the royal supremacy, 77, 142-5, 182, 185, 188; and subscription, 162-3, 165, 167-9; decline of, 183, 185-90; *see* Precisians; Disciplinarians; vestiarian controversy; prophesyings

Queens' College, 39, 64, 81

Recusants, 120, 122-30, 156, 162, 190

Regnans in excelsis; see Papal Bull of deposition

Replye to an Answere made of M. Doctor Whitgifte, etc., A (Thomas Cartwright), 95, 98

Rest of the second replie, etc., The (Thomas Cartwright), 99n

Restraint of Appeals, Act in; *see* Acts of Parliament

Ridley, Nicholas, 31, 36n, 37, 42, 45, 47

Ridolphi Plot, The, 126

Robinson, Nicholas, 155n

Rowse, A. L., 40, 105n

Royal supremacy, The; in the reign of Henry VIII, 4-13; defenders of, 15-24; and the Council of Edward VI, 31; in the reign of Elizabeth I, 54-7, 153; and the Puritans, 77, 96, 142-5, 182, 185, 188

St. Anthony's School, 26-8, 211

St. Catherine's College, 82

St. John's College (Cambridge), 43, 66, 74

St. John's College (Oxford), 224

St. Paul's School, 26-7

Sampson, Richard, 16

Sampson, Thomas, 52, 63, 73, 77, 93

Sandys, Edward, 104, 130, 155, 158; correspondence with Bullinger, 92; sympathy with the Precisians, 72, 147-8; difficulties with the Puritans, 96-7, 156, 173-4, 186

Saravia, Hadrian, 141, 207-8, 210, 214, 220

Scambler, Edmund, 95-6

Scory, John, 50, 102-3

Second Admonition to the Parliament, A, 94-5

Seconde Parte of a Register, The, 166

Seconde replie, etc., The (Thomas Cartwright), 99n

Seditious Sectaries, Act Against; *see* Acts of Parliament

Seminary priests, 127

Separatism, 157, 185

Separatists, 157-8, 187

Shakespeare, William, 3, 27, 181, 192, 197

Six Articles Act; *see* Acts of Parliament

Some, Richard, 209, 211

Somerset, Duke of, 35

Spanish Armada, The, 188

Stanbridge, John, 27

Statutes; *see* Acts of Parliament

Statutes of Repeal, First and Second; *see* Acts of Parliament

Stokesley, John, 17

Sturmius, John, 29

Submission of the Clergy, 5-8

Submission of the Clergy, Act for; *see* Acts of Parliament

Subscription; *see* Eleven Articles; Puritans; Thirty-Nine Articles

Succession Act, First; *see* Acts of Parliament

Suppression of monastic houses, 25

Supremacy, Act of, *Henry VIII*, 8; *Elizabeth I*, 1-2, 53-4, 60, 110, 164, 216

Survay of the Pretended Holy Discipline, A (Richard Bancroft), 188, 206

Sutcliffe, Matthew, 141, 207-8

Ten Articles, The, 34

Teversham parish, 61, 84

Thirty-Nine Articles, The, 55-6, 111, 144, 213, 216-7; form of subscription, 86-7, 91; and the Puritans, 91, 163, 177, 183

Thirty-Nine Articles, Act for; *see* Acts of Parliament

Throckmorton, Nicholas, 50

Tillotson, John, 119

Travers, Walter, 135, 144, 180; controversy with Whitgift, 176-9

Treasons Act; *see* Acts of Parliament

Treatise of Politike Power (John Ponet), 144

Treatise of the Church and the Kingdome (Robert Harrison), 157

Trent, Council of, 122

Trinity College (Cambridge), 29, 78-81, 84, 90, 94, 102

Trinterud, Leonard, 134

Tunstal, Cuthbert, 6-7, 52, 107, 121; defense of the royal supremacy, 17, 20, 22

Turner, Peter, 173

Tyndal, Humphrey, 211-2

Tyndale, William, 3, 134

Udall, John, 183, 185

Uniformity, Act of, *Edward VI*, 35-7; *Elizabeth I*, 53, 57, 59, 60n, 86, 110

Vaughan, Richard, 211

Vestiarian controversy, The, 63, 66-70, 72-7; *see* Precisians; Puritans

View of popishe abuses, etc., A, 91

Waad, Armigil, 51

Walsingham, Francis, 97, 130, 168, 174, 187, 195

Walton, Isaac, 225

Warham, William, 194

Wellow Abbey, 4, 25-6

Westminster Assembly, The, 213

Westminster Disputation, The, 53

Whitaker, William, 209, 211-14, 218

White, Francis, 223

Whitgift, Henry, 2-3

Whitgift, John; birth, 2; early life and influences, 3-4; at Wellow Abbey, 26; at St. Anthony's School, 26-9; education in Cambridge, 39-43; friendship with Andrew Perne, 44; ordination, 61; Fellow of Peterhouse, 44, 61; Lady Margaret's professor, 65; and the Precisians in Cambridge, 74-5; Regius professor, 78, 81; Master of Pembroke, 78n; Master of Trinity, 78-84, 94; Vice-chancellor of Cambridge, 81n, 84; controversy with Cartwright in Cambridge, 81-4; revision of the Cambridge University statutes, 83-4; Dean of Lincoln, 84-5; Convocation sermon, 86; and the *Admonition* controversy, 94-9; his *Answere to a certen Libel, etc.,* 95, 98; his *Defense of the Answere, etc.,* 98-9; literary controversy with Cartwright, 135-45; defense of the Prayer Book, 136-8; defense of the royal supremacy, 142-5, 182; Prolocutor of Convocation, 149n, 199; Bishop of

Worcester, 102-32, 154-60; dealings with Romanists and recusants, 120, 129-31; Archbishop of Canterbury, 161-230; his *Eleven Articles,* 161-8; the High Commission, 164-70; use of the *ex-officio* oath, 167-71; enforcement of subscription, 162-3, 167, 174-5; member of the Privy Council, 175, 195; controversy with Travers, 176-9; defense of episcopacy, 140-2, 178-9, 207-8; defense of the established Church against the Puritans, 132, 135, 137-8, 140-5, 161-74, 182, 187, 194-5; treatment of the Puritans, 167, 185-6; Puritan abuse of, 44, 165-6, 184, 186; and the *Lambeth Articles,* 208-20;

and the Croydon Hospital and School, 221-3; correspondence with Burghley, 75, 99-100, 169-72; correspondence with Hutton, 159-60; and Elizabeth I, 224-7; last years, 222-30; at Elizabeth's deathbed, 225-7; and the Hampton Court Conference, 229; illness and death, 229-30

Whitgift, Robert, 4, 25-6, 29

Whittingham, William, 72, 178

Wiggington, Giles, 79, 183, 186

Wilcox, Thomas, 89, 97

Wilson, Arthur, 166

Wolsey, Cardinal, 106, 184n

Worcester Cathedral, 111

Sacrifice in Greek and Roman Religions and Early Judaism. By Royden Keith Yerkes, Sometime Professor of Theology at the University of the South. 1952.

The Doctrine of the Atonement. By the Rev. Leonard Hodgson, D.D., Regius Professor of Divinity in the University of Oxford, Canon of Christ Church, Oxford. 1950.

Witness to the Light. By the Rev. Alec R. Vidler, D.D., Canon of St. George's Chapel, Windsor Castle. 1947.

Men and Movements in the American Episcopal Church. By the Rev. E. Clowes Chorley, D.D., L.H.D., late Historiographer of the Church. 1943.

Personalities of the Old Testament. By the Rev. Fleming James, D.D., Ph.D., Professor of the Literature and Interpretation of the Old Testament, Emeritus, Berkeley Divinity School, affiliated with Yale University Divinity School. 1938.

The Church in Japan. By the Rt. Rev. Henry St. George Tucker, Bishop of Virginia; a former Presiding Bishop of the Protestant Episcopal Church; formerly (1912-1923) Bishop of Kyoto. 1937. (Published under the title *The History of the Episcopal Church in Japan.*)

The Praise of God. By the Rev. Winfred Douglas, Mus.D., late Canon of St. John's Cathedral, Denver, Colorado. 1935. (Published under the title *Church Music in History and Practice.*)

The Social Implications of the Oxford Movement. By the Rev. William George Peck, Rector of St. John Baptist, Hulme, Manchester, England. 1932.

Pastoral Psychiatry and Mental Health. By the Rev. John Rathbone Oliver, M.D., Ph.D., late Associate in the History of Medicine at the Johns Hopkins University. 1932. (Published under title *Psychiatry and Mental Health.*)

Christ in the Gospels. By the Rev. Burton Scott Easton, Ph.D., S.T.D., late Professor at the General Theological Seminary. 1930.

New Horizons of the Christian Faith. By the Rev. Frederick C. Grant, D.D., Th.D., Professor of Biblical Theology at Union Theological Seminary, New York City; formerly Dean of the Seabury-Western Theological Seminary, 1927-38. 1928.

Some Aspects of Contemporary Greek Orthodox Thought. By the Rev. Frank Gavin, M.A., Ph.D., late Professor at the General Theological Seminary. 1921.

The Ethiopic Liturgy. By the Rev. S. A. B. Mercer, D.D., Ph.D., Professor Emeritus of Trinity College in the University of Toronto. 1915.

Biographical Studies in Scottish Church History. By the Rt. Rev. Anthony Mitchell, D.D., Late Bishop of Aberdeen and Orkney. 1913.

The National Church of Sweden. By the Rt. Rev. John Wordsworth, D.D., LL.D., Late Bishop of Salisbury, 1910.

Church Hymns and Church Music. By Peter C. Lutkin, Mus.D., A.G.P., Late Dean of the School of Music, Northwestern University. 1908.